AN ORDINARY COPPER

An Ordinary Copper

Reflections on policing since the mid-1960s

David E. Leach

ELSP

First published in 2015
by ELSP

www.ex-librisbooks.co.uk

Origination by Ex Libris Press
Bradford-on-Avon, Wiltshire

Printed by CPI Anthony Rowe
Chippenham, Wiltshire

ISBN 978-1-906641-82-5

Contents

Introduction

Every retired Police Officer has more than enough material to write a book. Many have actually taken the time in their retirement years to do so. In the main these have been the memoirs of very senior officers or the recollections of humorous incidents. The alternative tack, although not always declared, is to use the experience of years gone by to provide material for television and film script writing. It was, to some indirect extent, the television angle that prompted me to sit at the keyboard to create this work.

At a Classic Car Club dinner in the late 1990s my 'previous life' as a police officer came out in the conversation and I was asked if I liked the television programme *Heartbeat*. In jest, my reply was, "That was me!" My wife, Gill, hastily reminded me that I was no Nick Berry! As the conversation continued, with my reminiscing about the policing environment the lady who had asked whether I liked *Heartbeat* went on to pose the question, "Why don't you write a book?" This is my response. The idea as to how I wanted the book to be set out gelled quickly and I started this work then, at the turn of the millennium. With my taking on a Branch volunteer role with the National Association of Retired Police Officers (NARPO), the book took third place to other writing so has had a long gestation.

What follows is one man's recollections of his personal involvement in a Service, which, despite all the frequent criticisms, remains the envy of many other Countries. Nothing is perfect, certainly not the British Bobby or the organisational infrastructure within which he or she works. The Police Service in Great Britain being made up of human beings inevitably has its failings. The most notable of these, probably, being its inability to adequately present its real worth. All that said, it remains noticeable that there remains no reluctance on the part of police services in other parts of the world to acknowledge the long established expertise of the British Police Service. That this is often referred to as Scotland Yard is a minor annoyance to the other Forces throughout the country but it is recognition of past successes not equalled in many other countries.

That most people in the Great Britain realise the benefits of the police that serve them is not, greatly, thanks to what has been presented by politicians, media reporters or the most senior officers. The impression is given by the police officer who comes face to face with the citizen and that impression can be both negative as well as positive. That, overall, there remains substantial faith in the Service must be a reflection that, most of the time, the front line officers are getting it right. While not perfect, just being pretty good provides enough reason for some to seek out the negative and this has certainly applied to much of the mass-media approach to too much of their reflecting of police activity. My concerns regarding the way in which the police service has changed, not in every way for the better, will no doubt be evident as we go through our reader/writer relationship. In case it is not I have allowed myself the indulgence of a personal commentary in the final chapter but, please, read the bits in between first! That the massive advances in technological support for policing have been somewhat counterbalanced by changes in attitudes in respect of the primacy of service provision is a sadness about which I would be dishonest if I did not have my say.

In the following pages, names are excluded. Not, really, to protect anyone but because everyone is entitled to their privacy. It will, in a few cases, be easy for individuals to be identifiable from reference to their role at the appropriate time. I sincerely hope that none of those to which this may relate will feel that they have been treated unfairly. If they have it must be because my perception was and has remained incomplete. Just as no-thing is perfect, so no-body can be either. Whatever failing I may relate as my perception of some of my colleagues has always, in my experience, been balanced in heavy measure by positive qualities. Of some of those outside the service to whom I may refer, this was not always the case but they deserve the benefit of the doubt in assuming that no one is entirely without positive worth.

I was privileged to work in an organisation that, throughout my time, provided the most comprehensive service conceivable. Nothing was too small to be irrelevant and nothing too big to be unaccomplished. In a changing world the police service has also changed. Usually a half a generation behind in terms of attitude, the police service in this country for decades provided a source of dependable tradition. Keeping up in technological terms should not, immediately, have meant losing the personal touch. Coping with change has become a required trait of the police officer but recognising tradition remains, hopefully, important. As in any other walk of life, adapting to keep up with the way life changes is important but to forget the wealth of experience of the past has the disastrous inherent danger that earlier errors will be repeated.

In relating my story the resort to jargon would be impossible to avoid. To any former police officer who may consider my reflections a worthwhile read, they will be fairly easy to identify. Indeed, to most others many of these terms have become familiar through the wealth of fiction relating to the police. To be safe, I have attempted to clarify them when they first appear in the text.

The Police Service gave me an occupation that, with one notable exception, always felt secure. It gave me a career within the same organisation that was also extremely varied. It helped me to continue my education beyond its sound but not academically outstanding beginnings. It brought me into contact with more people than I could ever number and made me some friends to last a lifetime. It introduced me, and my family, to pressures not capable of being imagined by many.

If anyone has pondered as to why this book bears the title *An Ordinary Copper* it is because they are too young to have had the pleasure of watching, initially in black and white, the Saturday evening programme *Dixon of Dock Green*. Jack Warner, a little confusingly, brought to the television screen the 'revived' character of a London 'bobby' from the cinema's *The Blue Lamp*. Every week, in half an hour, we would see this genial man administering justice in the even-handed manner for which the British Police Service was held in high regard. His little chats to camera at the opening and ending of each programme presented home-spun low-level philosophy with which all viewers could equate. George Dixon seemed to epitomise what the population wanted, arguably still do want, of its police officers. The title music started with *Just An Ordinary Copper*.

That I have chosen to write about it is probably my best acknowledgement of my debt to the police service. Given the value that I place upon my upbringing and love of my mother and father, that I dedicate this book to my wife, Gillian, is some small recognition of her central role in being capable of bringing up our three, much loved, daughters with my support being far too often absent.

1 Looking into the Barrels

It is not true. You do not sweat on a cool summer night just because you are in extreme fear for your continued existence. Looking through the windscreen of the Hillman Husky at the pair of twelve bore barrels, thankfully for the only time in my police service, I felt no warmer or colder. The trembling was nothing to do with temperature, real or imagined, it was the actual reaction to such severe imminent danger. I had managed to talk myself out of being shot across the bonnet of the car and now, totally irrationally, my greatest fear was the damage that a shattered windscreen glass could inflict. Painfully, I was to find out many years later about windscreen glass but at this moment the prospect of all those lead pellets should have been more central to my concern.

After several abortive attempts to get the thin metal registration number tag into the keyhole on the dashboard, I fumbled the key into the correct position and managed to turn on the ignition. The greatest fear, now, was that my adversary would react negatively when I started the engine. Would forget his apparent inclination to let me escape rather than pull the trigger. The petrifying moment of turning the key a further few degrees passed and I drove down the road with a more conscientious eye on the mirror than would apply ever again.

The evening, as I suppose do so many that are to turn out to be eventful, started as routinely as had any during my, then eighteen month, period of probation at Weston-super-Mare. With only three months of the full two years probationary service to go, I had already seen quite a bit of life in the police. Not that anything could, at that stage, be taken for granted. Somewhat irrationally, for it was possible to see others being persuaded to go much earlier, there was always the feeling that within the probationary period the security of a police career was somewhat tenuous. These concerns were, of course, not uppermost in my mind as my colleagues and I sat down for our briefing by the Sergeant, at 17.45 hours on that Friday evening. Briefings, for all shifts, were for my entire shift working career started a quarter of an hour before the eight-hour tour was to commence. This arrangement was to end, along with many other changes in conditions of service, during the second half of my thirty years – after I had been removed from routine shift work.

On the last day of June, I had attended the Old Pier where a collecting box belonging to the RNLI had been stolen. The reverse of the Crime Report had spaces to be completed when the follow-up visits had been carried out. Usually this was to be done about fourteen days after the first report of the crime. Tuesday and Wednesday had been my Weekly Rest Days and Thursday had seen me attending the Probationary Training class at Bridgwater Police Station. This evening was my first opportunity, following the passage of those two weeks, to make another visit. The Sergeant who had briefed us had a special respect for the RNLI. He may, also or alternatively, have had a bit of an eye for the relatively young widow who devoted much of her time to the voluntary task of looking after the Lifeboat Station. Whatever his reason, he chose to accompany me on my follow-up enquiries.

Following the first hour spent in dealing with accumulated paperwork and allowing the Sergeant to complete his mid-tour refreshment break, we set off in the Hillman Minx. He did not comment upon my immediate call to Information Room to advise them of our patrol and crew but intimated that he would not have bothered.

The amalgamation with the Bath Police at the beginning of 1967 had, also, brought a restructuring of the Force area. Nothing as sweeping as those that were to follow, much later in my service, but it had resulted in the Divisions acquiring 'letters' and those vehicles equipped with radio receiving alpha/numeric call signs. Previously all vehicles with radios had, simply, carried a unique two-digit number for their identification at the Information Room at Taunton. As an aside but of some interest, in those early days of my service the numbers starting with one hundred were all allocated to fire appliances and the Somerset Fire Service shared our only VHF radio channel.

We had collected a carbonated copy of a telephone message sheet before we had made our way across the yard and it informed us of a domestic dispute in a house leading away from the sea front. It turned out to be no more than a dispute over the husband's failure to present the housekeeping money and, on this occasion, the old standby phrase of "parties advised" actually summed up the police action considered to be appropriate.

As we rounded the small one-way system near the Grand Pier, the Sergeant suddenly stopped. After we had pulled in, onto the promenade, I followed his example and got out of the car. I was somewhat taken aback when he drew my attention to a speedboat beyond the end of the pier. His instruction was that I should report the helmsman for exceeding the speed limit. I knew Probationary Constables were expected to know such things as that there was a 5-knot limit within the bay. But the demarcation line for this speed limit was only really identifiable from each end of that line. That the driver of the boat was within the line was not really in doubt but proving it at Court would not be so easy. We got back into the car and he drove me to the Knightstone slipway to await the arrival of the boat. Whether he was wholly impressed by my decision to caution the, at least apparently, contrite young man was not certain.

Having visited the Old Pier and the Sergeant having enjoyed the widow's cup of tea while I made enquiries of some of the stallholders, my purpose in being in his company was complete and I was dropped off at the front of the Winter Gardens to patrol on foot. About twenty minutes later, I rounded a corner into Regent Street to find a more mature Constable standing near the junction beside the black Hillman Husky police car. I joined him in watching a scruffy looking man staggering, sometimes on, sometimes off the pavement. He appeared not to like anyone who came anywhere close to him because he uttered the same two swear words at each encounter.

Through the haze of alcohol fumes, he was informed that he was being arrested for being Drunk and Disorderly and, because I was the junior man, he was my prisoner. He was reluctant to accept the situation but was loaded into the back seat of the Husky and taken to the Police Station. There, the Station Constable opened the heavy iron-barred gate into the cell passage and, when I returned from securing him, minus belt and shoes, slid the charge register across the table for me to complete.

Refreshments were normally taken at ten o'clock on the six-till-two late shift but our combining to complete our pocket book entries and the other paperwork in respect of the prisoner took us half an hour beyond that time. The canteen had all of the accoutrements for cooking and a number of Formica topped tables and laminated wood and tubular metal chairs. It did not, at any time of the day, have a cook. Although Weston-super-Mare was the largest divisional station it did not have enough staff to warrant such an extravagance. Consequently, much of the three-quarter of an hour refreshment break could be spent cooking so on most breaks, other than breakfast on early turn, sandwiches were the norm. In July, 1967, our wedding was only months away and I was about to occupy the rented flat that we had found but was enjoying the final few sandwich packs prepared by my landlady.

Upon our return to his office from the canteen, the night duty Sergeant had, evidently, forgotten us when allocating his patrols and took the easy option of allowing us to continue with the Husky as a Crime Car Patrol for the remainder of our shift. When performing this role, the detail normally contained in the Pocket Book was, instead, written into a thin bound 'log book', in order that the Detective Chief Inspector (DCI) could read it the following morning. Only matters that may be required to support evidence in court needed to be included in the Pocket Book. Much was to be included in the Pocket Book on that night.

At 11.15pm, my older colleague having retained the key, he drove out of the yard and we spent the first quarter of an hour drifting around the central area of the town. In the County Force, even after amalgamation with Bath, each group of Constables that provided shift cover was known as a Section. This term was also applied, outside of the larger towns, to geographic areas that were the responsibility of one or more Sergeants. Even in a station the size of Weston, all of the members of the other sections were known to everyone else. At various stages of the four-week roster of shifts, we at least met at the changeover times and the shift system provided several overlaps of four hours during which it was not uncommon to be working with a man from another Section.

In the 1960s female Constables were relatively few in number and worked within their own Policewomen's Section under their own, female, Sergeant. They covered most of the day but only worked beyond midnight when there was some specific reason, taking turns to be called out should their presence be required during the night. These woman officers provided a valuable resource to the Police Service, as they were predominantly dedicated to specialist duties, particularly relating to women and children. Legislation in the 1970s was to result in Policewomen's Sections being disbanded, as being gender discriminatory, and the expertise slowly dissipated. Many years later the loss became so obvious that Units were set up to cope with these, often sensitive, matters but with both male and female officers involved.

The first call came over the personal radio, from the Constable in the Station Office, and was to deal with a complaint of excessive noise from one of the hotels just back from the sea front. The proprietor was a local Councillor and a Magistrate, so was very keen to rectify the matter as soon as it was drawn to his attention. Having satisfied ourselves that all of those present were either residents or, really, guests of the owner, we radioed the result to the Station Officer. We were confident, such was not invariably so, that on this occasion the noise level would remain at the lower level after our departure. Our Councillor would not want the embarrassment of a second visit.

Midnight passed and our next intention was to make our way out to the small industrial estate. There we would, more faithfully, be performing the Crime Car role in providing a supplement to the one man on the Bournville Section who would also be working until two o'clock. The significant police area on the inland side of the town was named after the small Section Station that had been built, along with a large estate of houses, after the Second World War. Although the Bournville Section boasted a brand new Ford Anglia estate, most of the patrolling was either on motorcycle or pedal cycle. After ten at night, the one Section Sergeant having long before departed to his adjoining police house, the late tour Constable would be allowed to use the car. On this night, however, we knew that there was no six-till-two late Officer. My colleague chose, on this occasion, to take the longer route along the sea front and around the residential area to the south of the town in order to get to the Oldmixon estate across the railway bridge near the Uphill junction of the railway loop that allowed trains to avoid the Station if required.

The Oldmixon industrial estate contained many smaller industrial units but two that were of more significant size. These two, on opposite sides of the estate, each had a watchman. Watchmen had, by 1967, not been redesignated 'security officers'. It was a, probably unintended, generous gesture on the part of these larger companies that more calls were received from these watchmen about suspicious activity around the smaller business premises than relating to those buildings that they were employed to protect. It was also a fact that their existence, not quite in view of each other, was particularly solitary, even boring. When some form of police transport was seen approaching it was an automatic reaction to switch on the kettle as an inducement for the driver to spend a few minutes chatting over a cup of tea.

Crime patrol of the Oldmixon was not to happen that night. Instead, a call on the car radio directed us to a garage, on the approach to the village of

Banwell, on the main Weston-super-Mare to Cheddar road. Working as hard as it was able, the 1600cc Rootes engine propelled us to the location in just under ten minutes. The caller to the "Disturbance" had been a veterinary surgeon and he and his wife were standing in the doorway of their combined home and business premises to the rear of the filling station forecourt that he had used as a reference. Walking up their driveway from the garage the cause of their concern was lying prostrate on their lawn emanating whimpering sounds that should, more expectedly, be coming from the Jack Russell terrier that was seated near his head.

The vet explained that the man's other dog had been involved in a road accident earlier on the Friday and had been brought to him by the unknown driver of the car involved. It had been immediately evident that the injured dog was beyond repair and he had "put the animal to sleep". The man had heard from a drinking mate at a local pub what had happened to his pet and had arrived on the vet's doorstep to demand an explanation.

Our efforts to placate the man were either not heard or ignored for some time. He, then, suddenly jumped to his feet and was prevented from advancing upon the vet by the way in which we placed ourselves between him and his intended target. After telling his wife to retreat into the house, the vet advanced in his dressing gown and stood behind us. For some considerable time, he gave repeated explanations between our heads to the wiry man with the Jack Russell. Through this time the man repeatedly rose unsteadily to his feet, only to realise he could not maintain equilibrium and collapse to the floor. No length or depth of explanation was likely to make him understand why the vet had "killed" his dog. His own culpability, in that his dog had been alone and some distance from his home, was unlikely to register with this man, either in his current state or any other time.

In spite of his evident lack of satisfaction he, eventually and by dint of our combined slow movement in that direction, found himself on the ground beyond the vet's gateway. Having reached this point, he turned away and walked, more like an automated reflection of his National Service marching training, to the edge of the main road and sat on the grass verge. The little terrier remained in close and attentive contact. The vet thanked us for our assistance and rejoined his wife, who had not been wholly obedient but had watched the proceedings from her doorway. The door closed behind them and our attention returned to the distressed man.

My colleague sat on the grass verge beside him and remonstrated with him to return to his home. His repeated identification that "it will look different in the light of day, after a good night's sleep" was, evidently, not working. Nor did his getting to his feet and turning the persuasive tone into a more authoritative instruction have the desired affect. Not happy to leave him on the edge of a main road, we returned to the Husky and observed him for a while, expecting that any traffic passing would have to miss him by negotiating our repositioned car.

There was, however, a limit to how long we could remain in this situation. A call to the Information Room, repeated to the station office, brought back the address of the name that the vet had given us for his intruder. When it appeared that the man had no intention of moving, we decided to see if there was anyone at the address and found that his wife was awaiting his return. A brief explanation and the donning of a raincoat over her nightdress brought us quickly back to the place at which we had last seen him. He had disappeared.

Following her advice, we took the lane beyond the veterinary surgery and soon came upon him, with the faithful terrier at heel. Our first inclination, if only we had followed it, was to leave him to continue this alternative route to his home. His wife was not persuaded. Having taken the trouble to respond to our calling at her door well after midnight, she was determined that she was going to have her say. Upon leaving the vet, my colleague had handed me the key ring and I decided to turn the car so that some light would be cast upon the man. It was he who pulled forward his seat to let her get out from the back seat of the Husky.

If hearing of his dog being 'put down' had caused him to grieve, seeing his wife approaching caused him severe grief. Instead of bringing him to some semblance of rationality, his wife's appearance threw him into an uncontrollable rage. He had been carrying a short length of stout rope with a brass clasp at each end – a leash, we had correctly assumed, for the Jack Russell. Now, he swung it about his head. Our immediate concern for his wife was misplaced, as he strode past her without acknowledgement. We, the bringers of impending domestic chastisement, were his targets.

One brass clasp in hand, the few feet of rope provided considerable momentum to the other end as it struck the front of the Hillman. One headlight was extinguished immediately and several blows to the bonnet and the driver's side of the car then came within his sights. My colleague had got out and I followed across his seat. As he rounded the back of the car, I gained my feet and was almost fortunate in seeing the clasp approaching. Only almost, because it struck the blue light in the centre of the roof and the shattered Perspex showered me. I must have been foolish enough to open my mouth, probably in amazement, because I had to spit out a sizeable piece of the blue plastic.

In the dim red light at the rear of the Husky I caught a glimpse of the wife running away down the lane. The Jack Russell had, apparently, changed his allegiance and was keeping pace with her. In the semi-darkness, we grappled with a man who, permanently or temporarily, was remarkably stronger than he looked. With a complete lack of restraining reason the flailing arms and legs evaded our combined attempts to gain a grip and he sprang to his feet, even more quickly than he had on the veterinary surgeon's lawn. As we reached our feet he was several yards along the lane and in the complete darkness beyond the reach of the rear lights.

The effort to update the Information Room failed. With the blue light, had gone the aerial from the roof of the Husky. Near where the whole situation had started, was a telephone kiosk and a quick report was passed, using the peculiar emergency system to contact the Station Office in Weston. Weston-super-Mare must have been one of the final places in the United Kingdom to be joined to the national scheme of things by Post Office Telephones. Instead of dialling '999', there was a button, exactly like those on buses to notify the driver of a desire to get off at the next stop. Pressing this button alerted the Telephone Exchange where the Operator would make the appropriate enquiry as to which Emergency Service was required.

With others being informed of our situation, we drove back to the home of the man who had turned from being the subject of our concern to the target for arrest for criminal damage. As we approached, we could see in the single headlight beam that he was getting into a small van that had been parked outside the gate of his garden. I stopped to see what he would do next, reversed rapidly as he came backwards towards us, and, in contrast to what had always happened when I had performed my probationary attachment to the Road Traffic Department, sought to avoid allowing him to get near me. Thankfully, a 950cc van was no match for the 1600cc Husky and we decided that now was a good time to regroup.

Back at the kiosk, the intended telephone call was not required as a Hillman Minx was just arriving from the Weston direction as we came out of the village. The night tour Sergeant, accompanied by another Constable, got out and formulated a plan. They would follow us back to the house and await the man's return. The plan had to be somewhat amended when we saw that the van had returned to its parking place. I stopped a few feet behind it and the Minx a few feet behind me.

In the light from the window above the front door of the house, the wife was visible and was crying uncontrollably but conveying no coherent explanation as to her current predicament. Realising that she was in distress, perhaps real danger, my colleague and I approached the front door. The Sergeant remained the few feet away beside the gate to the small front garden. At that stage I had no sight of the Constable who had been with him and assumed that he had remained with the car. In the moment that it took to reach this situation there was no noise other than the sobbing from the window above our heads.

My colleague knocked loudly on the door. There was a slight delay. When the door flew open our man stood with a twelve bore double-barrelled shotgun across his chest. Rapid persuasion was all that my colleague had to call upon in this situation but the man was not in the least receptive. Retreat was the only sensible option and, walking backwards, we separated at the gateway. The Constable who had accompanied the Sergeant had concealed himself beside the gate, hidden by the low privet hedge. He had, apparently, hoped that if the man had made to run away he would be in a position to make a surprise interception. Even then, I did not see him until he rose, revising his intention, in a vain attempt to grab the gun. Instead, the man swung the barrels in the direction that the Sergeant and my colleague had taken and, in the process, struck the Constable on the head with the barrels of the gun.

As I was nearest, other than the Constable who had been rendered semi-conscious, the attention of our man with the shotgun was diverted toward me. In the few seconds available to them, the Sergeant and Constable with whom I had started out on this sorry saga, seized their opportunity, leapt forward and dragged our injured compatriot away. The man was switching his gaze and the barrels of the gun between them and me. But I was still his closest potential target so I received the greater part of his attention. Realising, as did our adversary, what my colleagues were doing, I withdrew around the front of the Husky, feeling the cold metal of the bumper against my left leg as I slowly reached the driver's side of the car.

The noise in the semi-darkness culminated in the slamming of doors and the 1725cc engine bursting into purposeful life. The headlights did not come on but, in the fleeting glance that I thought was all that I dare risk, the car was silhouetted by its own reversing light as it sped, backwards, up the road. Goodness knows why but I felt relieved that they had managed to get away. It was not a particularly caring thought, just another irrationality. Their departure meant that it was just him and me. And he had the gun!

What I actually said was not very clever. It was a repetition of similar phrases all meaning much the same. "Don't do anything you may regret." Was, definitely, repeated more than once. Anything that he may regret? At this point it was my regret, should I be spared to harbour any, which was motivating my one-sided conversation. The man said nothing. His breathing was heavy and pumped in and out of him in very short bursts. In retrospect, he may have been as stressed as I was by the situation. At the time, I could not believe that to be the case.

The fumbling for the key and expectation that the engine firing up would cause the most unwanted reaction was over. Having, unbelievably, been allowed to make my escape, I sat in the Husky with the driver's window open and the radio loudspeaker turned off. There was, not unexpectedly, considerable radio traffic audible on the earpiece of the handset. For minutes that seemed like hours, I sat in the darkness with my straining eyes fixed on the distant small van. Where my colleagues had gone was no more than a guess. I presumed that someone was at the other end of the road but, also, that our injured colleague would have been taken to hospital. I could only just see the little van but I was relying upon my ears for any clue as to whether the armed man had decided not to remain near his home. At a distance which gave some comfort, I heard two loud bangs and was in no doubt that it was the shotgun that had caused them. In later years, I may have considered that our man may have shot himself, perhaps also his wife, but at this time I was only thankful for the distance being adequate for my safety. It transpired that he had fired the gun into the air from his front garden to reinforce his immediate triumph in our having moved away.

One of the two Inspectors, then the full complement of that rank at Weston, had been summoned from his bed and was heard directing the Sergeant to meet him at the garage where our troubles had started. There was no mention of me. It occurred to me that no one knew where I was or what had happened to me. The temptation to send a message to Information Room was not sufficiently strong for me to lose the ability to hear every sound outside of the vehicle. Then I remembered that, although it was evidently receiving signals, the radio would not transmit.

The choice was removed by hearing the call sign of the Husky on the radio. "QH, QH – Alpha Two – Your location. Over." Speaking as quietly as I thought may carry across the airwaves, I responded. The Information Room had not heard but repeated their call before simply stating their message without knowing whether I had received it. The direction was to return, via the village, to the garage and, as I reached the main road I found a traffic patrol car across the junction. The driver responded to his crewmate's direction and eased the Zephyr Six backwards to make room for me to pass. The crewmate had been standing at the side of the car, also listening as much as watching, and he enquired after my health as I crept past the front of the patrol car.

When I reached the garage forecourt the Inspector made no such enquiry as to my health. This was a peculiarly stressful situation for him and he was not really too bothered as to what impact it was having on me. He had, apparently, decided to await daylight for another approach to the house and sent me and my original colleague, who had already related the earlier build up to this situation, back to Weston Police Station. We were not sorry to be obeying that instruction.

At dawn, the man suddenly 'broke cover' and came out of his home and into the little van. He was forced to stop by the patrol car blocking the end of his road and arrested with much less difficulty than had been expected. The sequel for me was to be my first appearance at Assize Court.

When, eventually, I was allowed to go off-duty, I returned to the 'digs' to which I had moved only a short time earlier. My landlady from the start at Weston-super-Mare, driven by her son of about my age, moved twice in eighteen months and ended up where they wanted to be, on Beach Road. The prospect of graduating from a lodger or two to a full-blown hotel was taking shape. Although she looked after me well and at reasonable cost, I tired of the constantly changing faces of the holiday visitors. My current landlady, one I shared with a colleague with whom I had joined, was a younger divorcee with two junior school aged children. This brought a pleasant 'family' atmosphere and she spent some time with me that morning helping me to reach base after a long and stressful night's duty.

When the trial date was announced it, perhaps inevitably, clashed with the planned honeymoon after our upcoming wedding. Not entirely unsympathetic, my Sergeant told me to see the senior Detective Constable who was the exhibits officer for the case. He helped me formulate a report in which I identified that should I be required to attend the Court I would be forced to return from Jersey, with my new wife, and the costs would have to be reclaimed. The DC knew exactly the right button to press and the case, perhaps for other reasons in addition to my report, was adjourned to a slightly later date.

*My final digs at 60, Beach Road, Weston-super-Mare –
before moving to our first rented flat in the town*

The same DC spent time with me just before the case was to be heard and gave me advice that was to prove very opportune. While giving my evidence, our man's barrister, with not a lot else going for him, tried to imply that the actions of my colleague and me on that night had provoked his client. To achieve this, he said "I put it to you, Officer, that … " and described a lengthy and wholly fictitious set of supposed circumstance relating to our confrontation with his client in the lane. I stood, as the DC had advised, completely mute in the witness box. The barrister repeated the whole process and again I said nothing. The Judge, as the DC had predicted would happen, looked at the barrister and asked him if he would "kindly formulate his supposition as a question – in order that we may proceed". The DC had warned me that "I put it to you" was a precursor to a supposition and not a question requiring a response from a witness. At the close, our man was sentenced to five years imprisonment, a sentence that reflected his previous record, and my colleagues and I were commended by the Judge for our actions on that night. In my case one of the two commendations I was to receive during my probationary service – a reward not to be repeated throughout my later years of service.

2 How it started

Throughout the earlier years of my life, my mother had always had in view for me a career in the Merchant Navy Service. Her father, who died before I was born and after whom I was named, had started his time in that service under sail and she had been born and brought up in Holyhead so had always had a love of the sea. I appeared, even to myself, to be going along with this way forward for a career but there had been an early signal as to what my later decision would be. When about five or six, I was given an appropriately sized policeman's helmet and truncheon for Christmas and spent many teatime sessions at the gate of the factory in Wellington directing the mass of traffic, mainly foot and pedal cycle, as they disgorged in large numbers. I was to be reminded many times by my parents' contemporaries of those days when, much later, I became a real police officer.

In 1962, as I was approaching seventeen, the decision was made and I applied to the Somersetshire Constabulary to join that Force as a Cadet. The process, which included a written examination taken at the local police station with one of the Sergeants invigilating and the Training Inspector visiting our home to ensure that I was from the 'right sort' of family, brought me to the interview day in Taunton. During that day, with others who were seeking admission as Cadets and Regular Officers, there were more examination papers, interviews and a full medical.

Having stayed on for a further term at school, in order to achieve the English Language 'O' level, I reached the first day of the Christmas holiday. A buff envelope arrived in the post that Saturday morning. It contained the unwelcome news that I was not being offered a post as a Cadet. Hasty arrangements, largely driven by my mother, brought me to a clerical job not far from our home. In retrospect, I have never since regretted what, at that time, seemed a devastating setback. The company I worked for over the next two years and ten months educated me, academically and practically, in many aspects of business that would become invaluable in my later police career, and beyond.

At nineteen, I was mid-way through a two year business studies course on day release sponsored by my employer so I delayed my application for the Regular Force until that course was completed, just as I was reaching twenty. Again, the process was long and much the same as for the Cadets. As had been the case in 1962, the final interview of the day was with the Chief Constable, flanked by his deputy, then the only Assistant Chief Constable for the Force, and the Chief Superintendent Administration, one of the few of that rank at that time. This time the result was what I hoped for and I received my joining instructions.

On Monday, 18th October, 1965 I drove the few miles in my Austin A35 to the Somersetshire Constabulary Training School at Canonsgrove, just south of Taunton. There I met with the other six new recruits with whom I was to spend the next nearly four months. We were a very mixed bunch. The eldest was on the upper limit for recruits at that time, 30 years of age, and the youngest had just reached the lower limit of 19, having been successful in his earlier application to become a Cadet with the Force. The thirty year old and one other, not quite his age, had been in the Army but the rest of us were around twenty years old at that time.

There were two Training Sergeants at Canonsgrove, ably assisted by an ex-Sergeant who seemed to run most aspects of that establishment. Training at the centre was under the command of a Chief Inspector who worked from the Headquarters only a few miles away in the middle of Taunton and the Inspector who had conducted my second 'home visit' a few months earlier was the resident Senior Officer. Later there was to be significant expansion at Canonsgrove but this was not very long after it had been acquired by the Constabulary and our accommodation was in a dormitory in the top of the old house. Although my home was only about five miles away, through a tortuous set of country lanes, I had been accommodated in the dormitory. I thought it unwise (as indeed it would have been) to question the need for that arrangement.

In the two weeks we spent at Canonsgrove before being sent to the District Training School (DTC) at Chantemarle in Dorset, we were educated by the two Sergeants and, occasionally, the Inspector and handed masses of books and papers for the thirteen week Initial Course. We were taken to a clothier between Highbridge and Burnham on Sea, in a very uncomfortable Ford Thames 15cwt personnel carrier to be measured by a small team of middle aged ladies who evidently enjoyed their work. Meanwhile we were issued with 'off the peg' uniforms, with the promise that our personal measurements would be better accommodated by the time we returned, early in the New Year. The only items we had to purchase for ourselves were boots, for which there was a small allowance, and socks (black) and underpants (colour optional) for which there was no allowance! To the best of my recollection, the boot allowance was 1/6d (7 ½ p) a month and we were advised, appropriately, to have two pairs so that one could be 'bulled' for parades.

One other important, vital really, event before we were sent off to Chantemarle was our being paraded before a group of Magistrates in an imposing room in the Shire Hall, across the road from the Police Headquarters at Taunton. Each of us, in turn and according to our 'collar' number was sworn in as a Constable. With Testament held aloft in the right hand the oath was read from a card which had evidently been held in the left hand of many recruits over the years. While, especially closer to the end of my service, the importance of the Testament was to grow less, the relevance of the content of the oath remained central to what I saw as the whole purpose of the office I then entered. The independence of the office of Constable, sadly eroded in recent years, was, to me and throughout my career, the essential core of what the British Police Service represented.

At that time, and right through until our amalgamation of 1974, the Force pay day came around every four weeks. We were told of the days, not too long before, when Constables had to parade to receive their pay, whether scheduled for duty or not, but that the Force had moved into the modern era with pay being sent direct to bank accounts. Until I joined the police, I had found no need for any other account than a Post Office Savings Book, which contained precious few savings. The advice was to open a current account with the Westminster Bank as this was the bank used by the Force and the money would be in the account a day earlier than with other banks. Several of us had, previously, been paid weekly and there was an offer of a small advance to bridge the gap before the first pay day but my PO account and assistance from my parents would see me through. After all, there is little opportunity to spend much money when time is totally committed to work. With meals provided, the only expense was the occasional mid-morning treat of a piece of cake with the coffee that was provided.

In addition to having the pay explained, we were presented with a series of possible deductions. These included the Police Federation, Force Club, Force Lottery, Convalescent Home and others that time has dimmed from recollection. None were high cost, with the Police Federation being the most expensive, and there was little opportunity offered to decline any of them. There was a culture, developed over the many years that the Service had been in existence, for mutual support and new recruits were expected to make their contributions from the outset.

With much effort being expected to make a sound start on learning the Definitions of the Law, from a small booklet provided by the Police Mutual Assurance Society, and Judges Rules, those two weeks passed very quickly. We were allowed to depart a little before five o'clock on the Friday, with strict instructions to be at Chantemarle by 6 p.m. (1800 hours) on the Sunday. Although we had all spent the middle weekend of those two weeks at home, it was not until that Friday teatime that I brought home all the uniform and equipment with which I had been issued, with precious little spare space in the little A35's boot. My mother insisted upon me standing near our back door for a photograph of me in my uniform.

After checking and double checking both the content of the boot and the route I must take, I set off early in the afternoon for the journey to Chantemarle, the District Training Centre (DTC). I was not the only one to arrive early, making what would become a familiar approach along the lanes leading to the old manor house. There was ample space for parking under the trees on the opposite side of the entrance driveway and, after finding the right door, it took several trips to unload my belongings. The dormitory to which the duty Sergeant allocated me was over the rear entrance, which was used as the main one throughout our stay, and a 'duty student' escorted me up the winding stairs to the first floor. There was only one of the seven beds in the dormitory already taken, a Gloucestershire man had just beaten me to it and was unpacking his gear in one of the corner beds. After introducing ourselves, I followed suit and took another corner bed. There were five beds and one double bunk in the room and the bunks were what were left for the last two that arrived together from the Bristol Force.

The rooms were all called after local landmarks and I noted that the one next to us also bore the name of one of the two Inspectors from the staff of the centre, so knew that we were to be closely supervised. At the rear of the house there was a former stable block which had been converted into offices around an enclosed yard. Beside that was the dinning room and behind it the more modern classroom block and gymnasium. We were, as we arrived, instructed to assemble in the 'reading room' within the old house and, by six o'clock we were all seated awaiting the introductory message. The Inspector on duty, not our neighbour, was from Somerset and his talk was brief. We had been split into two groups and numbered 159A & 159B, I was allocated to 'B' and our Class Sergeant was from the Bath City Police. We were informed of the location of the bar, just behind the reception, and small enough to emphasise that we were not expected to be filling it too often. As we trooped out, back to our dormitories, we were directed to take a bag from a couple of boxes and found that we had a couple of sandwiches and a packet of crisps to settle us for the night.

Next morning, we all assembled in the dinning hall for breakfast. The fare on offer, to be eaten off scrubbed wooden tables while seated on less well scrubbed wooden benches, was well cooked but not overly generous in portions. Breakfast was an egg and slice of bacon, sometimes the changes were rung with a sausage substituting for the bacon. Our eldest Somerset recruit, was appalled when, as we were eating our food, we were all called to stand for the entry of the Commandant, a Chief Superintendent from a Force in the Home Counties. He remarked that such was not expected even in the Army. Later we would become a little more understanding, if no more appreciative, of the slender rations offered, when we were informed of the minute sum allocated by the Home Office for our feeding. To the best of my recollection the sum quoted was 17/6d (87.5p) per man per week, to provide three meals a day and a small packed supper. Even in 1965 this was far from a generous allowance and the catering staff must have worked some real miracles to achieve what they did.

From breakfast it was straight to the two classrooms in the new block allocated to our intake. Now we were alone with our Sergeant from Bath and there began the process of getting to know what he required and hoping to manage to achieve those requirements. Much of what was demanded was contained in talks from him and, occasionally, other members of the staff but the real slog was the rote learning of the definitions and Judges Rules which we had made a start on at Canonsgrove. It was evident that not all Force initial courses had been thus focused, as some classmates from elsewhere had no idea what was about to hit them.

Not all my fellow students were prepared for the requirement to remain for a couple of lessons each Saturday morning, with the LeMans start away from the car park when released. Throughout my secondary education, my school had held lessons on Saturday mornings and my employment since had featured such working, so it seemed quite in order to me. It meant, of course, that it was mid-afternoon before I reached home and that a late-afternoon start was required for the return on a Sunday. With Christmas intervening and a 'long-weekend' (not working the Saturday morning) in mid November, not many nights were spent at home in those thirteen weeks.

I travelled home every weekend except that for which I was allocated as a 'duty student'. I was doubly lucky with the weekend that had been allocated from the first full day of the course. It was not a weekend upon which a new intake of students was arriving and, even more important, it snowed. Those who had returned to their homes for the one night and who were sufficiently wise, started arriving back earlier than normal on the Sunday afternoon. Those who did not, received short-shrift from the duty Sergeant for arriving late. The real benefit of that enforced stay over a weekend was the time it permitted, outside of some security patrols around the complex, for some 'cramming' for the forthcoming examination.

The classroom routine was broken in a number of ways. Some aspects of dealing with incidents were better illustrated by practical exercises and these were set up around the training school driveways and in various offices and other buildings. They were all, as may be expected, fairly basic but seemed complex to we new hands. Each exercise was used as a learning ploy in respect of the, all important, police pocket note book. We had been issued with special ones for the course and our notes about the set piece incidents were closely scrutinised by the Sergeants and, occasionally, the Inspectors. On occasions we would have to give 'evidence' on one of the incidents before a 'court' and the Chief Inspector (Deputy Commandant) was as strict as any Judge in demanding the evidence be appropriately presented.

Other breaks from the classroom included physical training, drill and, on Wednesday afternoons, organised sport in which all had to participate in some way or another. One of my Somerset colleagues, who hailed from Gloucestershire, was a keen rugby player and had been nominated to arrange a team for a match at Dorchester against the Army Junior Leaders. Having played rugby at school, although never well, he came to me on the night before the match and told me of the late injury to one of his selected team. I knew he was not just imparting the information and it was quickly followed by the request that I fill the vacancy. I, somewhat incautiously, agreed and was then informed that the vacant slot was in the role of hooker. With no time for any additional training I found myself at the Army playing field at Dorchester in my rugby kit on the following afternoon.

My props were one of our own, Somerset, contingent and a man from the Exeter City Police. Both of them were older than me and much bigger than my 10 ½ stones. The Somerset man was one of our ex-Army men and had spent some time, so he said, in the French Foreign Legion. The Exeter man, perhaps more reliably believably, had been an officer in the Rhodesian Police. At that time, seeing the way that the wind was blowing in that long-suffering African country, quite a few of those joining the police service over here were returning from Rhodesian Police service. I think all of them had been at least Inspectors and our Exeter man a Superintendent but all had, rightly, to start again as Constables in this country. This, experience, aspect seems to have been discounted in current Government thinking! A little later similar mature recruits arrived in many British Forces from Hong Kong, although the UK relationship was yet to last many years they often realised that they wanted to be back here for their long-term futures.

Our young Army opponents all saw this as an opportunity to have a legitimate 'bash' at a 'copper' and the game was, to say the least, very physical. Hidden in the middle of each scrum I was both crushed by the combined weights all around me and my opposite number was rather indiscriminate in his kicking. My advantage was that my props were so much bigger than I was that both my feet were available to collect the ball and we won possession more often than not. I cannot recall the result, I was more interested in all my abrasions and bruises. Eventually, and it seemed far more than an hour and a half, the final whistle blew and we all, me certainly, were glad of the hot shower.

The occasion was followed by an Army meal and an evening in their Mess. During the excessive rounds of bitter our team leader, our man from Gloucestershire, put two shillings (10p) worth of sixpenny pieces in the 'one armed bandit'. On his last pull on the long lever, the rolling drums fell just right and the machine started chuntering as it spewed out its jackpot. With the tray soon full the sixpenny coins were falling all around and several of us helped him to retrieve them. We set about counting while our hosts set about demonstrating their displeasure at a visitor taking the jackpot to which many of them had been contributing over some time. With the total being checked at £25, he decided to keep the peace and spent half of it on a round of drinks for everyone in the room. He still managed to pocket more than one of our week's wages.

The most enjoyable recreation for me was the weekly bus trip to Yeovil swimming baths. Despite much cajoling on the part of my physical education teacher at school, I was still unable to swim but the efforts of the staff at Yeovil baths achieved the objective. We were split between swimmers, the majority, and non-swimmers. The PTI from the DTC instructed the swimmers for the, all important Royal Life Saving Society Bronze Medallion, while the staff at the baths tried to get we others to manage a length or two. At that time, along with many other aspects, the RLS Bronze Medallion was a requirement for successful completion of the police probationary two years of service. At least, by the end of the course at Chantemarle, I was a swimmer.

Drill was considered an important aspect of training, as much for its coordination and discipline aspects as for its appearance when on duty. At that time there remained a few Forces where Sergeants marched their Constables out to their Beats and this could, of course, only be appropriate in the larger stations of the City Forces. Of greater practical importance, although it must have appeared really comical to any onlooker, was the incorporation of traffic point duty training. There were, fortunately, few onlookers with the grounds of the DTC being quite isolated but the prisoners from HMP at Dorchester who were brought in daily to tend the gardens must have had a good laugh at our expense. Small 'squads' of four would march about the roads and we all took turns at manning points at junctions to direct these squads as though they were cars. Although hilariously funny when a wrong signal was given, it was a relatively safe way for the Sergeant Drill Instructor get across the rudiments of this, in those days, important police function.

Although there were regular physical education sessions in the gymnasium, the more interesting sessions were those in which we were taught the more appropriate ways of defending ourselves and making arrests where there was some resistance. The PTI, from the Wiltshire Force, was suitably fit and found little difficulty in dealing with the student he had selected for any particular demonstration. Until, that was, he selected our colleague with the, at least claimed, experience in the Foreign Legion. The attempted demonstration turned into a massive and elongated struggle to which, eventually, the Sergeant had to call a halt. It proved that perhaps the most vital element in these holds was that of surprise.

Each week, a copy of the General Orders of each Force was posted on a notice board in the old house and there was the expectation that all would ensure they were read. In the final couple of weeks this was of some greater personal importance as it was anticipated that the, seemingly long, awaited notices would appear for our first postings. For the City officers, this was of little more than casual interest but for the County officers, especially those with wives and children, where we were to start our police careers was of some significant importance. Although quite a few Forces did post this information, Somersetshire Constabulary did not. We were, therefore, to enter the somewhat more relaxed last week of the course still ignorant as to where we would be going after the, two week, local procedure course back at Canonsgrove.

In that final week at Chantemarle a group of, I thought somewhat unfortunate, trainee nurses were brought in to balance the gender at a dance in the gymnasium. We also went out for an evening, when the two Sergeants each made a short speech to wish us well and let their hair down, just a little. There was a 'passing out' parade, for which it was too cold for anyone to take that title literally, with large loudspeakers reproducing the music of a military band. Some parents and married officers' wives were in attendance to witness the spectacle but, with no available personal transport other than Dad's little motorcycle, there was no representation from my family. With the final interview with the Commandant, there had been only one other in the first week of the course, the final day arrived and we all performed the last LeMans get-away.

Back at Canonsgrove we were not to be in the attic dormitory for the local procedure course but were farmed out to landladies in Taunton. I was still allocated such accommodation and, again, chose not to enquire as to whether it would be more cost effective for me to go home each evening. With such a short journey, my mother suggested that I invite my six colleagues back one evening and, somewhat to my surprise, they all agreed. My sister, then twelve, was quite excited at such a large gathering in our living room and my father made polite conversation while she helped my mother with the teas and snacks they had prepared. The other evenings of that fortnight were spent in one of the local pubs.

In the first week of that short course, we were all paraded in our new uniforms along the corridor outside the Chief Constable's office, a few miles down the road from Canonsgrove. When the signal was given by his secretary, we were marched in single file into the imposing office. For some reason, I was last in the line. When we came to a halt, there were six chairs, one behind each of my colleagues and, at the Chief Constable's invitation they occupied them. The Inspector and two Sergeants had followed in behind us and taken up the three seats at the back of the room. Seeing that the only vacant seat was a wing-backed chair at the end of the large desk, I walked behind my seated colleagues and occupied it.

The Chief spoke generally about what were his expectations of us and then started with the man to his, left telling him where he was to be posted. Five more postings were delivered and the faces of my colleagues told their own story as to how much, or little, they appreciated what had been decided for them. The Chief then swung his head back to me and, with no hint of amusement, commented upon "the one who has taken the Superintendent's chair" and told me that, like the rugby enthusiast officer from Gloucestershire, I was to go to Weston-super-Mare.

That fortnight went quickly enough and closed with the imposing figure of the Assistant Chief Constable entering our classroom, followed by one of the Sergeants. The Sergeant had, under his arm, a copy of a book the size of a family bible with which we had already grown familiar as we had stuck amendments in the copies with which we had been issued. Force Standing Orders was, indeed, a weighty tome and was made even more so by the amendments that appeared, quite regularly, in the weekly General Orders. Some of these amendments would be of only a few words and could be drawn through and amended by pen but others comprised whole new paragraphs and these were pasted in at the appropriate location. Standing Orders was, in fact, a compendium of 'shut stable doors'. Most of the wisdom it contained emanated from some time in the past, perhaps very recent past, where something had not gone as well as the high standards within the Service demanded.

The ACC stood behind a table at the front of the room and the Sergeant, almost ceremonially, placed the Orders on the table in front of him and joined his colleague at the side of the room. In the middle of his speech, evidently designed to minimise, as much as possible, his workload as the disciplinary authority for the Force, he reached the point where Standing Orders came into focus. He stated that these Standing Orders must be known by us all but that they were "for the guidance of wise men and the blind obedience of fools". He went on to explain that the sheer breadth of what a police officer may encounter made entries in Standing Orders for every potential eventuality impossible. He went on to state that we would find ourselves having to make decisions about which Standing Orders either made no mention or did so but the recommended course of action did not fit all of the current circumstances. If we made a decision that was outside Standing Orders that transpired to look wayward, he would be "down on us like a ton of bricks" but if our decision was in good faith, he would "back us to the hilt". Although a firm man and strong disciplinarian, he was, to my knowledge, faithful to those statements.

3   Learning the Ropes

Despite a deliberately slow run along the A370 and an unnecessary detour along Beach Road, I arrived at the front of Weston-super-Mare Police Station over an hour early. The seemingly, to my young eyes, ancient Station Sergeant directed me to the narrow alleyway leading to the car park 'yard' at the rear and told me he would see me at 1400 hours. He also told me where the canteen was located, in a more modern small block on the other side of that back yard. There was no such rank as Station Sergeant at that time, except in the Metropolitan Police, but it was common practice for Sub-Divisional Commanders to identify one, often the oldest, of the Sergeants to fill this role on a day shift during weekdays. This served the twin purposes of relieving the older man from full shift work and, more importantly to the Chief Inspector, ensured a continuity of the administration of 'his' Station.

There was some coming and going between the main, older, building and the two doors in the newer block. One of the doors led to the canteen and the other, so I was soon to learn, to the Road Traffic and CID offices. Although there was obvious lunchtime activity in the canteen, I remained beside the A35 but did not have to do so for long as my colleague, and by now good friend, had also allowed far too much time for his journey around Gloucester. We entered the canteen together at just after one o'clock, to be met by a small group of people, some in uniform and some not, a few of whom were women, only one of whom was in uniform and wearing stripes on her arm. Unlike the canteen in the Headquarters at Taunton, there was no cooking staff and one Constable was busy toasting some bread under the grill of the standard domestic cooker. A lady in an overall welcomed us in and declared that there was a pot of tea that had recently brewed. She was the station cleaner and had a major task in such a large complex of buildings, assisted only with the heavier waste bin emptying by the station handyman and car cleaner. This latter old gentleman focused his attention upon the Hillman Minx, acknowledged by all as the Sub-Divisional

Chief Inspector's car, the few other cars in the station fleet and, most regularly, the Divisional Chief Superintendent's personal Vauxhall Cresta.

Although Weston-super-Mare had been of little importance when the Somersetshire Constabulary had been formed in 1856, its popularity as a seaside resort and a retirement location had expanded it greatly. As a consequence its policing requirements had made it the largest Division outside of the Taunton Headquarters. It was, in 1966, the only one of the five territorial Divisions recognised as warranting a Chief Superintendent as its Divisional Commander. The Headquarters Administration, Traffic Department and CID at Taunton also had Chief Superintendents at their head. The other four Divisions, Taunton, Bridgwater, Yeovil and Frome were all commanded by a Superintendent. All Deputy Divisional Commanders were Chief Inspectors, even at Weston-super-Mare, as were all Sub-Divisional Commanders. The structure of both Divisions and Sub-Divisions reflected population rather than geographic area and some were much larger in territorial terms than others.

With a rather strong cup of tea each, we were welcomed by the various officers and few civilian staff in the canteen. One had evidently heard of my impending arrival and made a point of introducing himself as a much earlier recruit from Wellington. Although we, as did all, were to experience some considerable leg-pulling from the start, we also were made very conscious of being invited to join a large group where camaraderie played an important part. The hour passed quickly and we presented ourselves to the Station Sergeant dead on 1400 hours, having stood outside the station office for several minutes before hand.

We were escorted directly back across the smaller front yard and up the stairs to the Chief Superintendents office for, what proved to be, a very rare meeting with our Divisional Commander. His welcome was brief and we were soon back down the stairs and being told of the 'digs' that had been identified for each of us. My colleague was to be accommodated with a young family that already had another Constable as a lodger. I was allocated to an older lady, who was a widow and with a son just a little older than me, who had never before accommodated a police officer. My friend from Gloucestershire's Tutor Constable was on duty but mine was not. The duty Borough Sergeant took over from the Station Sergeant and declared that he had just the job for the three of us before my friend's tutor would take us to our 'digs'.

The public of Weston-super-Mare were treated to the most unusual sight of three uniformed Constables 'patrolling' from the Police Station, across Alexandra Parade and down to the Hospital. I cannot say why, even after the passage of so many years, but I did not feel anywhere near as self-conscious as I expected as I walked out in the public eye in police uniform for that first time. The near constant wearing of the uniform during the long months of training had, I suppose, made me feel 'natural' with that appearance. We soon reached the General Hospital and went around the side of the main block to a much smaller building at the rear.

Inside the double doors there was a long room with three tiers of square doors along the opposite side from the entrance, recognisable to me from the much larger refrigerator door in the canteen where my father was caretaker. We passed straight through to our right and into a much larger and higher room which contained three large ceramic topped tables. On the one farthest from the door lay the body of an elderly lady beside which stood two men in grey coats and another in a white coat. Our 'combined' Tutor for the afternoon was greeted by the Doctor in the white coat and gave the nod to the other men to start the Post Mortem examination. Other than seeing my old Grandmother lying in state in my aunt's home before her funeral many years earlier, this was only the second dead body I had seen.

I will spare the reader the more gory details but I found the examination quite fascinating, especially when the doctor showed us the heart vessels which had brought about the elderly lady's sudden death. My colleague was not so intrigued and chain-smoked throughout the entire procedure. Back at the station our tutor Constable showed us the forms and how they should be completed for the information of the Coroner. At that time any Constable, usually the first to arrive at a death, became the Coroner's Officer for that case. Quite some time ago this function was taken under the direct control of the local Coroner and this created a few job opportunities for retiring police officers.

The Station Sergeant provided us with the addresses of our respective landladies and was at great pains to ensure that I realised that our joint afternoon had been a one-off. I was to be tutored by a Constable on another shift and would be reporting for their duty time on the next day. We had already been instructed in the fact that all officers were expected to report for duty in advance of a quarter of an hour before the scheduled shift start time. This period was for briefing and in order to ensure that Constables were setting out on the beats as the hour was reached. It had also been made clear that, provided that the 'exigencies of the duty' allowed, a well favoured expression as I was to discover and really meaning 'the job must come first', the mid-shift refreshment period was not to exceed three quarters of an hour.

With my 'digs' on Milton Road and my colleague's in the village of Worle, half a mile farther out from the centre of the town, we followed in our own cars as his tutor lead the way in the station Hillman Husky. We stopped only long enough for him to be sure I knew the correct house and they disappeared along the road. A tall lady came to the door and we introduced ourselves. She showed me to the room she had prepared and identified that she was expecting a weekly payment of £4.10s (£4.50) for my lodging. Through the period of training, with our food and accommodation largely provided, I had discovered that the £1,000 a year policeman, relatively recently shown in banner headlines in the newspapers was one with over 22 years service. My, lunar monthly, 'take-home' pay was £51, so the impending abstraction to my landlady of £18 did not seem too bad.

My landlady explained that her son worked at an off licence in the town and did not get home until just after seven o'clock. She hoped that awaiting tea until after his arrival would be convenient and I had no real concerns when it should appear. It transpired that she was a good cook of basic but wholesome meals. She understood, from the Station Sergeant's earlier visit, that packed meals would be required for my breaks and her most favoured meal of the week turned out to be Sunday tea, when crab was the usual offering. She was particularly understanding of my wish to head back to Wellington at every opportunity and often granted deductions from the amount I paid her when I was away for more than the usual couple of rest days.

The evening was to have been spent sorting out all my gear from the boot into the wardrobe and dressing table in my room but this operation was cut short by my colleague's arrival on the doorstep. His excuse for asking me to go for a drink was that our different shifts may make this difficult in future. Although there was a bar behind the partition in the canteen at the police station we had been made aware that this had not been in use for many years. Instead we headed back into Worle and went to a local pub for a couple of hours. It had to be no longer as I was scheduled to be at the station to meet my own Tutor Constable on early shift and wanted to be there well before 6.45 a.m.

Only a short time before my joining, the allocation of rest days had changed. The average rostered working week had been reduced from 44 hours to 42 but this had, in fact, been accommodated by creating a new rest day (eight hours in each four week cycle) what was referred to as an Additional Rest Day. Instead of taking this day off duty it was rostered for working and we were paid for the extra day. Most officers seemed to think this a good idea as the money was welcome and, with my having only just had my proposal accepted with the plan to marry in eighteen months time, I was glad to have some prospect of saving.

Having set my alarm clock for 4.20 a.m., I arrived at the station and parked the A35 just before 5.30. The night duty Sergeant was busy writing in the small partitioned office at the end of the parade room, beside a similar office shared by the two Inspectors, but not at this time in the morning! I did not disturb his thoughts and sat at the large table in the middle of the room, consciously positioning myself at the end opposite the Sergeants' office door. Within minutes the early turn Sergeant arrived. Not knowing what was expected, I stood as he walked through the room. He said nothing but walked straight through to the office he shared and closed the door to hold a more private conversation with the man he was relieving. Soon after the other members of the shift started arriving, the first of them identifying himself, in a strong Scottish accent, as my tutor Constable for the next fortnight.

I already had my pocket notebook open and had entered the date, drawing a line under what had been recorded on the previous day. Beside it I had my Information Book, a similar sized but ring bound booklet, just right to fit into the breast pocket of my tunic. Our Sergeant came out of their office at dead on 0545 hours with a large clip board and a large lever-arch folder under his arm. Consulting the sheet on his clip board, he started to identify the beats to which he had allocated each of the five Constables seated around the table, most of whom had not been seated long and none of whom had done more than nod to me. He started with my tutor and me and took the briefest opportunity to wish me welcome and identify me to the others. This was a rare occasion upon which he used my name, for we were all most often referred to by our Force number. He had allocated us to Number One beat, the main streets in the middle of Weston-super-Mare. My tutor asked if we could have an hour 'report writing time' in order that we could get my Information Book up to date. The Sergeant instructed that we check the beat first and take an hour 'after tea' for the information book. As the Sergeant was reading the latest information from the lever-arch file, my tutor was updating his information book but told me not to do mine and he showed me how he set out the lighting up and tide times that the Sergeant had announced.

So, dead on six o'clock, the pair of us walked out from the front yard and into the well lit streets of central Weston-super-Mare. As we did so the night shift patrolling Constables were coming in to go off duty, ensuring that they were not back too early as this would incur their Sergeant's wrath. A relatively small beat in size, it contained all the main shops and we shook the door handles of pretty well every one in the following hour. We also went into a number of much darker alleys between shops and I noticed how sparingly my tutor used his torch. When I enquired as to why, he pointed out that our purpose was to try and catch people who were up to no good and the light from a torch was a sure give-away as to our presence. He also explained why the Sergeant had insisted upon our leaving the station before getting my information book up to date. The whole purpose of the quarter of an hour briefing time before the change of shift was to ensure a continuity of patrols and it was not unknown for burglaries to take place at six in the morning, in the hope that all the police officers would be in the station.

That morning, we found no criminals nor any doors or windows insecure. The only people we saw were the butchers and bakers as we patrolled the back alleys behind their shops. I was, not long after, to discover that these were the most likely traders to offer cups of tea but their offers were politely declined by my tutor on this occasion. At seven we and what seemed like most of the others approached through the alley into the rear yard and went to the canteen. The cleaner I had met the day before said, "Good morning David", I was impressed that she had remembered my name. She had brewed fresh tea in the large, rather battered, pot and my tutor had the chance to introduce me, by first name rather than numerals, to the others. They all seemed somewhat more awake after 'airing the streets' and we enjoyed a quarter of an hour of idle chat in which the Sergeant took only a minor part. He did redirect two of the men to whom he had allocated the more outer beats to patrol in the Hillman Husky and go out to Sand Bay to check the pubs and holiday camp. He had been made aware that the Constable scheduled for the eight o'clock start on the Bourneville Section, the area around the outskirts of the town and surrounding villages, had an urgent court file to prepare. He spoke to my tutor and told him that he had better take me around the offices to meet the Officers and staff, "When they get up".

The lever-arch file had been left on the parade room table and I started transcribing the items my tutor directed into the four sections of my information book. Part One was for serious criminal circulations and 'all ports warnings', although the only ports in the Division were at the extreme ends of Portishead and Burnham on Sea, these circulations related to the more serious criminals and had to be included. Part Two was for stolen vehicles and a fresh list was prepared from the Police Gazette (known to all as 'PGs') and South West Criminal Records Office sheets (known as SWerCROs) at the latter end of the night shift. Part Three was for suspect vehicles, those believed to be used by criminals and Part Four a general section for everything else, such as people reported missing. My book fully updated, and we having been joined by a police woman and a dog handler, each starting their eight to four shift and briefing themselves from the files, we set off to meet some of the others I had seen moving through the front yard and arriving from their cars in the back yard.

Soon I had been introduced to the three typists, one for the Borough, one for the Divisional Administration Department and one for the CID. There were few others about the station except the Traffic Sergeant and a couple of Constables reporting on duty and a couple of CID officers. The Borough typist also acted as, ex-officio, secretary for the Chief Inspector Sub-Divisional Commander. He had not been available the previous afternoon and she told us that he would see me at 10 a.m. We were allocated refreshments at 0915 hours, so I had eaten the sandwiches my landlady had prepared the previous evening before knocking on the Chief Inspector's door. Within a quarter of an hour I was back through his door, feeling somewhat chided. With no word of welcome, I had been warned as to what his approach would be should I err.

During our short patrol before the seven o'clock cup of tea, my tutor had tried to inculcate into me the procedure for keeping conference points. With these being set at hourly intervals during daytime shifts, we had not been allocated one but he pointed out a couple of the telephone kiosks used for this purpose. At briefings the Sergeants announced these locations and the timings and his expectation was that, should he choose to pay a visit, the Constable would be waiting at that kiosk at the given time. There was, in the Sergeants' office and the station office, a list of the numbers for these kiosks and, if necessary, the telephone would be used to update or direct the Constable. There was a double reason for these conference points. Not only did they provide a means for the Sergeant to ensure that the bulk of the beat was patrolled but also they were an hourly, at night half-hourly, provision to ensure that the Constable was safe.

Although we had no point in that hour before breakfast, my tutor introduced me to the peculiar system at Weston-super-Mare, which, as I mentioned earlier, must have been one of the last local telephone areas to go on to subscriber trunk dialling. Instead of, as was common elsewhere, dialling 999 for the emergency services, the kiosk had a prominently marked button just like those then common on buses and right in the middle of the notices above the telephone and coin box. Pressing this button had the same affect as would elsewhere the dialling of 999 and the operator would make the customary initial enquiry of "Emergency - which Service please". By a local and long-standing agreement, we used this facility to contact the station switchboard and my tutor demonstrated the facility for me. When the operator came on the line, the words "request a police flash call, please" were used after announcing your Force 'collar' number.

By mid-day, I had received my conducted tour and hoped, with very little confidence, that I would remember all the names with which I had been bombarded. We reported to the Sergeant and he agreed with my tutor that we should have the use of the Husky for him to show me the wider geography of the Sub-Division. After a quick cup of tea in the canteen and he already having taken possession of the Husky keys from the peg in the Sergants' office, we went to the car, which was always when not in use reversed against the wall in the front yard. He retained the keys and I was a bit disappointed that I was not going to be allowed to drive. He told me to 'book on' with the Information Room at Taunton but, when I looked a little concerned, he accepted that perhaps he should demonstrate the procedure for me. It was as well that he did, for I would have got it entirely wrong. During my teens, at school, I had ended up in the Signals Section and the procedure adopted by the police was nothing like the Army procedure I knew.

After waiting for a break in the transmissions he pressed the switch incorporated into the telephone-type handset. "QH99 - over", the female voice from the Information Room (in Taunton HQ) responded instantly, "QH99 - go ahead - over". "Mobile PCs 139 and 247 - patrol of Weston-super-Mare Sub-Division - QH99 - over". The female voice responded, "QH99 - all noted - out".

In the couple of hours left for my first full tour of duty, I received a 'whistle-stop' tour of the outer parts of the town and my tutor took special care to point out the beat boundaries and the telephone kiosks at which I would be expected to stand for my conference points. How little of this I was able to absorb would be demonstrated more than once over the remainder of my fortnight working alongside him but he proved to be a patient and conscientious guide.

Whether it was because he had misplaced his issue flat cap or simply through choice, I never discovered, but it was fortunate that the roofline of the Husky was unusually high and that this was added to by the sagging of the well-worn seats. I felt more conspicuous seated in the old Husky with my helmet on than I had when in the more open view of the public while on foot. At that time, and for many years to follow, the idea that a police officer would not wear either helmet or cap was beyond countenance by any rank of more senior officer. The Sergeants at Canonsgrove and Chantemarle had been equally enthusiastic regarding the correct wearing of our uniforms. Being properly and uniformly dressed was for much of my years in service considered an important part of the image expected by both fellow officers and the public.

The truncheon pocket was adjacent to the right hand normal pocket of the trousers and it was Somerset practice for the strap to be concealed in that pocket, along with the small pouch containing a 'field dressing' and triangular bandage. The whistle, mine still had 'ARP' engraved on it from its World War II first issue, was carried alongside the information book in the left breast pocket of the tunic and the chain passed through the nearest button hole, being hooked around the shank of the button. But, the visible part of the chain had to be as short as possible and the remainder hanging inside the tunic. The reasoning, here, was that the chain could not be grasped by anyone in any confrontational situation. Tunics were worn at all times unless the Divisional Commander gave permission for 'shirt-sleeve order'. This was no concern in that cold month of February but was often to be so later in the year. When shirt-sleeves were allowed, the sleeves had to be rolled up and I still find it looks odd to see Officers wearing shirt sleeves down to their wrists. It would be some considerable time before the open-neck became acceptable and this was only enabled by the, thankful, abandoning of the detached collars with those uncomfortable collar studs.

That, first day, run in the Husky was to prove to be a rare opportunity and the entire remainder of our time together was spent on foot patrol. Although it was evidently common practice, he did nothing to educate me as to where I could find cups of tea during our patrols. When, after a few days, I enquired why we did not seem to be finding these 'tea stops' he pointed out that finding them for myself would be a good way for me to practice making contact with the public. I, later, realised that, while this was a valid point, there was another reason. The 'sharing' of tea stops with colleagues was somewhat an abuse of the hospitality being offered and there were some Constables who would overstay their welcome. There seemed, in 1966, to be a ready willingness for members of the public, particularly small tradespeople, to invite patrolling Officers in for cups of tea but some Constables did abuse the welcome.

Starting with him on the Tuesday on early tour, we only had the following two days, Wednesday and Thursday, before it was his Section's 'long weekend'. The shift system was quite easy to assimilate, being spread over an eight week period but the rest days only over four weeks. Effectively the first lunar month was spent on the straight, night, late and early shifts (eight hours each starting from 0600 daily), while the other four weeks brought six (1800) till two (0200) lates, ten till six days and eight to four days. The two Sergeants on each Section arranged their shifts between themselves within that roster but the Constables were seldom allowed to exchange their duties unless there was some pressing reason and only then with a Sergeant's approval.

The full benefit of the longer of the two weekends, from two o'clock on Thursday till ten o'clock (actually 2145 hours) on Monday was lost to me, thanks to my newly acquired ability only to be able to swim. The expectation that the Royal Life Saving Society's Bronze Medallion must be gained before the completion of the two-year probationary period had expired was strong enough that attending the Divisional training on a Friday was a must. I, therefore, could not head home to Wellington that Thursday afternoon but had to wait until after the swimming training on the Friday. That this Friday was one of my precious Rest Days was of no significance to anyone other than me.

With the hour and a half session in the Knightstone Baths over, Friday teatime brought me back into Wellington in the A35. My mother, father and sister wanted to know what I had been doing and I was a willing informant over tea. Then off to collect the girlfriend with whom I had exchanged so many letters over the past four months and a rare return visit to the coffee bar we had helped to create at the youth club. Again, everyone wanted to know what I had been up to and I do not think that I gilded any lilies in the telling.

Soon, it seemed, I was back on the A38 and A370 to my lodgings. Never, before, having stayed up beyond midnight other than at New Year, I was unsure how I would accommodate working right through the night. As a precaution, I went to bed for a few hours that Monday afternoon to be sure I was prepared. With my sister at school, girlfriend and other members of the family at work, I began a routine of leaving around lunchtime on Mondays after my weekends at home and managed a few hours sleep before the start of my night shift weeks. This would change later, when our first child was born, as I had become accustomed to odd hours and a small child in the house is not conducive to sleeping in the afternoon.

I discovered, and it remained the case throughout the years I worked the full shift rotation, that I probably enjoyed night shifts better than any others. At that time, notwithstanding it was the middle of the, so called, rebellious 1960s, all licensed premises were closed well before eleven except on Saturday's when an extra half an hour was allowed by the Weston-super-Mare Bruster Sessions through the Summer Season. By midnight the streets were virtually deserted and anyone walking or driving their car was viewed with some suspicion, a Constable's trait not long in the acquisition.

Although it was mid-February, we were allocated to a sea front patrol on one of those seven, consecutive, night tours. It surprised me to discover that there were actually people resorting to the sea front shelters and I was introduced to the arrest procedure for the first time through this patrol. The normal practice of patrolling alone, at all times, made checking up on anyone suspicious difficult. With two of us it was easier for one of us to stay with the 'suspect' while the other walked to the nearest telephone kiosk to contact the Station. On one such occasion, our dishevelled sleeper was found to be wanted on a warrant from a court in the Midlands and the Sergeant arrived in the Husky to take him in. The Sergeant did not lose the opportunity to educate me in the, quite brief by later standards, recording procedure and I had the opportunity to get my evidence, such as it was, into my pocket book. Contact with the station that had circulated our man as wanted brought the promise of an escort to fetch him later that morning.

Also in that week, right at the start of a shift, the Sergeant sent us out to a road accident on Alexandra Parade. A driver had moved out over the 'Give Way' markings and collided with a taxi coming, uncharacteristically slowly, along the major road. The opportunity had arisen for me to deal with my first road traffic accident and to complete all the required paperwork for the recording of the accident and the potential prosecution of the errant driver. It was an unfortunate coming together for our driver as his elderly car turned out not to have a current tax disc (known officially as a Vehicle Excise Licence and by the police as a 'V.E.L.'), insurance or MoT certificate. Quite a small compendium of various types of report for me to complete for the first of countless times.

Although it was made plain from the start that I would only be with this Section for my tutorship period, it was the time in which I became inculcated in the many police terms and practices. Much as I had expected but perhaps even more so, the camaraderie within the police station and out on patrol was second to none. There was much, mostly good humoured, leg-pulling and it soon became apparent that some officers were 'rated' by their peers more highly than were some others. Being 'rated' as a 'good copper' by fellow Constables and immediate supervisors was important to self-image but the rating systems were not necessarily the same. Constables saw the practical 'coppering' aspects as the most important, essentially how reliable was the individual out on the streets. Supervisors looked, largely, for the same qualities but had the additional requirement that the individual did not bring them any 'grief' by their attitude and approach. Being industrious, especially 'thief taking' (being good at catching criminals) was recognised with approval by all fellow officers but being both confident and modest at the same time was important to remaining one of the team. Supervisors at all levels also highly approved of good crime detection rates but they also had the requirement that no corners were being cut and that the paperwork was completed to their satisfaction.

One of the favourite leg-pulls for new probationary Constables was encountered during the checking of sea-front shelters during night shifts. There was one, almost fully enclosed, shelter on the seaward end of Knightstone Island, really a small promontory to the north of the beach. Just as they had checked many other shelters, probationary Constables would be encouraged to visit this one alone. Upon entering the shelter they would be met with a tirade of abuse by the regular occupant. This woman, well into middle age, was the town's regular 'bag lady'. She was to be pitied, as she either could not or would not live in any of the several properties she was said to own. Instead, she walked the streets by day and slept in this shelter by night. No one else would take precedence in 'her' shelter as she would aggressively chase others out. Each month she would, with all her portable possessions in numerous bags, take the train to Bristol to visit a firm of solicitors and collect the rent from her properties.

There was only one regularly manned traffic point in Weston-super-Mare at that time, although there were numerous such locations when the Bank Holiday traffic flows had to be controlled. This 'centre point' was at a five road junction where Regent Street, the main road down to the pier, met the old and new High Streets. It was made into a forerunner of the mini-roundabout concept, later to become prolific, and this was signified by a round platform about a foot high. When the Sergeant felt he had enough Constables, one would be allocated to the 'centre point' during the morning period as the shop workers were coming into town and at other times when there was sufficient holidaymaker traffic to warrant it. The task only fell to the younger and probationary Constables. The only excuse beyond a crime in progress that any Sergeant would accept for abandoning this point was the approach of our 'bag lady'. Just as she would scare any young Constable out of her shelter, so too would she heap abuse upon any Constable directing traffic at this point. Why she had this aversion no one knew, for she did not seek to shout at Constables while on normal patrol. But, the Sergeants recognised the validity of avoiding the spectacle of a young Constable being abused in such a public fashion.

Patrolling the streets at night, my tutor showed me all the small back alleys and means of rear access for the many shops and offices. The newer development at the Boulevard end of the High Street had flat roofs and provided a vantage point from which much of the area could be viewed without a Constable being too visible. The physical checking of all property on the given beat was considered a central task at all times when it was dark, even on the first part of winter early shifts. Although it only happened to me once and more than two years later, any report of a burglary by a proprietor arriving at his or her shop or office and that had not been reported by the patrolling Constable would result in him being raised from his bed to give account. There would be no question of any financial compensation for this temporary recall to duty!

Until 1972 overtime was only paid, outside the Metropolitan Police, when the Chief Constable had declared a 'special occasion' or the duty was being paid for by some other agency. These 'special occasions' at Weston-super-Mare were limited to the Bank Holiday weekends at Easter, Whitsun and in August. The 'special duty' occasions were very limited and usually involved stopping vehicles at Ministry checks or attendances at Wincanton or Taunton Race meetings. Normal overtime was calculated at time and one quarter and Bank Holidays at time and a half. This was recorded on a buff card and the entries initialled by a Sergeant. As the time on the card accumulated it was available to take as time off but only if the Sergeant considered that he could spare the Constable being absent. In practice Constables all accrued quite large amounts of outstanding 'time on the card' and it was often not possible to get time off when it would really most suit the Constable. The special arrangement for Bank Holiday weekends is worth a mention. All Officers would work a twelve hour shift on both the Sunday and Monday. Four hours on the Sunday would be overtime at 1 ¼ and on the Monday the whole shift would be overtime at 1 ½. Hence a total equivalent to twenty three hours normal hours in overtime would accrue, of which eight hours would be paid at the standard rate, leaving fifteen hours to be taken in time off. Although only eight hours pay was added to the monthly salary it was a welcome addition to a far from considerable income.

After the Sunday night, at the end of my second week with my tutor, I was to move to my own allocated Section within the Borough. They were on late shift and I had met the two Sergeants and most of the Constables on the shift changeovers before my time to start working with them. Having started the week of night duties with my tutor on the previous Monday, they would be starting their rest days after the Sunday night shift. With my change to the other Section, I had to wait until the Wednesday before a day off. It also meant that I experienced the first of what would become many 'quick changeovers' by ending one shift at 0600 hours on Monday morning and being back on duty at 1345 hours that day. With my tutor's help, I had packed quite a lot of the basics of police patrol work into those couple of weeks and was looking forward to being out on my own.

4 Going It Alone

The two Sergeants on my 'own' Section were very different in both appearance and personality but seemed to compliment each other well. One, the elder of the two, had been in the Royal Navy during World War II and had served as a Constable in several places for eighteen years before he was promoted. He was a chain smoker, frequently lighting his next cigarette from the stub of the last and spent most of his time with the cigarette in his mouth, even when talking. The consequence was a well filled uniform that showed the tell-tale traces of ash, which he seemed to spend an inordinate amount of time flicking from his tunic. The other had reached the rank in the dizzy haste of just under ten years as a Constable and he was tall and slim and, for that time rare, a non-smoker. With a year longer in the rank and at least ten years ahead in age, the ex-sailor was, without doubt, the 'senior' man.

For the time, both of these Sergeants had a relatively 'laid-back' approach to supervision. They were demanding but not, like so many, focused upon making life for their subordinates as intolerable as possible. The Section had ten Constables and I found that I was privileged to be joining an extremely contented and industrious team. With very little ceremony, I was introduced at the first briefing but, then, immediately expected to blend in and do my fair share of whatever was required. Thus, on that first afternoon, I was allocated Number One beat, the centre of the town. Although the latter part of winter and traffic likely to be light, I was instructed to man the Centre Point from 1630 hours for one hour and to take my refreshment break at 1800. This was, I think, a ploy on the Sergeants' behalf to enable one of them to come out and ensure that I was capable of performing the task.

I had been equipped with two raincoats and an overcoat but, as it was dry and looked like staying that way, I had written 'fine & dry' in my pocket book at briefing and decided that the overcoat was best to keep out the cold breeze. As I walked through the front yard and made my way out onto Walliscote Road, I, for one of a very few times, felt a little self conscious. It was not that I was appearing before the public in uniform, I had done that with my tutor, it was the realisation that, now, whatever came my way it was down to me, alone, to be up to the task. The four months at Canonsgrove and Chantemarle were recent memories and I hoped that the mass of information I had consumed would stand me in good stead but knew that the first real test was yet to be experienced.

With a point at the Winter Gardens telephone kiosk at 1500 hours, I started by meeting the public 'head on' with a short patrol up Oxford Street, through New High Street, across the Centre Point junction and along the main High Street. The initial impact was good. Many of those I passed, at the carefully rehearsed and unhurried pace my tutor had adopted, wished me 'Good Afternoon' and I soon realised that everyone I had encountered before I reached my conference point, via the well kept Winter Gardens, actually wanted to see me on patrol. Well, not me, but the well recognised uniformed police presence.

As I emerged from the side of the Winter Gardens and made my way to the telephone kiosk near the front door of the building, I congratulated myself on the choice of the overcoat. The breeze I had experienced since leaving the Station was both stronger and appeared much colder here, with its uninterrupted blast across the miles of open water of the Bristol Channel. Not to be caught out on my first solo patrol, I reached the kiosk at 1455 and stood beside it. There were a few cars and vans travelling along the sea-front road but no sign of any pedestrians, it was far too cold for a casual stroll on this afternoon. Just in case one of the Sergeants should decide to appear, I resisted the temptation to enter the kiosk to get out of the wind. I also took the risk of getting my hands cold as I ensured that my patrol, thus far, was recorded in my pocket book. Although I had expected to stand there uninterrupted for the required ten minutes, at dead on 1500 the telephone inside the kiosk rang. Was this to be my first challenging assignment?

"Hello, young'un. Lost yer tongue?" It was the senior Sergeant's voice and I imagined the cigarette ash dropping into the mouthpiece of his telephone handset.

"Sorry, Sergeant - P.C. 247!" Had I failed at the first hurdle?

"That's better, could have been speaking to anyone who happened to be passing." He was evidently not aware how cold it was on the sea-front that afternoon. "Nothing for you, now, just thought I had better make sure you found your way there!"

"Yes, thank you, Sergeant." I thought of remarking on the cold wind but decided against it.

"Don't forget your point after, at the Post Office." My second conference point had been allocated as one of the three telephone kiosks outside the main post office.

"No, Sergeant." The conversation was brought to an abrupt halt as he returned his handset to its cradle.

I continued along the windswept front to the Grand Pier, crossing to the Promenade so that I could see that there was no-one on the beach. The large gates at the front of the pier were shut but the small gate at the side of them was open. As I walked across the front of the large gates a small man appeared in a doorway just inside the small gate and gestured by lifting his hand to his mouth as though holding an invisible cup. With another three quarters of an hour to my next conference point and feeling the bite of the wind despite my heavy overcoat, I was glad to accept the unspoken offer. His little area behind the ticket office was warm, almost enough to make breathing difficult, and his cup of tea was, evidently, poured from a pot that had been brewing for some time. Suffering the occupational hazard of a dislike for strong tea - everyone assumed policemen liked their tea very strong - I sipped the cup slowly and took on board all of its warming qualities.

I thought that ten minutes was enough of a risk that one of the Sergeants may be out patrolling and expecting to be able to find me but my host was pleased with the company, any company, and would have engaged in conversation all afternoon. Taking my leave with much thanks, I had my back to the wind as I made my way down the, virtually deserted, Regent Street and away from the sea-front. Half way along, I turned into the side alley used by some shops as their unloading area and met a few of the assistants wheeling in the contents of a small pantechnicon. Soon I was back in the old High Street and, here, the usual bustle of shoppers moving quickly from the warmth of one shop to that of another, hiding from the cold air.

After so many had simply passed the time of day, an elderly lady came up to me with a much more urgent expression and I knew, before she reached me, that she had something important to impart. "Officer!" she had a slight tremor in her voice which I could not determine between her age and her current state of apparent alarm. I had not been called 'Officer' before! "Yes, Madam," I made strenuous effort to ensure I appeared completely composed, "How can I help you?" "There's a disgusting man in the side of that shop window, Officer" she grew more agitated as she said the few words, "Please do something!"

My elderly 'informant' had, at once, demonstrated her trust that 'the policeman' would take action and that she was content that whatever action he would take would be appropriate. She had no knowledge, not even any concern, regarding what offences the man may, or may not, be committing or whether any aspect of the Law could be invoked. She had been offended, when she went to the side window of a shop that had created greater display area by virtue of a small alley off the main street. Fortunately, for my informant disappeared as soon as she was sure I was taking action, the man was still performing the activity that had offended her when I reached the corner of the shop window. At the inner end of the small alley, he was supporting himself against the brick wall opposite the display window with his back towards me and there was a growing line of urine creeping from between his boots.

I resisted, successfully, saying 'What's going on here, then?' but needed to ensure an initial air of authority. Instead, assuming the deepest voice I could call up from my, quite young, presence in the Congregational Church choir back in Wellington, I said, "What do you think you're doing? Immediately, I realised it was a somewhat redundant question, but it sufficed. He turned towards me, more in the way of rolling along the brick wall, hastily buttoning his flies and folding his ex-army greatcoat across the front of his several layers of holed pullovers. In the process, he dropped the bottle he was holding and its mauve contents were lost beside the stream of urine. Still near the opening of the alley, I could smell the metholated spirits and a complex mixture of other odours. "I think you had better come with me, don't you?" I, then, remembered that this was, in fact, the execution of my power of arrest and that the Judges Rules 'caution' was required. I quoted the caution to a totally unreceptive pair of ears reflected by a scarcely perceptive pair of very blurred eyes.

I further complied with the Judges Rules by informing him of the reason for his arrest. He, probably, recognised the word 'drunk' but, equally probably, lost the 'and disorderly', said nothing but shuffled towards me. Although no taller than my 5 feet 8 ½ inches, he was quite a few pounds heavier than my 10 ½ stones but I followed the instruction in the 'practicals' at Chantemarle and I held him by the upper arm. The theory was that taking hold of the person being arrested signified their detained status. On this occasion, I was pleased that my black leather gloves meant that I did not actually have to touch that disgustingly dirty coat.

So, alright, I had made my first arrest - now what? We appeared, together, on the pavement in full view of the small crowd that had gathered to witness the event, a crowd that did not include my elderly lady, and I had to make a decision. Should I seek the assistance of one of the shopkeepers to call for a car to transport us or should I walk my prisoner back to the Station. In retrospect perhaps the former would have been better but I chose the latter. With much support and to the accompaniment of much, but totally incoherent, mumbling, I walked him along the High Street and across the car park behind New High Street to the front door of the Police Station.

The Station Sergeant looked across the counter and gestured for me to take my prisoner straight into the cell corridor. There, assisted by the, to me elderly, Station Constable, 'my man' was placed in the 'drunks' cell, the one with a board bed that was only an inch or two above floor level. My senior colleague's assistance was more verbal than physical and he ensured that it was me who removed the prisoner's outer clothing and boots, leaving them in a pile outside the cell door. When I returned to the front office the Sergeant was already making out the detention sheet and the few papers I had found in the man's pockets were rendered redundant by the Sergeant having already written down the man's full name. "Better go and make your book up, 247!" was all the Sergeant was inclined to say.

Across in the briefing room, my chain-smoking Sergeant was standing in his office door as I entered the larger room. "Made your first arrest, then, young'un." He grinned with the half cigarette tilting upward at the corner of his mouth. "Some will do anything to get out of doing Centre Point!" The grin was still there so I did not consider myself being chastised. "Make sure you get your book right and let me see it." I sat alone at the large table and wrote in my pocket book all that had happened. As I was doing so I was conscious that the door of the other small office at the end of the parade room had opened. I looked up and saw the stockier of the two Borough Inspectors, a fellow countryman of my Glaswegian prisoner, standing in his office doorway. I immediately stood up but he gestured for me to sit down again. "So you've arrested Campbell Stuart?"

"Yes, Sir." "And on you'se own." "Yes, Sir" "Well, 247, there's obviously a bit more about you than meets the eye." He, too, grinned and returned to his desk, closing his office door behind him.

His comment was somewhat lost on me until after I had made the obligatory telephone call to the South West Criminal Records Office in Bristol, had my pocket book checked by my Sergeant and returned to the Station Office to collect the teleprinter pages from SWCRO. My prisoner warranted two of the perforated pages from the teleprinter roll and almost all of his many arrests for being drunk and disorderly included the additional charge of assault on police. Why he had chosen to 'come quietly' for me I will never know but his doing so had done no harm for my early credibility with the supervisory officers on that day.

My refreshment break was drawn forward by half an hour and I was back on number one beat for the rest of the evening. The Sergeant instructed me to appear at the Magistrates Court with my prisoner the following morning and to report to him when he returned to duty for the two-to-ten shift that Tuesday afternoon. He ensured that I was aware what I would require to give as my evidence and showed me the papers that I would need with me. Having just returned to that shift with the minimum eight hours since my last night shift with my tutor, I was now departing at ten in the evening to return for ten the following morning. My anticipation was that I would be in court for the morning and then expected to work my whole two-to-ten shift. Certainly different from the nine-to-five existence I had left a few months earlier.

The Station Sergeant repeated my Section Sergeant's briefing when I appeared before him at nine thirty on the Tuesday morning. They, evidently, wanted to ensure that I did not let the side down in front of the Magistrates. My prisoner was the only one who had been detained overnight in the cells and looked only slightly less disgusting after his night's sleep and a wash supervised by the Station Constable. The old hand accompanied us up the stairs to the Court, although the prisoner was still showing no sign of his previous predilection for assaulting police officers. In court I sat with him in the 'box' while those appearing in responses to summonses gathered on the benches beside it. These errant members of the public had all made some effort to ensure their appearance was clean and tidy and made my prisoner look even more dishevelled.

My prisoner had declined the offer of the assistance of a 'duty solicitor' and pleaded guilty to the charge but my supervisors had seen to it that the Magistrates would hear my evidence. The Magistrates showed an open tolerance to this slight waste of their time, appreciating the importance for me that I should 'cut my teeth' with such an easy first appearance before them. After they had heard me and enquired as to whether my prisoner had anything to say, to which he simply said, "No!" The Chairman of the Bench sentenced him to a fine of £5.00 and looked at me, enquired, "Has he any means." Thanks to my double briefing, I recognised the meaning of the enquiry and identified that he had in his possession at the time of the arrest the sum of two shillings and three pence. The Chairman returned his gaze to the prisoner, changing his expression to the most severe he could manage, and said, "Unable to pay, one month in default." The prisoner, evidently totally familiar with the situation, said nothing.

By eleven o'clock, I had been briefed again by the Station Sergeant and was exercising my police vehicle authorisation to drive the Hillman Husky to Horfield Prison in Bristol. The Station Constable welcomed the excursion as escort for my prisoner and had made it plain that he did not want to drive. Driving with one hand and holding the radio handset in the other, I told the Information Room at Taunton of our mission and they volunteered that they would inform the Bristol Constabulary of our reason for being in their territory. Before we reached the outskirts of Worle, both the escort and the prisoner were asleep and I followed the directions I had received to reach the gates of the prison. My passengers were awake as soon as I pulled up outside those imposing gates and I left them while I spoke to one of the warders through the small hatch in the door inset into the larger double entrances.

The large doors were swung slowly open and it was evident that they were of considerable weight from the effort required. I had returned to the driver's seat before the gates were fully open and drove into the area between them and the iron grill gates beyond. The slow process was reversed and the huge solid doors shut behind us before the grills were swung open for us to continue on into the area beside the reception block. For the first of many times, I was to experience the weird sense, similar to what I imagine to be claustrophobia, as we delivered our prisoner into the safe keeping of Her Majesty's Prison Service. Thankfully in short time we were out through the security bay and back on our way to Weston-super-Mare. However many times I found myself in this and other prisons I never got used to the feeling akin to isolation they invoked in me.

We arrived in the front yard at our home station just as the, chain smoking, Sergeant for my Section was reporting for duty and checking through the Information files to ready himself for the late tour briefing. Apparently confirming my expectation of a long shift, some cigarette ash was dropped during my instruction to take my "First Refs." In shorter time than permitted, wanting to show some enthusiasm, I was back in front of the Sergeant not long after the rest of the Constables on the Section had set off for their allocated duties. "You can have a rest now, 247!" What did this mean? "We've got a full crew, so do number three beat this afternoon and you can go off duty at 1800." "Thank you Sergeant."

As I was donning my overcoat, I took a quick look at the map that my tutor had obtained and upon which he had crayoned the beat boundaries. Beat three was a large area to the south of the Station and the Sergeant had been generous in allocating conference points in Drove Road and at the Sanatorium. I set off at about half past two on a now bright but still cold Tuesday afternoon. The old houses along the first part of my near deserted route gave little distraction to my reflections on a busy first twenty four hours as a 'solo' policeman. Much more prominent in my thoughts was the prospect of being able to get away back to Wellington at six o'clock, instead of arriving home at nearly midnight. With only the long weekend since I had arrived at Weston-super-Mare and our communication being through the constant exchange of letters, it would be good to surprise Gill by getting home before she was asleep.

Things changed as I approached the small row of shops in Sunnyside Road, with mums and their prams and pushchairs interspersed with more elderly residents, and Weston had more than its fair share of them, out shopping. One of the older hands had pointed out to me the 'right' way to patrol, my tutor had followed the practice but not spoken of it. In daylight it was seen as sensible to patrol near the kerb, where everyone, motorists and pedestrians, could see the uniform. When it was dark the favoured system was to patrol close to the building line. This was virtually demanded by the practice of trying door handles on all commercial properties but also enabled an officer to see what was going on without being too conspicuous. A useful situation should anyone be considering some anti-social (although that phrase was then unknown) behaviour.

As I walked, at the regulated slow pace which was considered appropriate,

I saw ahead of me an elderly gentleman who was approaching along my same track. Well before I reached him, I deviated slightly to afford him 'right of way' but he, too, deviated so that he was still likely to confront me. A second deviation on my part was, similarly, met with him resuming my same line of travel. Throughout this short time he had been looking straight at me and just before we were in danger of colliding, he stopped and wished me a good afternoon. In the conversation that followed, one which he evidently intended to have, he quickly acquainted me with the fact that he had been in the police. As the conversation progressed, I discovered that he had been the last Chief Officer of the Tiverton Borough Police, with the rank of Chief Inspector. Intrigued, but not wishing to show my ignorance at the time, I later discovered that the Borough Force had been combined with the Devon Force in 1943. The old gentleman had served as its Chief Officer from 1925 until its closure.

Having, dutifully, made my conference points at the telephone kiosks in Drove Road and at the Sanatorium, the last leg of my patrol was naturally along the Beach Road. The afternoon passed quickly, with just a few instances of conversations with motorists about minor infringements noted in my pocket book. The small group that comprised the other half of my Section were just completing their briefing by the other Sergeant as I walked into the Parade Room. The two-till-ten Sergeant took a quick look through my pocket book and ensured that it was several minutes after six o'clock before he allowed me to depart. With my tunic substituted by my sports jacket and all my other required items in the little boot, I set off in the A35 back to Wellington. With very little traffic, even on the A38 trunk road, it was well before seven thirty when I arrived at Gill's mother's house and we enjoyed an unexpected couple of hours together. My parents were surprised to see me arrive just after ten, thinking that I would not be leaving Weston-super-Mare until that time.

The full day off on the Wednesday gave me the chance to meet my sister from school in the car and to do likewise for Gill when she finished work. Thursday was slightly different as I had to make my way back to Weston to get to bed at a sensible time before the week of early shifts was to start on the Friday morning. During that week and somewhat unexpectedly, I walked into the end of Locking Road from Alexandra Parade to encounter an interesting, even amusing, display. Only yards from me, a young man was struggling with a Vespa motor scooter. I stopped, as did a few other people, to watch him attempting to mount and start the machine. It quickly became evident, although it was only lunch-time, that this young man was considerably the worse for having consumed some significant quantity of alcohol.

Several times he, and the machine, fell to one side onto the pavement. Anticipating, correctly, that his next fall may be in the opposite direction, I stopped the traffic and went over to him. He abusively identified that he did not want my interference and again tried to mount and start the motor scooter. I told him that he was being arrested for being drunk in charge of a motor vehicle and sat him on the pavement while I placed the machine on its stand. This time the decision as to what to do next had been taken out of my hands and the Hillman Husky pulled up behind me as the traffic restarted its flow. The Sergeant stood with the door open and passenger seat folded forward while I pushed our unwilling and unable scooter rider into the back seat. There was a garage only a short way along Locking Road and the Sergeant made arrangements for them to hold the Vespa pending our dealing with the young man.

The duty Police Surgeon, a local GP who received a retainer to act as such, attended and went through a number of checks to identify whether that the young man was drunk. He certainly was unable to perform most of the simple tasks, such as walking in a straight line and touching the end of his nose without difficulty. Later, in the Magistrates Court, it was brought home to me just how important the Road Safety Act, then nearing finalisation in the Houses of Parliament, would become. This young man could scarcely stand up and only did so because he had the scooter upon which he could lean. His whole demeanour would have made it quite easy to prove a conviction for being drunk and incapable but not to secure his conviction for being drunk in charge of his motor vehicle. While the test of opinion for being drunk and incapable (sometimes called 'simple drunk') rested with the Constable that for drunk in charge of a motor vehicle required a qualified Doctor's expert opinion. Even with that expert evidence, and in my only case of its type, a conviction was unlikely.

The general acceptance, even within the police service, the Magistracy and the legal profession, of drinking and driving did not alter with the Road Safety Act. I was to have personal experience of the difficulties conjured out of the air by the legal profession during the early years of the 'breathalyser'. All manner of 'wrinkles' were devised in order to evade conviction no matter how obvious it was that the driver was guilty of this offence. The saddest cases, of course, were those when other road users had been injured or killed by the actions of the driver who escaped conviction. Although the target of much criticism the police service came out of this period with integrity intact while the legal profession came out of it with a tarnish that would last forever in some wrecked lives. Later, but too much later, drinking and driving would become widely socially unacceptable. One day, perhaps, speeding will follow suit - until then the ridiculous arguments regarding the roadside cameras will persist.

It was not long before the Easter Bank Holidays arrived. There was no special arrangement for the Good Friday and this was proven appropriate as it was a quiet day. Easter Sunday and Monday were, however, different. We were all working a twelve hour day of some sort, starting variously at 0600, 0800, 1000, 1400 and 1800. With Weston having grown for over a century in popularity as a day-out destination for many Bristolians and a large number from the Midlands, the town became flooded on Bank Holiday weekends. Officers were sent from all other Divisions except Bridgwater, which had somewhat lesser (in those days) resorts of it own. The strategic potential bottlenecks for traffic from both north and south were all covered permanently through the day, with much arm waving. I found that this was the job for the younger officers like me and, after that first Easter Sunday, my arms felt like they reached my knees. In compensation, I had both lower tunic pockets full of boiled sweets, as almost every coach driver held one out as he drove past.

The sea front was heavily policed following some years of experiencing large groups of youths gathering. In the mid-1960s, these were the 'Mods' and 'Rockers', who seemed bent upon mutual destruction. The mods rode motor scooters, often laden with many mirrors and auxiliary lights, and dressed in long 'parka' jackets. The rockers rode motorcycles, usually of a somewhat larger engine capacity, and wore leather jackets. For both groups, until some years later, helmets were optional. The police had a duty to prevent the types of breach of the peace that their confrontations created but the real concern was the safety of the older people and family groups wanting to enjoy their day by the seaside. Whatever duty performed, these long days passed quickly enough.

On the May Bank Holiday weekend I arrived for the six-to-six, early, shift and was sent directly to Hutton Moor to allow a night duty Constable to get home. On the Sunday, a man from South Wales had brought his neighbours' two children across on the 'steamer' to the Old Pier. That a single middle-aged man should take two children away for the day did not seem worthy of a second thought at that time. Some of what took place had to be conjecture but it appeared that he had noticed a large advertisement near the exit gates of the pier for 'flights around the bay' from the Weston Airfield. Having taken the bus or a taxi out to Locking, the flight was coming to an end when the light aircraft crashed upon approach to landing. The pilot, the man from south Wales and both young boys were killed. I remember, as daylight dawned on what looked as though it was going to be another beautiful Bank Holiday Monday, surveying the smashed aircraft and identifying the scattered parts of the remains of those four people. My saddest reflection was not really for those who had died but for the parents back in Wales who had, yesterday, expected their sons to come home full of stories of their day out.

My probationary period was to have two crashed aircraft, with none for the remaining 29 years of my service! One wet and chilly early shift, I was directed to go with another Constable, with only a few years more service than I, to check Sand Bay. I cannot recall what prompted this unusual attention but was glad of the warmth of the Husky's heater. While coming back from the bay through Worle village, there was an unusual radio message, "All units north of the County go to Felton - aircraft crashed on houses!" My colleague brought the Husky into raucous life as he headed up the A370. There were no other immediate responses on the radio, so I made mine, "QH99", I gave our Force numbers, "on our way - 99, over". "Thank you 99." Almost immediately there was a transmission from a Traffic car from Flax Bourton, the crew having probably been in the station in anticipation of their cup of tea. Tea was certainly to have a lengthy interruption that morning. With two units available, the Information Room directed us to approach from the A38 and the traffic crew from the Winford village side.

Felton is a very small village right beside what was then Lulsgate, now Bristol airport. Our expectation was of the aircraft having failed to make the runway but that was to be entirely wrong. The fortunate aspect was that the initial report was not entirely accurate. An Army Air Corps helicopter had crashed in the lane behind the short gardens of a row of houses at the northern edge of the village. Close enough but no damage was caused to the houses because the wreckage was, for the most part, contained by the stout hedgerows on either side of the lane. The real good fortune was that no one had been in the lane at the time of impact, for the rotor hub was several hundred yards on the A38 side of the main mass of wreckage and the splinters of the blades scattered all along the lane in between.

Because of the extent of the damage, initially there was confusion as to what type of aircraft was involved but the size of the heap of wreckage and the rotor hub narrowed it down. There was probably a mighty sigh of relief over at the control tower at Lulsgate when it became evident that the crash was nothing to do with their operations, although it was their 'in house' fire tender that was first on the scene. The gradual and welcome arrival of daylight helped in the attempt to identify the aircraft and enquiries by the Information Room staff were bearing fruit. The Army thought they had made the right connection but it was only when we found the pilot's helmet that we could be sure. The markings on the helicopter were simply lost in the wreckage and the, thankfully limited, fire that had followed the crash. The helmet was marked and confirmed the identity of the Army Captain pilot, this brought assurance from the Army that the others were a Brigadier and his Corporal 'batman'. They had been returning from a visit to the Army ranges in Pembrokeshire.

At the Inquest, the Coroner issued his commendation to those of us first on the scene, acknowledging the difficult task of establishing the identity of the machine and the distressing state of the bodies. I must confess that I had not found the incident at all distressing, nor did it appear that any of my colleagues had suffered such concerns. As with the many sizeable and severe road accidents I would attend, there is a job to be done and the focus is directed at that job. I always found far more distress when there were serious injuries but none when it was evident that those involved had not survived. As with my thoughts regarding the families of the crash victims at Weston, so in all such situations, it was for those who were about to get the bad news that I felt most concern.

There was one other aspect of my introductory education that was accomplished during my period of probationary service and it related to a matter that the police were soon to lose from their list of responsibilities. Back in the early days of the new Somersetshire Police force (and all others), local Justices of the Peace had realised that one of the tasks they had, previously, appointed inspectors for could be handed to this wider law enforcement organisation. From those early days in the mid-19th century, police officers had carried responsibility for enforcing legislation in respect of animals and contagious diseases. Some of the legislation relating to restrictions in the event of disease was quite manpower demanding and few serving officers were discontent at the removal of livestock inspection to designated inspectors in the late 1960s and early 1970s. Indeed, those with the right amount of service at that time seized an opportunity for a post-police second career.

In 1966, though, the responsibility for all matters relating to most aspects of law enforcement remained, squarely, with the police. A telephone call from a local veterinary surgeon started the ball rolling and with not a little sense of urgency. The suspicion of the veterinary man was that he had discovered a steer on a local farm, at Bleadon, which he suspected had been suffering from anthrax. Anthrax was, still remains, a seriously infectious and devastating disease and the dead animal lying in the middle of the field showed all the, somewhat distasteful, signs of suffering from the disease. Indeed there have been instances in more recent years of threatened terrorist attack in the form of releasing the spores of this disease. Standing Orders had a large section within the Diseases of Animals chapter and went to great lengths to describe a thorough procedure intended to restrict the chance of an infected animal becoming the source of an epidemic. To the modern eye, the one aspect that those Standing Orders neglected to cover was any precaution necessary on the part of the Officer dealing with the situation.

The Sergeant took me and a copy of standing orders to the farm at the bottom of the field, quickly inspected the dead animal with the veterinary surgeon and very worried looking farmer. He, and the vet with his small glass files of fluid samples, departed, with the less than reassuring words, "There you are 247, you know what to do so get on with it." In detail, the Standing Order contained a description of the procedure and lists of items required. Effectively, the animal being treated with suspicion had to be cremated where it had fallen. The quantities of timber, coal and paraffin were relatively easy to arrange, with the farmer more concerned as to who would pay for it. The size and depth of the hole required was daunting until I struck upon the fortunate circumstance of the large, close by, building site for the latest extension of the Oldmixon estate.

A word with the foreman brought a JCB bouncing across the field and the farmer's wife did not seem to at all mind that yet another mug of tea was now required. With the full authority and apparent breadth of knowledge of one who had just read the appropriate page of Standing Orders, I briefed the JCB driver. By the time that the coal merchant arrived in the gateway at the bottom of the field, the hole was dug and the front bucket of the JCB served to make transporting the items from the lorry easy. With British Railways well into replacing their main line sleepers with new design concrete ones, the coal merchant had a good stock of old wooden ones. These were well soaked in creosote and long enough, because the JCB driver had adhered to the measurements related to him, to just bridge the hole. Some chains from the back of the barn enabled the carcase of the steer to be lifted by the JCB onto the pyre. Last to arrive, and just in time, was the 'Esso Blue' man, in his then familiar little van. Many at that time relied upon paraffin heaters and these vans were seen regularly delivering the fuel. This was an unexpected extra order and the Esso man staggered up across the field with his jerry cans.

With the whole assembly, farmer, wife, JCB driver, foreman and Esso Blue man, watching I lit the edge of the pyre. The paraffin soon spread the flames right across the animal's carcase and the draught of air being drawn up from the hole beneath soon developed into an inferno. Mindful of the foundations that his JCB had not created that afternoon, the foreman squeezed into the cab on the JCB and they departed. Not long after the Esso Blue man realised that he was spending too long on one delivery. Eventually even the farmer and his wife decided they had many more important things to do and I was left alone. Mrs farmer brought me more cups of tea as the afternoon drew on and Mr farmer stood guard for me while I availed myself of their loo a couple of times but that was a long afternoon. I was watching the level of activity across at the building site as the fire dropped into the hole when the railway sleepers gave way. Luckily the incineration process, accelerated by the fat in the animal, was completed and I could see that their lost time in the afternoon had prompted the JCB to still be operating beyond what would normally have been their end of day. Another request and a very quick job for the digger brought the infilling of the hole on top of the mass of hot ashes.

The worst aspect had been that the incineration of this beast had been the equivalent to the most gigantic barbeque, although barbeques had not become fashionable by that time. The smell of all that beef burning only served to emphasise the fact that I had not been enabled to enjoy my mid-shift refreshment break. No one at the police station had considered it appropriate to check on my progress and certainly not to show any concern regarding my refreshment. In later years the 'fashion' for operational feeding of police officers grew immensely but at this time police officers were expected to show their own initiative and to sustain themselves wherever they may be performing duty. Having been grudgingly allowed a lift and after a brief report back at the station, I went off duty just in time to catch the fish and chip shop before it closed - probably one of the best bags of fish and chips I ever enjoyed.

My first day carrying the Stornophone personal radio – recorded by a cameraman from The Weston Mercury – by kind permission of the Weston, Worle & Somerset Mercury.

In the summer of 1966 we were issued with Stornophone personal radios and on the first day I was on patrol in New High Street I was approached by a reporter and cameraman from the *Weston Mercury*. With the ideal means to verify their story, I confirmed with the station Sergeant that the Chief Superintendent had, indeed, given consent to my being photographed with the new equipment. Too late, anyway, they had got their photograph while I was checking and it appeared in the next edition. These radios were somewhat cumbersome in that they needed the aerial to be extended to transmit back to the station but they revolutionised patrolling. No more conference points, once the supervisors started to trust the new radios. For some few weeks we stood at telephone boxes with a radio strapped to our chest – just in case the technology failed!

One second half of a 6p.m. to 2a.m. shift I was allocated to the 'southside vacant houses'. Weston-super-Mare was predominantly flat land to the south of the town centre but very hilly to the north. It was an established practice at that time, one that had been taking place for many years, that people leaving their premises empty, to go on holiday or for any other reason, reported the fact to the police station. These addresses were included in the 'Vacant House Register', a loose leaf folder that, in Weston, was split between north and south. The north side duty suited me better as it involved the use of one of the two LE Velocette motorcycles. These machines were water cooled and remarkably quiet so ideal for patrolling residential areas at night. I had, however, been given south side and this was a pedal cycle patrol.

With my list of addresses drawn from the station register and my refreshment period over, I plotted my route and went about checking the empty properties. With the new Stornophone strapped to my chest and points just done away with, I planned to start farthest out and zigzag my way back for the 2a.m. finish. Almost half way through, at about half past midnight, I received a call that the burglar alarm had been activated at the Drove Road Working Men's Club. Only a couple of streets away, I informed the Station Office Constable that I was on my way. I also heard the Sergeant say that he would be attending in the Hillman Husky. As I rode, as fast as my pedalling would enable, through the open gateway into the car park of the Club, a shadow of a figure was directly in front of my line of travel and running away from the building. I grabbed him with one hand, trying to maintain a hold on my bicycle with the other. We both, and the bike, ended up in a heap in the middle of the car park, almost immediately to be illuminated by the headlights of the Husky.

We placed him in the back seat of the Husky and I kept half an eye on him while the Sergeant checked the building. He found that a window had been broken and some pieces of glass heaped up beside it from the jagged pieces around the window frame. My prisoner had, evidently, not got into the building as he had been trying to clear the broken glass so that he could climb through without injury. He denied that he had broken the window, stating that he had heard the noise and came into the car park to investigate. He fell short of an explanation as to why he ran away when the delayed audible alarm had started up. Our problem was that, with his torch, the Sergeant could find no fingerprints on the moved glass yet our man did not have any gloves in his possession. Back at the station, he slowly came around to the idea that he had been caught 'bang to rights' for attempted burglary and, eventually, quite proudly informed us how he had fooled us with the absence of fingerprints. He had placed his socks over his hands to remove the pieces of glass and stuffed them in his pocket when he ran after the alarm started sounding. While we had him in the back seat of the Husky, he had replaced his socks on his feet without me noticing. Another small lesson learned!

The length of this chapter already dictates that I occupy another, Chapter Five, with the probationary attachments that were part of the two year training process. That separate chapter will also allow for some description of the post initial training courses provided in conjunction with the 'on the job' training of Probationary Constables in the 1960s.

Just one other incident is worthy of a mention before this chapter closes. One late evening, early in a night shift and with no Bourneville Section Constable on duty, I was sent with another Constable of about my age in the Husky to an address on the new Oldmixon council house estate. There a very distressed woman in her early 30s ushered us in to the house. The house was well looked after but had been rendered quite a mess by her drunken 'common law husband'. Besides the extensive damage he had caused in the living room, including the destruction of the small bar quite popular with residents on this council estate at the time, the most memorable was in the kitchen. Most houses built before and after World War II were equipped with a pantry and it usually had a 'cold slab' for the storage of what later would occupy the domestic refrigerator. The lady of the house had prepared some home-made jam and it now stood in a heap on the slab with the broken jam jars mixed in with it. Having done the damage, the man of the house had departed into the night. Our scan of the premises brought the realisation that most of what he had damaged was his, at least their, own property but he had broken a window, which 'belonged' to the Council, so was eligible for arrest for causing criminal damage.

My colleague and I were neither of us large but we knew that the errant householder was extremely so. Nonetheless, we set off in search of the culprit, not really too keen as to whether we find him. It took a remarkably short time before we saw him walking along Winterstoke Road. My colleague turned the car and we drew up facing him and he stopped as we did. Our expectation was of an almighty struggle with no certainty that we would come off best. We got out of the car and walked slowly towards him. As we got nearly within 'grappling' distance, he sank to his knees and burst into, seemingly uncontrollable, tears. "I'm sorry Officers, I know I shouldn't have done it." Meek as a lamb, he walked with us back to the car and sat himself in the back seat!

Through from my arrival in Weston-super-Mare, I was in 'digs' with the same lady although at three different addresses and then, for a short while, with a younger lady with two small children. Some weeks before our intended wedding date a flat being occupied by another police couple, in this instant both were Constables, became vacant as they were allocated their 'first police house'. I moved in to ensure we had tenancy and we bought two of everything to equip the kitchen, two plates, two knives, two forks, etc. The only larger scale purchase proved soon to be necessary and was a refrigerator bought in the Curry's 'ten pound sale'. That piece of equipment was to last, in our use and then my parents', for well over thirty years.

The Chief Constable inspects the prepared trial UBP cars and chats with the first crews at Canonsgrove

Through the summer of 1967 and following an experimental project in Lancashire, Taunton Division had some old Hillman Minx and Husky cars re-sprayed in 'panda' colours. The scheme seemed to meet approval within the Force as much as it had obtained the fullest backing of the Home Office. Almost as though synchronised with our wedding and taking up occupation of the flat in Trevelyan Road as husband and wife, the Unit Beat Policing System reached Weston-super-Mare.

5 Probationary Attachments

So much was crammed into the probationary period between my joining in October 1965 and reaching that milestone of 'confirmation' two years later that Chapter Four needed to have excluded from it some aspects which can be viewed as directly related to the training process of that period. Scheduled into the training programme of those two years and timed to come after about a year of patrol experience, were a number of attachments to the specialist departments. Also part of the programme were the Continuation Courses at the one year and near to the end of the two year probationary period. I will deal with the various aspects distinctly but, to maintain cohesion in each area, only in approximate chronological order.

For a reason that is difficult to gauge at this distance but one which the supervisors saw no good reason to discredit, there was a very real sense of foreboding throughout the probationary period which only seemed to reach more of a crescendo as the second anniversary approached. The visible fact was that those not likely to make the grade and, hence, not have their appointment confirmed were weeded out much earlier than at the two year stage. Indeed, those who survived the two years intact all progressed to having their role as a Constable made, as it was then but is looking less certain as I write this in 2014, permanent. But, the vulnerability myth survived, probably still does! The particularly long probationary period was a very sensible preparation for the next twenty eight years which most officers expected, then, to serve. It gave both recruit and other officers, especially supervisors, a defined but adequate period in which expectations of performance were slightly, but only slightly, less and enabled each officer to 'grow' into what was, when done properly, a very complex job.

After about eight or nine months of general patrol duties the Intermediate Continuation Course was reached. This was a two week course but was not available at the, then, South West District Training School at Chantemarle.

Instead we had to make the, then epic and even now not easy, journey along the south of the country to the old army barracks above Folkestone in Kent. Structured around the time of this course came the probationary attachments. These comprised a month with CID, two weeks with the Traffic Department and one week in the Administration Department. At Weston-super-Mare there was also a month on the Bourneville Section, the large semi-rural area surrounding the main town of Weston-super-Mare and so called because the police station was on the edge of the large council estate of that name and built soon after the Second World War. After spending most of the remaining time in the Borough the Final Continuation Course, of another two weeks duration, was scheduled quite close to the end of the probationary two years and, in our case, again necessitated the long trek to Folkestone.

Alongside these specific training opportunities ran that which I mentioned in Chapter Two and again referred to briefly in Chapter Three. This was the requirement for successful completion of the probationary period of gaining a Bronze Medallion from the Royal Life Saving Society. Despite the many efforts in the pool at Wellington School, at the Blue Horizon nearby and hours splashing in the river Tone, scarcely to mention the close encounter with a career in the Merchant Navy, I joined the police at twenty years of age as a non-swimmer. The recognition of the vital nature of gaining the Bronze Medallion was probably the spur required but to expect to start from such a baseline was not realistic. The weekly trips while at Chantemarle had brought me to the, still lowly, status of 'swimmer' by the time I reached my first posting at Weston-super-Mare.

Life Saving Training was provided by a relatively young Constable, who had only recently taken on the task from a much older officer who had retired. As I mentioned in Chapter Three, the requirement to attend these weekly sessions at the Knightstone Baths was only suspended when on annual leave. Hence, regardless of shift, the training was maintained. As a consequence, the move from non-swimmer to proud holder of a Bronze Medallion was accomplished in the necessary period and in good time to know that this would not be the cause of any failure to have my appointment confirmed. There was to be an almost immediate sequel to this already meteoric escalation from the non-swimmer status of the first twenty years of my life.

The Constable who had assumed the role of Divisional Life Saving Trainer was far ahead of what was, later, to become quite a significant exodus of officers.

He decided that he was going to use the degree which he had worked for in his own time to take him into the legal profession. The significant pay rise of the early 1960s had not been followed by any sensible annual reviews and police pay steadily fell in real and comparative terms right through until the late 1970s. In that time many good officers were lost to the service as they refused to see their families become reliant upon state benefits. The announcement of his decision had been preceded by a winter, the one immediately after our marriage in 1967, in which, when our duties allowed, we had shared transport to attend a sub-aqua course in Bristol. In addition, I had continued to attend the Life Saving classes, in my own time, to gain my Instructor's Certificate. It was, therefore, not surprising that he recommended me as his replacement. Hence, in that first two and a half years of police service I had gone from non-swimmer to Divisional Life Saving Instructor - perhaps it was because no one else wanted the job! The only benefit for the instructor was that all attendance was classed as duty time and, as there was no provision for payment, a comfortable build-up of time-off accrued, to be taken when the Sergeants permitted. This marginal benefit was to last less than a year, before the longed-for first police house coincided with the equally desired transfer to Traffic.

In the September of 1966, as far as I can recall, all of the old Somerset contingent from Class 159 at Chantemarle were posted in General Orders to attend the Intermediate Continuation Course at Folkestone. My longest and most consistent colleague and working on the same Section had a somewhat larger car than the A35 so we determined that he would drive to Folkestone. At that time there was an expectation that all would report on Sunday evening and not expect to leave until Saturday lunchtime. It was, therefore, inevitable that we all were committed to remain in Folkestone for the weekend between the two weeks

PC 247 at Folkestone for the Probationers Intermediate Course in 1966

of the course. The accommodation was exactly what may be expected from a former army barracks, with large dormitories with a 'turtle' stove for 'central' heating. Although only just into autumn, it was cold on the top of the hill above the town and the bucket beside the turtle stove was kept well filled from the bunker of coke at the end of the quadrangle between the four, two storey, accommodation blocks.

At one end of that quadrangle was the back of the 'guard house' which we were all expected to man at some point, the roster being presented on the first morning of the course. The training received was no more than a repetition of what the 'powers that be' considered the more vital aspects of the thirteen week initial course back at Chantemarle. Trips out into the town were permitted in the evenings, provided it was not your turn to man the Guard House, and it was a somewhat less regimented regime than the earlier experience. There was still a perceived need for a few drill sessions and, more appropriately, some energetic games sessions in the old gymnasium.

At this distance in time there is only one thing, person in fact, which differentiates the two courses almost a year apart. On the run-up to the Final Continuation Course in the late summer of 1967, the transport arrangements were discussed between those of us listed to attend. For whatever reason, one officer from Weston-super-Mare who had been a month different in attending the Chantemarle course was scheduled to be with us and, he being without a car, we agreed that he would accompany me in the A35. The antics we encountered such as dormitory pillow fights and 'apple pie' beds were repeated, as were the evening excursions into the town. Our colleague, however, did not take well to such frivolities. This made him, of course, become more a focus of such antics than would otherwise have applied and this served to reinforce his disdain. The aspect he was most against was the association with girls from the town when on evenings out. Although I had no intention to do any more than join in the general banter, he kept reminding me, as though it was necessary, of my impending wedding! I was to work alongside our colleague again a few years later when I found that he had cheered up - a bit!

First of the probationary attachments, and seen by most as the more important, was that to the Criminal Investigation Department (CID). My friend from the Forest of Dean and I had our CID attachments at the same time and turned up at the offices above the canteen across the back yard in good time. We were welcomed in by a man in his thirties, whom we both believed to be a CID officer and, with no badge of rank available, hedged our bets by calling him 'Sir'. He immediately declared that he had not been 'knighted' but did not reveal that he was actually the civilian clerk. That situation was clarified by the Detective Sergeant when he arrived shortly after us. While the time spent with senior detectives was very useful from the point of view of assembling more complex crime prosecution files, the memorable moments were few. I do recall attending the scene of a burglary that had occurred over the previous night and the splendid view from the roof of a hotel in Sand Bay. That I make this comment probably reveals how much, I should say little, was memorable.

There was one interesting episode but it was scarcely crime detection. There were two Constables with somewhat more service who were each performing their, three month, Aide to CID, the necessary precursor to any intention to seek a permanent posting in the Department. With one of these officers I was detailed to collect a prisoner from Windsor, where he had been arrested and detained on a warrant issued from the Weston CID office. We walked the short distance to the railway station and obtained our tickets against railway warrants issued by the Divisional Administration office. The journey involved a change of trains at Bristol and another at Reading, so it was drawing towards evening before we reached Windsor but the local CID had got the timing right and were awaiting our arrival. Time being what it was, we accepted their suggestion that we go to a pub near the castle walls for a meal before collecting the prisoner.

When we had dealt with the paperwork I was handcuffed to the man and we were driven back to the railway station. It was now getting dark but our local colleagues just deposited us at the gates, told us that all trains went to Reading and we walked onto the platform. We boarded the first train that arrived and settled down in the corridorless, old-time commuter train, compartment. After a couple of stops, I grew suspicious that the stations through which we were passing were not at all familiar. An enquiry of a railwayman on the next platform confirmed that we were heading in the wrong direction so we crossed the bridge and caught the next train in the correct direction.

Inevitably this brought us to Reading extremely behind schedule and we sat in the British Transport Police office while my colleague sorted out our transport arrangements. There were no trains that night stopping at Weston-super-Mare, so we took the next train to Bristol Temple Meads and one of the night shift officers came up in the scenes of crime officers' Cortina estate to collect us. It was well after midnight when we lodged the prisoner at Weston but he had not been overly concerned, perhaps even mildly amused, at his elongated journey.

Of much greater interest to me was the two week attachment to the Road Motor Patrol (RMP) or Road Traffic Department (RTD), the terms seemed not to be prioritised and could be used without distinction. Both appear to have now been replaced by Road Policing Unit (RPU). I recall particularly well three of the officers with whom I was crewed, although I worked with quite a few in those two weeks. Having a probationer with the seasoned traffic man brought him two main penalties so the Sergeant would try to share it out as much as he could. The first penalty was that the Traffic Constable had to drive for the whole of the eight hour shift. The second, and much more to concern him, was that he would be expected to cram as much experience as possible for the probationary officer into their time together. The three officers of whom I have special memories were all very different and two of them would still be in their posts when, some years later, I became a full member of that department.

Ford Zephyr Six MkIII patrol car (taken at a Taunton Motor Club Cup competition)

The first Traffic Officer I will reflect upon was soon to be another joining the escape party from low police pay. He left to go into insurance sales and, at about the same time, another emigrated to Canada to join a police force over there. The future insurance man was particularly memorable for one remarkable attribute. Most Traffic Officers of the time carried a clipboard upon which to make rough notes before completing their pocket note books in more evidentially tidy fashion. This was not entirely in keeping with the pocket book being the 'notes made at the time' but never seemed to be challenged and, hence, was the way, in practice, things were done.

But not for this Traffic Officer. On the day we were together he, as did the other experienced officers, packed in as much as possible. This involved a run out to the A38 and concentrated upon stopping a number of heavy lorries and either reporting or cautioning the drivers for a range of driving or vehicle related offences. After about two hours he drew the Zephyr Six up on a wide lay-by, with its front bumper just in from the edge of the carriageway. He, then, produced his pocket book and I did likewise. He dictated all that had happened in that preceding period of time, including all the precise times, vehicle types and registration numbers, drivers' names and companies to which the vehicles belonged. This feat of memory left me utterly amazed and I would never meet another person with that level of retention and recall. I was never to hear of him after he left the service but I hope that his, near unique, capability served him well wherever he went.

Another of the Constables was the one from my home town of Wellington. About fifteen or more years my senior he actually knew my uncle quite well through their joint involvement in the local rugby club in his earlier years. He was probably the most laid-back Constable imaginable without that appearance being combined with actual idleness. He gave the impression that nothing could ever stir him to anger yet his whole demeanour made it evident that he would be unlikely to entertain being 'messed about'. This produced a balance that brought him minimal personal stress and could be easily mistaken as revealing that he was 'bone idle' but his work record and productivity gave the lie to this potential view. A few years later, reflected in Chapter Seven, he was to reveal, momentarily, that he could show anger, but it was rare.

The recording of the activity of each Traffic Officer had started in the early 1960s with the nationally introduced Regional Experiment (RE) Scheme. The mandarins from the Home Office and the Ministry of Transport had combined to produce a dividing of the Trunk Roads into Sectors. The sectors were of about twenty five miles in length and the expectation was that each would have a traffic patrol car patrolling in all daylight hours, with sectors being combined for patrol at night. The cars used to patrol under the RE scheme were mainly the Zephyr Six Mk.III cars already in use in Somerset but they had been re-sprayed white (previously, they had been a variety of bark colours) and were fitted with large roof-mounted signs. There was an early precursor to the 'bean counting' to come at the end of the 20th Century as each officer had to maintain a record of his activity, submitted on a monthly basis, and known as an RT8. The RT8 contained a list of the various types of offences for which the Constable may have made arrests, reported drivers for legal process or administered verbal cautions.

The third Constable for whom memories of that probationary attachment flood back was, at that time, based with the small traffic contingent at Flax Bourton police station. One morning the Sergeant told me that I was to be crewed with him and that he was on his way to collect me. I knew, no one could not know, of his reputation. Rumoured to have been a young pilot in World War II, his skill at coordinating his actions was similarly applied to his driving of a Zephyr Six. More quickly after the Sergeant spoke than I would have imagined, the Zephyr more than breezed into the back yard. Our man got out and tugged at the back of his gloves as he walked away from the car, which was making frequent pinging noises as the metal of the engine started to cool. Anticipating the request that would otherwise have followed, I had brewed us a cup of tea and ensured that the Sergeant had his mug filled.

After a brief introduction, we headed out of Weston-super-Mare south towards the A38. Through the built up area, the needle of the calibrated speedometer in the middle of the dashboard remained at or below the 30 mph limit and my crewmate for the day spoke very little. As we reached the derestriction signs at Uphill he launched the Zephyr down the A370, overtaking everything in its path and in each of the long sweeping bends on that stretch of road keeping the car as close as possible to the limit of adhesion of the Michelin ZX tyres. I was conscious that he took the occasional glance across at me but my obvious enjoyment of his demonstration of driving skill was spontaneous and not for his benefit. With no reference to that ten mile dash but plenty of general and useful traffic related conversation, we turned on to the A38 and spent the rest of the tour of duty at more normal speeds. I, it appeared, had passed his form of initiation test!

The one week attachment to the Divisional Administration Department must have contained some information that was of importance to my development but time has dimmed any recollection as to what that may have been. Of greater interest and to prove useful in terms of geographic knowledge just over a year later was the one month attachment to the Bourneville Section. This was to be quite a large chunk of the Panda area I would join in 1967. For now, it brought much greater opportunity for mobility through the use of one of the two Triumph Tiger 100s allocated to that station. Although some pedal cycle patrols of the post WWII Bourneville and burgeoning Oldmixon housing estates were expected, the Sergeant knew that he got far more work from his Constables if they were more mobile over such a large area.

The Bourneville Police Station was contiguous with the Section Sergeant's house and had quite a small office. In addition to the two motorcycles there was a Ford Anglia estate which was used for patrols but only subject to the Sergeant not needing access to it. The area covered was the whole hinterland around the Borough and included several of the small villages surrounding the town as far out as Congresbury and Banwell. It included the, then busy, RAF Locking signals school and the Weston-super-Mare airfield with its offshoot of the Westlands Helicopter builders. Oddly, I was to discover, the airfield had, perhaps because of its Westlands connection, a small Royal Naval detachment from RNAS Yeovilton, comprising a Petty Officer and three ratings. They had the exceedingly boring role of 'being there' should there be some need for Yeovilton to have to use the airfield. Why this could not have been serviced from RAF Locking, only a mile up the road, only the Ministry of Defence would have understood.

This attachment came quite late for me and I was heading towards the end of my probationary period by the time I got to it. I risked the ire of the Section Sergeant by feeding him reports of offences under various Road Traffic Acts and Regulations for which I had reported people. The availability of the 500cc motor cycles enabled me to get close to my desired traffic patrol role. I would dash around the area to accomplish what I was able in respect of the outstanding enquiries picked up at the start of the shift and spend the rest of the tour, subject to being directed by radio to other matters, operating on the A370 either side of the Borough. There was, however, one traffic related matter which the Sergeant did not get to hear of and nor did anyone else until some years later, when I felt established enough to make fun of my own actions.

One early August morning in 1967 I had got my usual package of enquiries sorted and safely in the pannier and sat up on the side of the A370 at Hewish. Amid the flow of traffic in each direction, I saw a Bristol Omnibus single decker heading towards Congresbury and was surprised to see that it was displaying a registration number with an 'F' suffix. I went after the bus but it stopped at a bus stop just down the road so I rode to the front of it and spoke with the driver. He was as amazed as was I when I pointed out the registration number, the bus crews all worked on fleet numbers and, although he knew the bus was new, the driver had not even looked at the registration number. I noted his details and, thankfully, decided not to impede the journeys of the few passengers heading towards Bristol.

I rode to the Bus Terminus on Beach Road at Weston-super-Mare, thankfully not making any enquiry over the radio of the Information Room, and found the depot manager. He, too, was most concerned that one of their vehicles, freshly delivered the previous day on trade plates, had been supplied with the wrong registration number displayed. Telephone calls to the head office in Bristol did not bring an immediate answer but, eventually, there came the explanation that, for the first time, the registration numbers were being changed on 1st August instead of 1st January. That I was somewhat embarrassed is an understatement but at least the bus company managers were no more switched on to this change than me. A good lesson learned, if something seems inexplicable try to get the explanation first!

The probationary continuation courses were useful and my development from non-swimmer upon joining to life saving instructor just after confirmation was a pleasant surprise. The attachments were the best possible way to develop a rapid and wide knowledge of what the many variations of police work demanded. I was fortunate in the enthusiasm with which the experienced officers met my thirst for knowledge and gave freely their guidance and advice. At this quite early stage, I realised that there were lessons to be learned from those working alongside me whether they were examples to follow or to seek to avoid. Learning always seems a chore to the young but, in my early twenties, I had realised that everything encountered held a lesson to be filed away.

6 Unit Beat Policing

Perhaps inevitably, given the adherence to the earlier Minx and Husky Hillmans, the small car of choice for use in the new Unit Beat Policing (UBP) system in Somerset & Bath was to be the Hillman Imp. In its distinctive markings of all-over blue with doors and strip of roof between them in white, they looked the part. Many Forces went for the tried and trusted Morris Minor 1000 others for Ford Anglias and a few for Vauxhall Vivas or Austin/Morris Minis. The Imp was as good as any for performance but did have a slight problem in terms of front wheel adhesion. The building site foremen experienced a bit of scrounging as all of the five 'Panda area' crews realised that a couple of breeze blocks in the front boot worked wonders.

Behind the foldable back seats there was another small storage area above the rear engine compartment. This was used, along with some of the back seat, to store the many files which contained the latest crime information. It seems incredible now but we were expected to carry out foot patrols away from the car, and did so, leaving some pretty confidential paperwork unguarded by anything other than the flimsy car door locks of the day. On the front parcel shelf was a small wooden cradle, fabricated by someone at the Home Office engineering depot at Shapwick. This enabled the receiver of the Pye Pocketfone (this, two piece, radio replaced the cumbersome Stornophones along with the arrival of the Imps), to run from the car battery and be linked to a roof mounted aerial. The logic in this was lost on me, with my little knowledge of radio gained in the CCF at school. It was the transmitting unit that needed boosting not the receiver. Anyway, that's the way it was.

Working the Panda area was like nothing before. Working the most of the area that had immediately before September 1967 been the Bourneville Section, we had the slim advantage that the police station was still available to us. The advantage was slight because the expectation was that we would be on patrol at all times. The Panda car was our mobile police station. Innovatively, we were equipped with a small cassette dictating machine upon which to store our reports. Once a day, usually in the second half of the early shift, the driver would seek the duty Sergeant's consent and visit the main station in Walliscote Road. There he would deposit completed paperwork and recorded tapes and collect the next batch of enquiries for the area and the latest editions of Police Gazettes and SWCRO informations. Unless the arrest of a prisoner or a call from the duty Sergeant dictated otherwise, this would normally be the only time in the twenty four hours that the car was not on its patch. The other time could be when the driver was enjoying his three quarter of an hour refreshment break.

Example of the many Hillman Imp 'Panda' cars introduced in 1967 for Unit Beat Policing (taken at a Taunton Motor Club Cup competition)

For those engaged on the roster as Panda car drivers the considerable workload involved was in some way compensated by the relative independence that the work brought. Perhaps the biggest personal advantage was the arrangement by which the presence of the car on its given area was maximised. At a quarter to the hour of a shift changeover the driver about to go off duty would collect the next crewman from his home address. Although this may not be, in my case was not, immediately on the patrol area it would, even in a town the size of Weston-super-Mare, not be too far away. The officers would then travel together to the home of the officer being relieved from duty and, in the process, he would brief the 'fresh' officer as to what was worthy of note. While this would focus upon what was relevant to that Panda area it would not exclude any other matters of interest. It was, in fact, an excellent means for continuity to be maintained and ensured that officers were exceptionally well briefed. These quarter of an hour conversations and the day-time arrivals at each others homes quickly brought a considerable familiarity between the officers and their families and helped to foster considerable pride in efficiency on our shared area.

A further means of pooling knowledge and a way in which the Sergeants could maintain some input, was that much of what would otherwise have been recorded in individual officers' pocket notebooks was written into a shared log. The exception was, of course, those matters which an individual officer thought important only to him or that may necessitate his resorting to those notes for a court appearance. There were days when precious little needed to be recorded in the pocket notebook other that a reference to the area log.

The other advantage to individuals was the approval for officers to take their refreshments during early and late shifts at their homes. The Pye pocketfone ensured that the officer remained available during his refreshment break and it was not uncommon for the period to be interrupted by the need to attend to some call from a member of the public. On the night shift all five area cars would attend the main police station for the officers to take their refreshment break and the duty Sergeant would direct what times these breaks would be taken to ensure a street patrol presence at all times. The previous 'hands on' direction of Constables by the duty Sergeants was extremely diminished under the Unit Beat Policing system and this was one of the causes for it not being allowed to continue in its original, and best, form for more than a few years. The notion among supervisory officers of all ranks, although not routinely proven by what actually happened, was that Constables only performed at their optimum when they were being closely supervised. To some extent, of course, this was nothing more than a means to ensure the recognition of the importance of their role. The other reason for the eventual erosion of the independence that the UBP system afforded to officers was that some abused that freedom to take a lazy approach. Too many undertook precious little foot patrol away from the vehicle preferring, especially when it was cold or wet, to sit in the car.

Circumstances were to dictate that I would only be directly involved in the

Panda scheme for about fourteen months and, hence, it remained largely as intended for that time. The ability to deal with far more work and be mobile enough to rapidly attend all manner of incidents suited me and, fortunately, the others on my area well and the public in our large geographical area had no cause for complaint as to our visibility. As well as the officers crewing the car over the twenty four hour cover the scheme provided that there were, on our area, two Resident Beat Officers and a (somewhat notional) allocated Detective Constable. The detective still worked from the CID office but was our specific contact when required. The two Resident Beat Officers patrolled their respective parts of the area on either day or late shifts and afforded an even more recognisable face to their 'parishioners'.

With the villages of Locking and Hutton included in our area, the Bourneville housing estate and the burgeoning estate of houses at Oldmixon, as well as industrial expansion in that direction from the established trading estate off Winterstoke Road, this area provided considerable variety. The RAF policed themselves within the large area covered by the Signals Training School at RAF Locking but we called in to liaise (and drink tea) on a regular basis. Although the Resident Constables did most of the liaising with schools and business operators they would often call upon the Panda car to expand the children's interest for school sessions. At night, in the latter part of late tours and the first part of early shift, much of the patrol activity was directed toward crime prevention and detection across the whole area. While the public were more active the time for the Panda crew was largely occupied in responding to calls or dealing with files collected from the Station.

I recall only one occasion upon which I was held to have failed to maintain the standard required and the way in which this was dealt with was a reflection of the discipline of that time. Toward the end of a night shift and with little time available, I did not get out of the car to check each door in the twin ranks of shops, set in chevron fashion, on the Bourneville estate, instead turning the car for the lights to shine across their fronts. Later, after I had been tucked up in my bed for a couple of hours, I was roused by a colleague banging on the door. Both my wife (of only a few months) and my landlady (we were in the rented flat) were at work but eventually the knocking achieved its aim. Fully dressed, and my colleague having returned to his patrol, I made my way into the police station. There my failure to identify that the small window above the door of one of the shops was broken, when the car log showed that I had 'checked' those shops, was examined minutely. That the damage was minor and may well have happened after I had gone off duty did not prevent my sleep being disturbed.

Another potentially close encounter with the Discipline Regulations was brought about by one of the Sergeants embroiling me in his own shortcomings. It was normal for Sergeants to visit the Constables on their areas and an additional Hillman Imp was provided for them to be able to do so. On one morning, and not unique, a Sergeant called on the radio and instructed that I should "show me in the book at the police station". This I dutifully, later I realised stupidly, did and he subsequently signed the entry. Weeks later, I was summoned to the Chief Inspector's office and confronted by a Superintendent from Headquarters who was investigating a complaint. A prisoner in custody on the morning of my fictitious logbook entry had alleged that he had been assaulted by a police officer in the cells. Fortunately, for me, the prisoner had indicated a tall Constable as his alleged assailant and my contention that I had not gone near the cells was accepted. That I had not actually visited the station at that time was not actually challenged so my honesty was not further compromised. It was another lesson to be valued for the future.

On a more positive note in terms of my performance and early on in my time on the UBP area, I received a call to inform a woman in her mid-twenties to telephone Ham Green Hospital, near Pill. I was, fortunately, told that she was to be informed about the deterioration in her husband's health. I found that the address, just off Windwhistle Circle, was a top flat in a three floor block and discovered that there was no one at home. As it was late in the afternoon, I decided to wait on the small lay-by in front of the block, near which there was a GPO (General Post Office, for the younger reader) telephone box. Employing the time to get the information files up to date, I saw a woman of about the right age get off the bus in Windwhistle Circle and walk around to the entrance of the small block of flats. I intercepted her and passed on the request that she telephone the hospital.

In common with most people at the time, the woman had no telephone in her flat but went straight to the nearby kiosk. I returned to the panda car but waited to see what would happen. To some extent what I anticipated, although somewhat more severe, the woman collapsed on the floor of the kiosk. I ran to her and picked up the telephone handset. The nurse on the other end told me that she had just passed the woman the information that her young husband had died earlier in the afternoon. That I was appalled at the way this had been done was somewhat relegated to my more immediate problem of the woman. I made a short radio contact with the Station to tell them what had happened and managed to lift her out of the kiosk. They say that there is never a policeman about when you want one, well on that occasion it was equally true of members of the public - no one in sight! I managed, with significant effort, to carry her up the four half-flights of stairs and to the door of her flat.

By the time we reached her flat door she had started to come around and was able to help me find her key in the handbag she had never released from her grip, even when unconscious. I helped her in to her lounge and she sat, alternating between being totally distraught and simply bewildered. A few radio calls and the passing of some pieces of information I managed to elicit from her, got a message to her sister but it was the better part of two hours before the sister and her husband arrived. I returned, unusually, to the main Police Station immediately after this encounter and spoke with the duty Sergeant. The result was contact by the duty Inspector, before he went for his tea, with the Matron at Ham Green and, hopefully, the promulgation of instructions not to notify deaths in the same way again. Of some significance in our modern climate of cost-counting it is unlikely that my nearly half a tour of duty being spent on the aftermath of one 'death notice' would meet with approval. In the 1960s spending time caring for people was a genuinely accepted part of what policing was all about.

The year I spent on the Unit Beat Policing Area was extremely busy but largely involved carrying our routine enquiries, often for other Forces as a follow-up to people on the area having been dealt with by the police elsewhere. Most of those enquiries were forgotten almost as quickly as they were conducted but one, on Sunday late tour on 17th March, 1968, I have good cause to remember. I had checked through the outstanding jobs inherited from my early shift colleague and was not impressed to see that one was to serve a summons upon a man in Lonsdale Avenue on the Bourneville estate. This man's reputation for belligerence and aggression towards police officers we had all seen reinforced more than once and it was my expectation that the fairly newly acquired authority to serve a summons on a Sunday would bring me another earful.

The vista of the front garden would have indicated that I had reached the right house even had I not been here several times already. The front hedge, so thoughtfully provided by his council landlords, had been depressed into the ground rather than cleared so that he could get his car onto the front garden and keep it free from expensive police attention. It was risky enough when using it without the appropriate paperwork and its scant adherence to road traffic legislation requirements. I managed to avoid the smaller items of debris on the pathway to reach the front door. Summons in hand, ready to thrust it into his hand as quickly as I expected he would slam the door when he saw who was knocking, I tapped on the door.

To my total bewilderment, our man arrived at the door, took the summons without question and invited, no demanded, that I enter the house. The inside of the living room was totally in keeping with the front garden and I did not even think to enquire as to whether he had a licence for the large television to which he insistently drew my attention. On the screen were being played out the serious confrontation between the police and demonstrators in Grosvenor Square, London. I had known that the demonstration against the United States involvement in Vietnam was happening but not what was taking place. Perhaps a strong indicator that this demonstration was a turning point in terms of violence in support of political, or should it be pseudo-political, views was this inveterate criminal's reaction. He was totally appalled at the way in which the police officers were being attacked. A man who hated the police with a relish still saw the behaviour in Grosvenor Square that Sunday afternoon as beyond all reason. That no-one reacts in quite that way today is, perhaps, at the root of many of our social problems.

Although the Unit Beat Policing arrangements took me away from the old Borough Section my former Sergeant, he of the cigarette ash impregnated tunic, maintained an interest in my progress. In the new UBP set up the new role of Collator had been introduced and this Sergeant was appointed to the post. He, therefore, welcomed visits from all the area crews with their little snippets of information for his rapidly growing card index system. As often as seemed reasonable, I kept in touch and it was through him that I submitted my application for a Standard Driving Course. The observation he appended to my application report was suitably supportive. In the late summer of 1968, I received joining instructions for the Standard Car Course at the Regional Police Driving School at Devizes in Wiltshire.

The independence of operation which Unit Beat Policing offered me was a valuable grounding for the rest of my police career. At the age of twenty two and for the first year of our marriage, I worked the area I shared with the other car crew members on a virtual 'working from home' basis. At that time, and enjoyed by most officers and their families, being a police officer was quite substantially a way of life more than 'the job' which it was called by many, although not a term commonly used in Somerset. Bringing the police car home for refreshments, being collected and deposited at beginning and end of shifts made meeting each other's wives and families part of every day's activity. This extended, although the facilities were poor at Weston-super-Mare until the new police station opened in 1971, to social events. The biggest of these events was Force Family Day held at Mountfields and then at Canonsgrove each summer but there were more localised socials and, for most stations, an Annual Ball. I will return to the Police Ball in the next chapter and to Family Day in chapter eight. The essential ingredient, lost for more than one reason in today's policing structure, was of a strong bond that went beyond the confines of the working day.

In the year after my probationary service came to an end, I did some further reading to keep myself reasonably up to date and as I reached the three year service anniversary took the Sergeants promotion examination. Later I was to discover that I had been successful in passing that examination. Earlier there had been an additional requirement for candidates for promotion to sit and pass an 'education' examination but this requirement had been dropped at about the time that I joined the Service. I suspect that it had been considered that the academic aspects should come with any suitable candidate for Constable. I maintained my study for some years, increasingly mindful that I had not really committed myself as much as I should to the opportunity that my parents had afforded by supporting me through secondary education at Wellington School.

7 Traffic and Williton

Early in September 1968, General Orders identified that another officer based at Frome was to attend the same Standard Driving Course as I and we arranged by telephone that I would pick him up on the way through from Weston-super-Mare to Devizes. We had never met before but the administrators at the Regional Driving School saw fit to accommodate us in a shared room in Goldney House on the Wiltshire Police Headquarters complex. As was usual at the time, we were expected to report on the Sunday evening so that no time would be wasted for the start of the course on the Monday morning. Each course was run by a group of instructors in, what was referred to as, a 'wing' and there was an informal get-together with them on the Sunday evening. Each 'wing' had a Sergeant and four Constable instructors, in later years all the instructors would be afforded temporary sergeant status.

With five weeks of the course to run and the requirement for Sunday evening arrivals and Saturday lunchtime departures there was the prospect of quite a separation, especially as the course spanned our first wedding anniversary. With 1968 being a leap year, the anniversary was on a Monday, fortunately on one of the two weekends when the week started with a 'late run' to accommodate some night driving. Although only briefly, Gill and I did at least see each other on the morning of that first of thankfully many annual celebrations.

The normal programme, with a greater concentration of classroom mornings in the first week, was that each crew of an instructor and three students were allocated a different car for each week. The Constables who performed the roles of instructors were drawn from all Forces in the Region and, in those days when occupying police accommodation was the norm, even for many in the city forces, a small estate of houses had been established a short distance across a, seemingly seldom used, sports field from the driving school facilities. The normal period of secondment for the instructors was two years. In spite of this open arrangement and no apparent shortage of those from elsewhere volunteering to perform the secondments there was, perhaps inevitably, a greater proportion of Wiltshire Constables. Although certainly not apparent on the Standard Course with which we are currently concerned, the instructor from Wiltshire I had on my Advanced Course was certainly not of the same calibre.

Ford Zephyr Six MkIV and Regional Driving School crew –
author beside driver's door

The crew for my Standard Course was very positively lead by the instructor, who had arrived with the Canadian Air Force during World War II, met a local girl and joined the Wiltshire Constabulary. My fellow students were very different. One was, like me, keen to move to the Traffic Department and hailed from Dartmouth in Devon. The other had, it appeared, been sent on the course in a 'last ditch' attempt to enable him to drive any sort of police vehicle without being a liability and came from Gloucestershire. Our friend from Gloucester gave us much tedium, while the instructor sought to drum into him the most basic elements of the police system of car control, and some unwanted excitement, when he performed driving manoeuvres which scarcely did the driving school much credit.

Some instructors, ours was certainly one, 'kept their eye in' with a short drive either first thing in the morning or immediately after the break for lunch. These 'demonstration drives' were, from our Canadian, something to really seek to emulate. They inspired the Devonian and me but, probably, further demoralised the man from Gloucestershire. Each half of a driving day was, subject to the instructor having a drive, split evenly between the three students and each session usually equated to about one hour. The level of concentration demanded to avoid incurring the instructor's wrath made an hour just about as much as could be sustained. Two of us soon mastered the basics and spent each successive week expanding our new-found skills in keeping with the driving school's aim of 'making progress safely', which really meant driving as fast as the prevailing conditions would allow.

I will avoid boring the reader but the most alarming incident of a quite eventful course was on the exit from another housing estate, this time in Bournemouth, where the Canadian had taken the man from Gloucester for some more basic car manoeuvring. On leaving the estate, the main road was a dual carriageway with two lanes on each side of a wide central grass strip. The width of the central reservation allowed for our right turn exit to be accommodated in two segments, with room in the centre of the two carriageways to safely position the Wolseley 6/110. The Gloucester man awaited his opportunity to cross into the central area then focused his attention upon the traffic approaching from the left. When it was clear of traffic, he made to enter the carriageway. But, he had managed to engage reverse gear instead of first and we immediately shot back across the carriageway we had just traversed. I was seated behind him and, therefore, had the best view of the expression of dire panic on the face of the man who was making a valiant, and thankfully successful, effort to brake hard enough to avoid hitting us.

When the final week arrived there were written papers to sit and, after a weekly progress run with the Wing Sergeant, the, all important, Final Drive with the Inspector. Some indication of the standard required can be gauged from the fact that a recommendation for road motor patrol duties required a minimum of 92%. The Devonian and I both managed to comfortably reach the required standard and, miraculously, the Gloucestershire man managed to 'pass' the course. What mattered to me had been achieved and I returned to the panda area in hope that it would not be long before an opportunity to move to the traffic department would arise. It did, within a few weeks, but not in quite the form I had anticipated. There was a vacancy for a traffic motorcyclist at Weston-super-Mare, a posting that would not necessitate an immediate move from the flat. But I was not the only potential candidate.

As had been the case two and a half years earlier, a motorcycle instructor from Headquarters at Taunton was sent up to asses me and the other candidate, who was a transferee from a northern Force and several years my senior in both age and service. I did not think that I would take precedence over the other man and was not overly concerned as another course at Devizes would have been required, but was going to do my best to impress the instructor. When he arrived, I wasted the best part of an hour in the canteen while he took the other man on his assessment. He followed each of us in turn on his Triumph Saint while we lead the way on one of the two station Triumph Tiger 100s. My colleague looked too confident when I took over the Tiger 100 from him.

Following the instructor's directions, I set off to travel south from Weston on the A370. As I left the restricted area of the town, near Uphill, the road took a double bend up onto the small crest before several miles of long successive sweeping bends to the point at which he had directed me to stop, at East Brent. After the steady 30mph that negotiating the four wheeled traffic on a motorcycle allowed, I opened the throttle as I gained the short level section before the brief bends at the side of Bleadon hill. I had glanced frequently in the mirror attached to the handlebar fairing and seen that the instructor was following me at a reasonable distance. When I accelerated, the image in the mirror was so blurred by the vibration for which Triumph twins were renowned that I could not see clearly what was behind me. The speed at which I rode those few miles out to East Brent made concerns about anything approaching me from behind somewhat academic, so I did not worry about it. When I reached the bus stop at East Brent and pulled up, the mirror was empty, a glance behind revealed that it had not lied. Several seconds elapsed before the Saint appeared and the instructor, with no hint of amusement, directed me to return to the police station and "take it steady" on the way.

It was not a surprise to me when, a few days later, the Traffic Sergeant broke the news to me that my colleague was to attend the Advanced Motorcycle Course. More of a surprise was to follow only a couple of weeks later when I was summoned to the Chief Superintendent's office. He told me that I had been allocated my first police house and that the move was to the Road Traffic

First Police House – Williton in late 1968

'*Williton Police Station – photograph taken in 2015 – the only external change since 1970 are the models of cars outside*'

Department at Williton. After the immediate reaction of delight at getting the transfer into the department, my next thought was "where is Williton"? A quick look at the large Ordnance Survey map in the front office revealed only that it was too far away to be on the edge of the sheets covering the Weston Division, even though that then included Burnham on Sea. A look at the road atlas in the mini that had replaced the A35 shortly after our wedding revealed that Williton was quite near Minehead and at the junction of the 'A' roads from there to Bridgwater and Taunton.

Gill having secured an office job with a local transport company even before she joined me at Weston after our marriage, had suspected that our first police house and my achieving a transfer to Traffic would necessitate a move. This was to be the first of too many in too short a period of years but that, of course, was unknown to us at that time. We exploited the provision in Standing Orders for a police car to be used for a visit to the proposed new house and were, exceptionally, allowed to use the plain Hillman Imp allocated to the Policewomen's Unit. When we arrived at No. 1 Police House, Williton we were greeted by the couple who were about to move away from the house and somewhat concerned to discover that he had requested the transfer after quite a short time, on the grounds of a degree of incompatibility with their neighbour and his, more senior, crew partner. There was only a brief meeting with that partner who I was about to inherit before a return journey in which there were inevitable worries as to what it was I, we, had in prospect.

With the help of the colleague and friend from the Forest of Dean, we stripped out the seats of the new Ford Transit crew-bus and took our few personal belongings from the flat down to the house at Williton. Between hearing of the impending move and its date I was told by another officer of the discount deal offered by the Special Constabulary member at Flax Bourton who managed a large furniture warehouse in Bristol. We contacted him and visited the warehouse, allocating all our savings to a lounge suite, dinning room set and bedroom furniture to be delivered to Williton. On the A39, at St Audries, the Ford Cortina MkII passed us in the opposite direction and the partner I was about to join, patrolling solo pending my arrival, gave the Devizes left handed salute as he approached. With the statute of limitations well expired, I can reveal that it was only after we had unloaded and returned the Transit to Weston that I realised that removing the seats from the vehicle had breached its type classification and invoked the requirement for higher road duty as a goods vehicle!

After a busy use of the three 'moving days' allocated for a transfer our first police house looked like a home, provided you did not look into the other, empty, bedrooms. The rooms we had been able to afford to furnish were added to by the gift, from my parents, of a kitchen suite to go with the police supplied cooker. Buying reasonable quality at the discount available proved a good investment as most of this furniture, added to over time, was to move around with us frequently over the next few years. My new colleague and his wife, our next door neighbours in the pair of semi-detached 'standard Somerset pattern' police houses, proved to be as friendly as possible and their young children to be a delight. I could see why my predecessor was not compatible with my new crewmate but we hit it off immediately and it stayed that way for the relatively short time we were to work together. Indeed, we never afterwards lost touch.

To clear up the domestic aspects before moving on to the rural traffic policing experience, there were, especially noticeable in early December, two main matters that needed addressing in respect of No. 1 Police House. The first had been sorted out by our predecessors by the purchase, at very low cost, of a huge piece of fawn coloured cloth to divide the 'L' shaped main room. These 'standard pattern' Somerset police houses did have slight variations and in some cases this 'L' shaped room had a wall dividing lounge from dinning room. In the open versions there was a lot of room to heat in winter but by the introduction of a curtain rail along the prominent joist a heavy curtain served as a removable divider between the lounge and dinning room areas of the space. This large piece of cloth came from the Wansborough Paper Mill at Watchet, where the nap of the cloth was extracted to bind the paper then the cloth discarded. I suspect that half the area had curtains and even blankets that had once gone around the large drum in the paper factory.

Insulation already upgraded there was now the need to provide heat. My partner identified the need to minimise fuel costs and one of our first journeys in the Ford Cortina MkII patrol car, RYC 168 F, was to the sawmill at Dunster. After identifying my next (first at Williton) rest day and handing over 10/- (50p), at that time about the price of a hundredweight bag of coal, I awaited that rest day. Meanwhile, after a hopeless experience with the new-fangled Job Centre, that had quite recently replaced the Labour Exchange, Gill obtained, without their help, a job in Gliddons, the local agricultural engineers and based right beside the police station. Gill, thus, absent and my neighbours departed for the day, the small tipper truck arrived quite early. It was reversed up the slope at the side of the police station and into the yard. The rear was stacked full of off-cuts of timber and when it tilted the sectioned rear half of the load was joined by quite a lot of the top part of the front half. The Sergeant loaned me his wheelbarrow, but not his help, to get the yard cleared. By the time Gill came in for her lunch break, the timber had been stacked wherever I could find a sensible space.

With only a few weeks to Christmas and my new colleague having reserved the Christmas period for some of his annual leave, it was realised that the usual policy of new to Traffic Officers having to drive accompanied for the first six months would need to be amended in my circumstance. Arrangements were made for my colleague and me to go to Headquarters on a Saturday afternoon so that I could take the Traffic Inspector for a run in order that he may authorise me to drive patrol cars solo. Only one aspect of that run was in any way memorable, I stopped a car being driven with a bald tyre in Langport and reported the driver. On several occasions when attending the court over in the east of the county I found other offenders and created another 'evidential' trip across the county.

In the week before we had moved to Williton, a young woman was found at the bottom of some cliffs at Watchet but it was soon realised that it was no accident. This was about the last time that the long-established 'Murder Room' at New Scotland Yard (NSY) was involved in our area. Up until that time but soon afterwards abandoned, the Home Office insisted that to gain financial help with a murder enquiry any provincial Chief Constable had to call in the Murder Squad from NSY within 48 hours of a murder being reported. There was even a 1950s television programme based upon this practice, called 'Murder Bag'. A Detective Superintendent and Detective Sergeant were deployed to assist the local Force, with the 'tried and tested' system of statement cross referencing and, importantly, the central funding support. The need for the statement system was, not many years later overtaken by the computer system known as HOLMES (Home Office Large and Major Enquiry System) and the financial support became less certain. Most senior Detectives in provincial Forces welcomed the absence of the 'interference' most saw as the involvement from the Met.

I had to collect our Detectives from Bridgwater railway station one evening and return them to their lodgings in a pub in Long Street, Williton. The Detective Superintendent invited me for a 'night cap' so I returned the car to the Police Station and let Gill know where I was going. I had never seen such a wad of cash as my host took out to pay for my drink, not even among the gypsy scrap merchants and horse dealer fraternity. The murder was detected through local information and the culprit volunteering information which only the guilty man could know. The victim's location could have signified an accident but for the fact that her mouth was stuffed with tissues, presumably to keep her quiet. The man pointed out by locals in Watchet as suspect number one was the only one who volunteered the information about the tissues that the senior detective had been careful not to publicise. Another sequel, our Detective Superintendent rose to the Metropolitan Police rank of Commander, equivalent to a provincial Force Assistant Chief Constable, but later was successfully prosecuted and dismissed.

One morning, early in the spring of 1969, we were on patrol between Watchet and Washford when my crewmate pulled into the deep gated entrance of a field. Across the field there was a tractor heading around towards us with a chain harrow in tow. When he reached us the farmer stopped and there ensued a conversation which I fell somewhat short of fully understanding. My only real involvement, after being introduced, was to surrender the bulk of my current wealth, another 10/- (50p) note. This payment in advance was, I was told, for potatoes. Weeks went by and eventually we were hailed by the farmer as we travelled along the A39 towards Minehead one morning. We identified our next rest day and turned up at his field on that morning. With others, we spent a back-breaking day following the tractor with the spinner which excavated the potatoes and bagged the potatoes which we collected on a wooden sledge being drawn on the end of a long chain. Days later, his calculations completed, the farmer arrived and, after a further display of skilful reversing, we unloaded both our shares of the potatoes. With only the two of us to eat them and the bicycle shed at the side of our home packed full with a total of 18cwt, a bag accompanied us to Wellington on many of our journeys and, that year, kept quite a lot of our extended family well supplied.

In addition to the very occasional discovery of a brace of pheasants hanging on the door, I was never sure whether from the Game Keeper or a poacher, the shoot provided a rare and welcome addition to the budget. Standing Orders specifically allowed for a dispensation to the general ban against other employment for 'light agricultural work'. This was really to allow for the local Constable to help at busy times, such as harvest, but was quite liberally interpreted. At least at Williton, the interpretation included beating for the local shoot, for which the handsome sum of £1/10/- (£1.50) was paid and a sandwich and couple of bottles of beer provided at the lunch break. The other local advantage was the fortnightly, weekly was not possible with night shifts getting in the way, trip to the small chicken farm at Quantoxhead. Orders secured from the stations at Minehead and Williton and coffee consumed at the farm, a gentle - very gentle - patrol along the A39 ensued, with the rear seat of the patrol car fully laden with the two and a half dozen egg trays stacked one upon the other. We never received a call during one of these deliveries but I often conjured with the picture had we ever received such a call demanding an immediate response.

The history of the Williton and Minehead placements of patrol cars and crews went back to the aftermath of the terrible flooding disaster at Lynmouth in 1952. The poor response by Somerset in support of their colleagues in Devon had been criticised and these cars were placed on the extreme west of the Force area to provide emergency cover for whatever eventuality. The Section with which we were housed comprised a Sergeant and two Constables living alongside the old but selectively modernised police station at Williton, two Constables at Watchet and one each at Kilve and Stogumber. Although the local Sergeant had some responsibility for us our main supervisor was eighteen miles away at the Divisional Headquarters in Bridgwater. We saw quite a bit of the local men and something of their families, both the Constables in the large old houses flanking Williton Police Station each had four children. As did most Sections, Williton held an annual Police Ball at the Cleeve Hotel near Washford and we were involved with the section officers in its organisation but that was, really, the limit of the formal social events.

We spent by far the major proportion of our duty time away from Williton, with the Minehead Sub-Division being quite large and the Bridgwater Division really very big. The Minehead Sub-Division extended from the Quantock Hills west to the Devon border and many still have no conception that three-quarters of the vast area of Exmoor is in Somerset. The Borough and Glastonbury Sub-Divisions extended the Bridgwater Division eastwards to mid-way between Glastonbury and Wells and it included much of the Somerset levels, the entire Polden Hills and to within a few miles of Taunton. For the majority of the shifts my next door neighbour and I were crewed together. Although I suspect that I could understand that some could feel overpowered by the supremely confident nature of my crewmate and, therefore, perhaps why my predecessor had not felt comfortable with the partnership, I did not have that experience. Indeed, perhaps because we were so different and there was a fourteen year age gap, we got on extremely well and I saw the opportunity to pick up on his already more than ten years of experience on Traffic. As a small aside, the VHF radio frequency used by the police in that period was not too far away from that used by the old 405 line television sets. When we returned to Williton and booked off the air as we placed the Cortina GT in its garage, Gill heard that message over the television and would put the kettle on.

I have already remarked upon the nationally sponsored Regional Experiment (RE) scheme, whereby all major routes were divided into quite lengthy sections. The A38, then the main trunk road from the midlands to the south west, had two Sectors in Somerset, split at Edithmead, where the current M5 motorway junction at East Brent meets the A38 (now a roundabout, then a relatively inconspicuous junction except for a few weekends in the summer). In daylight hours, in keeping with the since closed national RE scheme, at least one patrol car would be allocated to each Sector but at night they would be combined. If we were both on duty during a night tour week, we would almost invariably be allocated to 'Sector Patrol' of the A38. This necessitated an eighteen mile journey to either Bridgwater or Taunton to start the patrol and, of course, a similar eighteen miles to get back to Williton in the morning. With the road mileage between the Bristol Constabulary and Devon and Cornwall Constabulary boundaries at close on sixty miles, just one patrol of the whole territory brought a high nightly recorded mileage. This was part of the thinking of the Traffic Sergeant at Bridgwater in those times of early management worries about costs. Our car, used almost exclusively by the pair of us, sat idle on our rest days, whereas the variety of cars kept at Bridgwater were often used by more than one crew in a day. Hence, giving us the tasks that called for higher mileages was a sound way of coming closer to evening out the Divisional Traffic fleet.

Even when, as was not unusual, my regular colleague chose to take his annual leave during our scheduled night tours, I could end up covering high mileages. Although it was common, then, for other patrols to be by a single Constable, night duty by Traffic Patrol cars it was considered should be by double crewed vehicles. This was made possible by our car being allocated to the nightly 'Crime Car' patrol. These patrols were mounted on each of the six Divisions, used a marked Traffic vehicle and were crewed by a Traffic driver and non-traffic 'observer'. In most instances the traffic crews were working out of the same stations as were the 'Borough' or 'Section' Constables. In our case, the non-traffic crewman could be from anywhere on the large Division. Most often it would be a Constable from the larger station at Bridgwater, even better but rarely from Minehead but quite often from the Glastonbury Section, either that station or Street. Where the latter applied, I had to drive the near thirty miles to Glastonbury or Street to collect my crewmate for the night, carry out the patrol of that extensive Division, usually taking refreshments in the Bridgwater kitchen, and deposit him back at his home station for a solo run back to Williton in time to go off duty at 0600 hours.

On one of the rare summer evenings when I collected my Crime Car crewmate from Minehead, he came armed with some, seemingly reliable, information from a local Automobile Association (AA) man regarding deer poachers. Near the AA box at the junction of the A39 with the Porlock Toll Road, our AA Patrolman had heard and seen activity which could only be people with a Land Rover shooting deer on that northern edge of Exmoor. With the only pre-determined commitment being the nightly 'static check' coordinated by the Divisional Detective Chief Inspectors (DCIs) arranged so that they took place at the same time at various locations across the County each night, we set off for Porlock Hill. At the top of Porlock Hill, the road to Exford turns off left from the A39 and a short way up the hill there was a large parking area for sunny day picnics with a magnificent view. We went to the edge of the parking area where a track appeared to go steeply down to connect back up with the A39 not far on the Porlock side of the junction with the AA box.

Lights switched off and, recognising how sound travels over the open moorland, the radio turned to the handset only speaker, we sat with the windows open waiting for something to happen. We anticipated that we would be there for some long time but were surprised that only half an hour had elapsed before a lone Land Rover broached the top of Porlock Hill and passed along the A39 beneath our unseen position. Better still, the Land Rover stopped near the AA box and moved slowly into the copse of trees on the junction opposite the box and at the top of the Toll Road. There was a slight delay, during which all was in darkness with the Land Rover's lights extinguished. There then followed a succession of times when the lights on the Land Rover were switched on and, on each occasion, loud cracking noises which sounded like the discharge of a rifle. It looked as though my crewmate's information from the AA man was good.

With the patrol car lights out and the handbrake off, we started slowly down the track before us, intending to retain for as long as possible the element of surprise. Our, most importantly my, eyes had become accustomed to the dim light from a partial moon but, as we descended closer to the A39 I saw that the middle of the track had been worn away by successive downpours of rain water and was gradually showing an increasingly deep 'V' formation between the wheels of the car. Wondering how we would extricate ourselves and realising that reversing back to where we had started would be nigh-on impossible, I breathed a big sigh of relief when I realised that council workmen had been piling gravel in the layby we were approaching and we were able to regain a relatively level surface before reaching the road. Now was the time to start the engine for a quick dash along the couple of hundred yards of the A39 to where our 'poachers' were operating.

Perhaps because of the adrenalin generated as I was pondering how we were going to get out of the 'V' shaped track, followed by the short but rapid dash, we entered the copse and pulled up behind the Land Rover with our headlights blazing. Initially all I saw was bodies jumping away from around the Land Rover in all directions. To identify who we were, I flicked on the blue light and Police roof sign as I applied the handbrake. We jumped out of the Cortina GT expecting to try and grab just one or two each as the rest made good their escape. Instead, they stopped in their tracks and stood looking at us. We, then, saw that they were all in the familiar uniform of the Venture Scouts! It transpired that they were down from Weston-super-Mare for an expedition weekend. The lights being turned on and off was to save on the Land Rover's battery as they struck the large tent metal pegs with their mallets. All present thought that the situation was quite amusing and the leader suspended his involvement with the tent erecting exercise so that he could get the primus stove going. We shared a cup of tea before they settled down for the night and we continued our patrol.

I learned a valuable lesson in respect of 'man management' one morning in the spring of 1969. My regular colleague, and neighbour, and I made our way up the A39 to Bridgwater, anticipating timing our arrival to coincide with the Borough section's seven o'clock brew. Just as we were approaching the entrance to the police station yard we received a call from Information Room directing us to a 'serious road accident' on the A38 at Pawlett, a few miles north of Bridgwater. We were there quickly, with little traffic to impede our progress and what we found was certainly correctly categorised as 'serious'. The current, at that time, project to construct the 'B' Station at Hinkley Point was underway and there was a fleet of old but roadworthy coaches, each driven by one of the workers, which came in to Hinkley Point each day from all parts of the county, picking up workers on the way. One of these coaches had stopped beside the small transport café at Pawlett to collect a few men waiting for their lift to work.

An eight wheeled rigid lorry laden with coal had approached the coach, traveling in the same, southerly, direction. The driver had, evidently, not realised that the coach was stationery until the last minute and his efforts to avoid a direct collision brought a serious glancing blow which removed the rear off-side corner of the coach. The lorry then veered across the road and into a loose group of trees, long since replaced with a solid fence, until it struck one tree and came to a halt with most of the long section of the chassis still across the road. The impacts with the coach followed by the more severe one with the tree split the timber sides of the lorry and most of its load of coal was scattered all over the road. The injuries from such a severe accident were mercifully low in severity. The rear offside corner of the coach had not been occupied and the most serious injuries were through men being thrown around by the impact inside and on the entry steps of the coach. Of all those present, the lorry driver had suffered the worst. The few local residents and people from the transport café looked after the injured but soon we were joined by a couple of ambulances, usefully both from the Bridgwater direction.

In those days there was no local radio but the BBC did run a West of England service as part of the Home Service Radio. We asked Information Room to request that the BBC broadcast that the A38, at that time a major trunk route, would be closed for some time. Fortunately, this section of the A38, although it had been there for some years, was an earlier by-pass for the village of Pawlett. With the cooperation of locals and a couple of motorists who did not seem in any hurry to continue their journeys, we diverted traffic from both directions through the village. With the Information Room staff making the appropriate calls, another coach eventually arrived and a lorry and JCB were on their way from Bristol to sort out the coal so that the heavy breakdown truck, also coming from Bristol, would be able to remove the obstructing vehicles.

Now for the lesson in man-management! The two of us were feeling quite content that since our arrival at fractionally after seven o'clock, we had set in train all that was necessary and appropriate to rectify this mini-disaster. At just before nine o'clock a black Hillman Minx, one of the many the Force owned, arrived with a Senior Officer at the wheel. He stopped the car in the middle of the road and got out to survey the scene. Unlike when we had arrived, it looked untidy but contained none of the earlier chaos but he immediately started challenging what actions we had taken with a succession of questions. My, older, colleague was polite enough at the start but grew increasingly tired of the Officer's attitude. Eventually, he invited the senior officer to get back into his car and return from whence he had arrived. I am not sure who was most surprised at this blatant insubordination, the Senior Officer or me. On reflection, it must have been him. He mumbled something about not ever having been spoken to like that before but as he did so he was getting back into his car. Lessons on how to deal with people come in two ways, approaches that are worthy of being emulated and those which should never be copied.

One of the advantages of the A38 Sector patrols, especially on night duty, was that we had legitimate access to the southern reaches of that road, where it passed through my home town of Wellington. Since before I had left school, my dear mother had made, as close as she could by that time, a return to the career she had hoped to follow and for which she had started the training in London in the 1930s. Being a night duty auxiliary at Wellington Cottage Hospital suited her far more than had the years she had spent when my sister and I were small operating a loom in the pattern weaving shed at Fox's Woollen Mills. On night shifts the local Constables all visited the hospital for cups of tea and, in the winter, a warm-up. There was a 'fair exchange' for this hospitality in that there was a settled and approved practice for the duty Officer in Wellington to attend the hospital when required to assist with the removal of a deceased patient to the tiny mortuary, known as 'Rose Cottage' in the garden of the hospital. There was a 'handy-man' for such tasks in daytime but only female nurses at night, and everyone seemed to think it just another part of the community service of a police officer to assist the local nurses with this task.

In the early hours of the morning on one night when we had parked beside the staff room window and placed the radio handset inside the window sill, our chat and coffee was disturbed by a call for Tango 32. I picked up the handset and answered, with a slightly 'coded' location of 'Wellington Road, Taunton!', for us to be directed to a Road Traffic Accident (RTA) on the A38 at Barrow Tanks, just a couple of miles from the Bristol boundary and about fifty miles away. We thought little of the distance as such journeys were not unusual but were more concerned at the potential for such a trip to make our anticipated return to Williton by 0600 hours seem unlikely. With very little other traffic on the road, we negotiated Taunton, Bridgwater and Highbridge, as well as all the smaller places in between, and arrived at the walled area between the Barrow reservoirs to find that, in the same time, the Section Constable had also just arrived, having travelled much less than half the distance from Clevedon. The articulated lorry had skidded across the road and jack-knifed to block the carriageway. Remarkably, there was so little traffic that only a few other lorries were waiting for the breakdown wagon to do its bit. The driver of the obstructing lorry was uninjured and the breakdown truck had beaten us to the scene, having only travelled the short distance from Bristol. Soon the damaged lorry was on its way behind the tow-truck and all had returned to normality. A quick run down the A38 and, via Bridgwater, along the A39 brought us back to Williton only a few minutes late to go off duty.

I will restrict myself to two more anecdotes linked to A38 patrols from Williton during 1969. We met up one night with a crew from Weston-super-Mare, also equipped with that Division's Cortina GT and known to us both, the elder being my probationary attachment mentor from my home town. Earlier, there had been a general transmission to inform all patrols of a Leyland 1100 car having been stolen from Bridgwater. While we were chatting opposite the A38 junction with the A370, an 1100 came at quite a high speed down the A38 from the Bristol direction. As it passed us we all realised that it was 'that' 1100. We were parked across the front of the Weston car so were, necessarily, first away. When we reached the Fox & Goose pub the 1100 was not to be seen and we could not believe that it would have gained on us that much. A brief stop at the crossroads beside the pub and down the road towards Mark there was a very brief flash of brake lights.

When we turned into that road the 1100's lights came back on and it sped off. The other crew took the slightly longer route and, correctly, anticipated the

1100's direction of travel, setting their car across the narrow road to block its way. The driver slewed around the patrol car, almost taking the older police officer off his feet. Incredibly, the 1100's front wheel drive dragged it into and out of the ditch at the side of the road. The Weston car was quickly moved out of our way and we followed the 1100 along a road towards a 'T' junction. Indicating firstly right, then left, the 1100 did neither but went through an open gateway and across a field, with us in distant pursuit. At one point the 1100 disappeared momentarily, a second or two later we went down and up traversing the same, fortunately dry, rhine. There was, now, nowhere for the driver of the 1100 to go except into the corner of the field. There the two occupants abandoned the vehicle and ran in opposite directions. My man ran back towards the rhine but I rugby tackled him in a short distance, having calculated the shorter route to intercept him. My partner was less fortunate in that his man took to the hedge but soon came to an abrupt halt as he had grabbed at some hidden barbed wire. We deposited the passenger, my prisoner, in the Weston Cortina, as we did not think that our colleague from that patrol car would be too well disposed towards the driver. Both were taken to Bridgwater police station and the 1100 recovered after they had been locked up for the rest of the night, for the CID Officers to interview them in the morning.

A sequel to this pursuit was that we noticed the next day that the Cortina was feeling a bit 'solid' over even the smallest bump in the road, although we also noticed that its road holding had improved somewhat. A trip to the Force garage at Taunton revealed that the rear leaf springs had gone past the point of no return and made the back axle virtually rigid. The sequel to the sequel was that we were compelled to use the, much disliked, Ford Zephyr Mk.IV from Bridgwater for a few days. This car had probably the softest suspension of any car I ever drove as a patrol car and was evidently too big for its engine. What made it most disliked by us was the length of the bonnet. Exiting Williton Police Station brought a very restricted view towards Minehead because of the beautiful thatched cottage that sat right beside the road. Getting the Mk.IV out required assistance as the front bumper would be level with the centre line of the road before the driver could see to his right!

The other Sector Patrol incident worthy of a mention came on the Saturday of the August Bank Holiday weekend in 1969. We received a call to go to a telephone kiosk and were told in that more secure manner that the Force had just been told by the Bristol Constabulary Information Room that the Royal Train was entering our area, destined for the Regatta at Dartmouth. With the train making unhindered speed south we hot-footed it to check the Whiteball Tunnel. Being close to my home territory, I soon found the private driveway which was the closest we could get the patrol car to the tunnel portal. Leaving the car, in those days, meant not being in communication, but we walked quickly along the trackbed towards the mouth of the tunnel. Just as we reached the, even darker, tunnel mouth, we could hear the massive diesel engines pulling the relatively short train up from Beam Bridge towards Devon. At that same moment, we heard voices in the tunnel! Not much could be done, the train was upon us in next to no time and clattered into the tunnel. We virtually held our breath but listened as it was evident by the noise disappearing that the train had reached the Devon end and departed.

When we reached the patrol car we chose not to relate everything, simply reporting all that the Information Room Sergeant would want to hear - that the Royal Train was now clear of our County. We needed a few minutes to collect our thoughts and decided to go up to the Devon boundary on the A38 for a quiet spell. No sooner had we parked the car in customary, nose to the carriageway, fashion than a patrol car approached from the Devon direction and stopped beside us. A short conversation with our Devon and Cornwall counterparts revealed that they had been instructed to attend the tunnel too and had also heard voices. It became evident that the funnelling effect of even such a long tunnel carried our normally spoken conversations through to the opposite end.

Away from the A38 and back in the local area around the Minehead Sub-Division, we often were kept busy by the 'squaddies' from Doniford Army Camp, long since turned into a holiday camp just a couple of miles east of Watchet. On Friday and Saturday evenings the little town of Watchet was awash with the young men from the Royal Irish Rangers who currently occupied that camp. As an important part of keeping in with the locals, the Regimental Police ran a three-tonner 'shore patrol' to 'sweep up' any strays but there were often the odd one or two left staggering around Watchet late at night. We would 'detain' them and take them to the Guard House at the camp gates rather than arrest them for being drunk and take them into custody at Minehead Police Station. Public tranquillity was resumed and the army much preferred to deal with their errant members themselves.

The young men from all over the United Kingdom who were stationed at Doniford found it appropriate to commit all sorts of minor criminal acts, most often relating to the use of motor vehicles, in all parts of the country. The consequence was that the senior of the two Constables at Watchet collected, every week, numerous enquiries from other Police Forces requiring that individuals be interviewed and, often, reported for offences. Every Wednesday, he would submit a list to the Guard Room and each Thursday would be offered the use of the Guard Sergeant's Office. Outside, regardless of the weather, those from the list would be on parade and called in one at a time for the interview to be conducted – with the Guard Sergeant in close attendance to ensure that the Constable was treated with his due respect.

For some years prior to 1969, the Force had allowed the Taunton Motor Club to organise a Divisional driving competition on the area then used for local driver training at the disused Culmhead airfield above Blagdon Hill, the buildings of which were used by the Ministry of Defence for communications purposes. Each August, the six Divisions fielded a team comprising a patrol car, traffic motorcyclist, 'panda' car, section motorcyclist and woman Constable in a Hillman car. This team of five competed in set-piece situations marked out on the old runway by cones and each contestant was scored by the Taunton Motor Club officials. The first item of the day was a 'concourse d'elegance' where the vehicles were scrutinised for their appearance and equipment. My crewmate had represented the Bridgwater Division for several years but was on annual leave that August so, with the Cortina from each Division being the chosen patrol car input, it was down to me (not yet even an Advanced Driver!). I had received permission for Gill to accompany me and we set out from Williton that weekend morning with a gleaming car which I drove very sedately all the way to Culmhead. Our 'concourse' scrutiny docked me a mark because we had lost the petrol filler cap only days earlier and had been equipped with a replacement that was in grey undercoat rather than white to match the rest of the car.

With the competition nearing its end, I was informed by the Traffic Inspector, rally enthusiast and new 'import' from Birmingham, that the competition was in the balance between Bridgwater Division and the Weston-super-Mare Division. With only the two patrol cars left to complete the final test the Division to receive the Taunton Motor Club Cup for 1969 was to be decided by the last two drives, that of my old former Wellingtonian colleague from Weston and mine. With the Inspector clicking his stopwatches along the top of his clip-board, I watched my older friend do a perfect run, not a cone touched. "That's it", said the Inspector, "You can only win by doing it quicker!" The MkII Cortina GT had an 'umbrella' handbrake which was fixed under the parcel shelf near the steering column and, when I entered the first section which necessitated turning the car in a gap only one and a half times as wide as the car was long, I grabbed the handbrake and slid around to avoid the time taken to perform a three, or more, point turn. With fingers metaphorically crossed, I reversed zigzag through a row of cones, drove back in similar fashion around them, did another handbrake turn and stopped astride the finish line. The Inspector was jumping up and down in a very un-officer-like fashion, but the Assistant Chief Constable was not looking nearly as pleased. Back down at Canonsgrove he did have to present the Cup to Bridgwater Division and the small Driver's Cup to me!

Ford Cortina GT MkII, identical to RYC 168 F used at Williton
(taken at a Taunton Motor Club Cup competition)

Before we leave Williton, just one more reference to Doniford Army Camp. A camp which I had visited as a cadet in the Wellington CCF as a teenager on several of our 'Field Days'. One afternoon we were told over the telephone by our Traffic Sergeant at Bridgwater that we may have to work on a bit at the end of our 2p.m. till 10p.m. shift as we were to collect the Divisional Chief Superintendent from an Officers' Mess reception he was attending at Doniford Camp. We arrived at the camp gates at 2100 hours and were admitted to park outside the Officers' Mess. After about a quarter of an hour the Mess Sergeant came out and invited us in, assuring us that our Divisional Commander looked as though he was not yet ready to leave.

We were taken in to a bar through which there was a constant flow of stewards collecting and delivering trays of drinks to the Officers down the corridor in the main room and a number of side rooms. Two well inebriated young officers came into the bar and tried to press us to have something other than the soft drink with which the Mess Sergeant had supplied us. Our protests were falling on deaf ears until the Sergeant tactfully ushered them away. We were then taken into a side room in which there were several Royal Navy Officers. In conversation with them we discovered that one, a Surgeon Commander from Plymouth, had been there many years earlier when my colleague was in the Royal Marines. A long time later, our Chief Superintendent appeared and we bundled him into the back seat of the patrol car. A confused radio exchange followed, with the Information Room staff wondering why we were still on duty. Then a rapid trip to Bridgwater and back brought us back to Williton with a few hours to take off the overtime cards at some later time.

As I have already mentioned, the time spent at Williton was often brought back to me when, in the 1990s, the television programme 'Heartbeat' came to the screens. The countryside across Exmoor was very similar to the Yorkshire Moors shown on the programme and the small Section's personnel had quite a few similarities to those found in 'Aidensfield'. The whole, and very enjoyable, episode was brought to a halt by the early recognition of a need to economise, one used many times later to reduce what the police are able to offer. It was decided that it would be more economically sound for the two crews both to be based at Minehead and for them to share a single patrol car. Our neighbours were allocated a direct swap with a Constable's family from Minehead and we were offered a flat above Minehead Police Station.

At that time Gill was expecting or first child and a visit to the flat made it evident that it would be entirely unsuited to bringing a baby into this world. The access was by means of a very restricted staircase direct from outside the building and the 'lounge' overlooked the exercise yard for the cells on the floor below. Much to the Divisional Commander's annoyance, I objected to the accommodation and, thankfully, circumstances made it appropriate for my Traffic Chief Superintendent to have good reason to support me. In early 1970, with the extension of the M5 anticipated down through Somerset in the next two to three years, he was looking for every opportunity to increase the number of trained Traffic Officers at Weston-super-Mare. Hence, only fifteen months after we had moved into our first police house and with Gill seven months pregnant, we were back to a house on Milton Road in Weston.

Through the time at Williton the Force had recognised that it was woefully short of qualified candidates for promotion, especially of Sergeants eligible by examination for the role of Inspector. The Divisional Training Sergeants were each charged with the task of presenting day sessions to assist officers with their preparation for the two examinations, those to Sergeant and Inspector. With my Sergeant's examination already under my belt, I joined the regular group traveling to Bridgwater for these voluntary sessions with a view to getting a pass in the Inspectors' examination. Voluntary sessions meant that you did them in your own time, although we were allowed to use a plain police car to get to Bridgwater. I was fortunate that this support enabled me to also gain the qualification to Inspector. Promotion Boards were held annually and there seemed an expectation that anyone with ambition would apply to attend. They, at that time, comprised the Chief Constable, Assistant Chief Constable and all the Force Chief Superintendents. The main objective on the day seemed to be for the Chief Superintendents to demonstrate to their colleagues just how uncomfortable they could make each candidate.

8 Return to Weston-super-Mare

That no other accommodation could be found other than the totally unsuitable flat at Minehead seemed doubly incongruous when we realised that 287, Milton Road had just been bought and re-roofed in anticipation of it becoming another police house, alongside the one that the Authority had owned for some years at 289. It had, however, formed a part of the intended build-up of Traffic Department personnel at Weston-super-Mare in anticipation of the M5 motorway. With me and the crews from Flax Bourton, plus several motorcyclists brought in to handle the higher number of abnormal load escorts for the motorway construction, when we arrived back at Weston in February 1970 there were eighteen Constables with, still, the one Sergeant. By the time we left Weston, again, in November, 1972 there was a Chief Inspector, four Sergeants and forty eight Constables.

Following the RE scheme, mentioned in the previous chapter, all patrol cars were white by the late 1960s. Well before late 1972 they all had 'dayglow' and 'scotchlight' tape on many of their panels. The cars which were up for replacement at just the right time were the Jaguar 240s (actually 340s for police use). The, scarcely altered, MkII body panels of these Jaguars would not have been as easy to 'mark-up' with tape as were the later XJ6 models. My new crewmate, for some time after the return to Weston, was a really gentle gentleman who had spent quite a time performing cycle patrols over wide areas of the Flax Bourton Sub Division, to the north of the Weston-super-Mare Division before moving on to Traffic. He had been one of the several moved down to Weston just before Gill and I arrived in Milton Road. He lived with his family in one of a group of police houses on Windwhistle Circle in the middle of the Bourneville estate and, except on night-time shifts, we took turns at dropping each other off for refreshments before taking the patrol car home for our own meal. This not only enabled a much more recognisable family life but meant that we each got to know the other's family members at the drop off and pick up times.

Talking of family, Gill gave birth to our first daughter, Tanya, just a few weeks after our return to Weston. I took her in to Ashcombe House Maternity Home that morning, with no expectation that I should be present at her birth. Not being on duty that morning had been handy but what to do now? I went in to the Traffic Office, still across the back yard, which was now being excavated to form the base of the new Police Station. One of the motorcyclists was doing some reports and, when I told him why I was there, he immediately sat me down and dashed off to the canteen kitchen to get me a cup of coffee. We are still in quite regular contact and I often remind him of that kindness, especially when I see him near to Tanya's birthday. At 287, in addition to the roof being retiled the garage, up the narrow alleyway between us and number 285, had a front constructed. The previous owner had built a substantial garage but recognised that without a front door it would not attract an increase in his rates. The Police Authority were not inclined to see such a partial structure and got the job finished to our advantage.

*The new Weston-super-Mare Police Station (taken in 2015
but only the entrance changed since 1970)*

Our neighbours across the alleyway had divided their house into two flats. They occupied one and an equally elderly couple rented the other. There was a space in the small garden beside their garage in which the other couple parked their Fiat 500 car. At refreshment times in daylight hours I reversed Jaguars and, more commonly, Triumph 2.5 PI patrol cars up to the back gateway.

Triumph 2500 PI MkII at Canonsgrove c. 1970

Our neighbour seemed to take umpteen shifts between first and reverse gears to get the little Fiat into its resting position. We liked our neighbours at Milton Road and the older couples both delighted in Tanya's arrival and early growing. The other half of the semi-detached pair, which now both belonged to the Police Authority, had three couples as occupants in the two years and nine months we lived there. Each had young children or babies, so Gill found quite a bit of common ground to chat about over the garden wall. Soon after Tanya's arrival we realised that a trip to Wellington in the Mini, with pram carriage in the back seat, chassis on the roof rack and everything else in the tiny boot, was not a good experience. I hunted for a replacement and found the ideal answer, a MkI Ford Cortina estate. It was already five years old but in good condition and the asking price at the local Ford dealership was £400. They offered £250 in part exchange, so I went to the bank, got an interview with the manager and was told that the National Westminster Bank could not risk loaning me such a sum - £150! At that time my salary was about £20 per week and my position as secure as could be but there it was, no loan. Instead I took the balance on hire purchase and paid double the interest.

Gill found a good friend in the then wife of one of my colleague in the Traffic Department and we still are in regular contact with her. She already had two small daughters and her and Gill spent many happy times together with the little ones. The row of shops a short way along Milton Road provided for most of our needs and there was even a take-away for the rare occasions when we thought we could afford it. Gill's favourite outing with the pram was beyond the shops to Aschcombe Park and she must have walked many miles over the years taking Tanya to get an occasional sighting of a squirrel. Being at Weston-super-Mare made us more popular to visit and, for the only time in all the years we had lived distant from our various relatives, those couple of years brought the most visitors. Before returning to the policing aspects of this phase in my Service it is worth mentioning the first, could be only, visit to Canonsgrove for Force Family Day. This annual event had started in the Mountfields era and carried over after the purchase and development of the Canonsgrove estate. Tanya was only a few months old and we had her in the pram, when the Chief Constable asked after our health and looked into the pram. He put his hand in and Tanya caught hold of his finger but was reluctant to let go. He laughed and commented upon how strong was her grip!

The mods & rockers of a couple of years before had, by 1970, been replaced by a single, weirdly attired, 'tribe' with shaved heads and known generally as 'skinheads'. Rather than seeking battles with any structured opposition, these young people seemed to want to demonstrate their physical superiority over anyone and to prove themselves about as anti-social (to apply a much more recently discovered expression) as they could. Whereas the mods and rockers had arrived on their various two wheeled machines, the skinheads came by all means, cars, motorcycles and, predominantly, train. Their weapon of choice was a bicycle chain, although knives were not uncommon. Searching them for weapons was legally complicated after they had left the railway station but, thanks to a raft of railway legislation, straightforward while they were on railway property. Hence we met them as they got off the trains and searched them, confiscating anything that could become a weapon of offence. All day on Easter,

Spring and Summer Bank Holiday Sundays and Mondays, we herded these unlovable people around the seafront, attempting to prevent them from spoiling too much the enjoyment of the families who had arrived for a day at the seaside.

Perhaps a demonstration of just how boring it was to carry out this task on so many occasions was our realisation that the Triumph 2500 PI had electrically powered windscreen washers that the control stalk operated independently of the wiper blades. With a small screwdriver the washer nozzles could be adjusted, even to the extent that they missed the windscreen altogether and sprayed water one nozzle to either side of the car's bonnet. Threading through the crowds of skinheads as we often did, a short burst of the washers brought a mass look to the heavens and confusion as to how it could be raining without a cloud in the sky. Not many of them seemed bright enough to work out what had actually just happened but the exercise did present many with a wetting to which they were evidently not accustomed. On one occasion, I was starting a 2p.m. till 2a.m. shift on a Bank Holiday Sunday with an Officer I knew well but with whom I was not often crewed. Before we had briefed ourselves we were called to help with a large group of skinheads heading into the town from the seafront. We drove from the back yard and across to Oxford Street where the road a couple of hundred yards ahead of us was thronged with the crowd running towards us. We stopped and each got out to stand either side of the Triumph, not quite sure what we were going to do next against such a horde. Before they reached us, much to our relief, they turned into the pedestrian precinct of Dolphin Square. With the many other Officers available they were pressed back on to the beach lawns where we could keep them under some level of control and away from the holidaymaking public.

Far more serious an anarchical element were the Hells Angels. Mostly on larger motorcycles but with a few cars and vans, these groups had developed out of similar manifestations in the United States of America and were, in the early 1970s a source of quite serious concern. By dint of numbers they brought worry, even terror, to any community through which they passed or upon which they chose to descend for a while. It was not unknown for them to 'invade' a petrol filling station and perform a mass departure without paying for the fuel they had poured into their tanks. Although some of the former 'rockers' had been somewhat unsavoury, many of the members of these Hells Angels groups took nastiness to a new level, not discouraged by the 'punk rock' craze of the time and later.

I have mentioned in an earlier chapter the Bank Holiday support system which the Force had developed for Weston-super-Mare. Except Bridgwater, where they had their own seaside issues, the remaining four Divisions each sent a contingent in personnel carriers to support the policing effort at Weston. One Bank Holiday Monday morning, with my affable regular crewmate, we came on duty at 0545 hours preparing for another twelve hour shift similar to that we had performed the day before. We were immediately sent to Shipham Gorge, a much less spectacular gap through the Mendip Hills to the west of Cheddar. On arrival, just below and opposite the entrance to a disused quarry, we found the night crew whom we were to relieve. As we chatted briefly before they set off for their well-earned rest, the noise that was building from the quarry was accompanied by a JCB digger appearing, driverless, from the mouth of the quarry. On its large rear tyres, it bounced across the road and one member from each crew dived into the drivers' seats to get the cars clear but it went fairly straight across the road and into a wooden shed, probably used by the Council to store road maintenance equipment.

Breathing a sigh of relief and with no chance of identifying those from within the quarry who had set the machine on its path, the night shift departed and reported the incident as they drove down to the A371. They had also identified that from our position opposite the quarry entrance we would be able to hear Information Room transmissions but may have difficulty in getting through to them. The Information Room Sergeant's familiar voice instructed us to remain where we were but report any movement away from the quarry. It was nearly ten o'clock when our boredom was suddenly interrupted by a crescendo of noise which signified that all of the motorcycles in the quarry were being started up. Soon there was a large cavalcade of motorcycles, with an old car and a van in their midst which poured out of the quarry and down the road towards the bottom of Shipham Gorge. When it was obvious that there was no one following a second old van, we joined the rear of the convoy and reported what was now happening as we cleared the steep sides of the gorge.

The convoy turned left just before reaching the A371 and followed the road that runs through the village and comes out near the bottom of Cheddar Gorge. They then went up Cheddar Gorge and 'occupied' the car park just around the bend after Gough's Cave. They immediately started to abandon their transport and walk the short distance back down to the cave entrance. We turned the car and drove down, surrounded by them, and pulled up just on the upper end of the cave entrance. Although so early there were quite a few ordinary visitors around the cave entrance and visiting the shops nearby. The Hells Angels just milled about and did not, as we had feared, attempt to force an entry to the caves or, for that matter, the small museum and shops. After reporting the current situation, I remained in the driver's seat while my colleague decided to seek to prevent any minor scratch damage to the patrol car by standing beside the front passenger door.

We were quite relieved that those of the group who were nearest to him seemed quite friendly and, after a while and feeling somewhat more relaxed, he was chatting with them and felt able to smile. I then noticed that there was a middle-aged man on the small bridge that spanned the entrance to Gough's Cave who seemed to be taking rather a lot of photographs. When I looked behind my colleague, I realised what had attracted his photographic interest. The young 'ladies' accompanying the Hells Angels 'Chapter' were gathered around the police uniform and had opened their denim waistcoats to reveal that they were wearing nothing underneath. One breast was pressed firmly against the glass of the rear door window and several others were also visible. I called to my colleague through the open front passenger window and he hastily got back into the car. Soon after, the whole gathering shifted back to their machines and we reported that fact to the Information Room.

While we had been stationary outside the cave, I had turned the radio to handset only and even that had the volume set low as I held it near my ear. I had heard Information Room relaying an instruction from the Deputy Divisional Commander, only quite recently upgraded to Superintendent at the same time as all the other Divisional Commanders had joined the one at Weston-super-Mare in the rank of Chief Superintendent. His instruction was for all the personnel carriers from the other Divisions and quite a few Traffic cars and dog handlers to assemble in the car park at the bottom of the Gorge and next to the local resident beat man's Cheddar Police Station. The cavalcade soon appeared in my wing mirror and processed past us and down the road towards the middle of the village. We tagged along behind.

At the bottom of the gorge there were police officers and vehicles so positioned that the only avenue open to the Hells Angels was to go through the 'in' access to the car park, which was walled off from the road. The 'out' gap was blocked by a patrol car and we stopped when we were blocking the entrance through which they had all passed. Inside the car park there were a large collection of various types of police transport, cars, dog vans, Land Rovers and Ford Transits all parked so as to provide a clear area in the middle, into which all of the Hells Angels had been 'corralled'. The Superintendent, heavily supported by a small army of other Officers soon found the leaders of the gang and made it plain that he would value their presence much more highly if it was elsewhere! Recognising that they were, for a change, outnumbered, they accepted the Superintendent's effectively 'running them out of the County'.

Having been with them the longest, it was decreed that we would, with a couple of motorcyclists from our 'home' station escort the group while they remained in Somerset. Radio traffic confirmed that the surrounding Forces were being put on warning and, as had been most likely, we tailed the group all the way down to the Dorset border. There quite a contingent of the Dorset Traffic Department took over from us and we departed back to Weston-super-Mare to enjoy a 'catch-up' refreshment break and a relatively quiet afternoon. As usual, there is a sequel. The Hells Angels ended up at South Bay and settled on the beach for that night but, unfortunately, saw some of the beach huts as ideal fuel for their camp fires!

Much more in the way of quarry patrols came our way in that early 1970s period. We were told that chemical analysis had identified that the explosives used in the bombing by the IRA at the Aldershot Barracks on 22nd February, 1972 had either been stolen from the explosives store at Wick Quarry in the south of Gloucestershire or from the store on the M5 motorway site at Tickenham Hill in north Somerset. The Police response to this information was to mount nightly patrols specifically to check the myriad of such explosives stores which then existed in quarries throughout the country. In our area, pretty well right across the county, there were quarries and, of course, remained the massive excavation taking place for the M5 route at Tickenham, near Clevedon. It has to be said, and has now been addressed, that the plethora of explosives stored in isolated locations throughout the quarrying industry at that time made getting supplies for any clandestine use about as easy as it could be. The stores were, for safety, well away from the daily working areas and the containers very strong steel boxes but their very isolation did not assist in any way their security from attack by thieves.

The Weston-super-Mare and Frome Divisions each produced a special patrol to augment those undertaken by the regular local patrolling officers. At Weston the timing produced a peculiar shift of 8p.m. till 4a.m. and the crew comprised a Traffic Unit driver with an observer drawn from the Borough foot patrol strength. It was quite a cushy number, discounting the potential for having to confront violent criminals (no one supposed that anyone stealing high explosives would be anything but violent if confronted) but a bit of a strenuous shift for the Traffic driver of the short wheelbase Land Rover used for the task. Driving up through quarries in the middle of the night was not easy, in fact quite dangerous, as there were pot holes filled with water in which it would have been possible to have 'lost' a double decker bus let alone a small Land Rover. We all assumed that a large puddle would be too deep to drive through it. I do not recall that these patrols brought any detections and it is, of course, impossible to know what contribution they made in preventative terms.

While talking of Land Rover patrols, an earlier apparently interesting diversion from the normal Traffic patrol came my way on a Saturday afternoon late in 1971. I was in the Traffic office, briefing myself for a solo 2p.m. till 10p.m. shift when the Sergeant told me to prepare the Borough Land Rover for a trip, with the ex-Birmingham Traffic Inspector from Headquarters at Taunton, to check up on the progress of the motorway construction. I spoke with the Borough duty sergeant to ensure that he would not miss the absent Land Rover, fuelled it up as it was common for such occasionally used vehicles to be left low on fuel. Having made the preparations, I brewed a pot of tea in the canteen adjacent to the Traffic Office, being sure to take the Sergeant a cup and, as though he had smelt it brewing, the Inspector arrived in his Triumph PI patrol car before the tea in the pot was 'stewed',

After the cuppa, we set off along the A370 to St Georges, just to the north of Worle, then still expanding away from the small village that it had been for a long time, north of Weston-super-Mare. At that point the route of the growing M5 crossed the A370 and that crossing was controlled by a set of long in use 'temporary' traffic lights. These lights were controlled by a man in a very small shed, almost akin to one of the sentry boxes seen outside of the Royal Palaces. I can only suspect that these crossing operators were quite lowly paid, yet for the contractors driving the tipper trucks along the track of the motorway they held the key to how many trips a day each driver/owner could make and for which he would get paid. They had a tally system operating to which all of the drivers subscribed, with the light operator accruing a small tip every time a lorry driver found that he did not have to stop when he approached the crossing. This had a negative effect for the normal traffic on the A370 as it meant that the flow was impeded for every works truck that appeared.

As a small aside, these lorries used by the contractors were, predominantly, 'time-expired' eight wheeled road vehicles which could legally cross the public road at St George, and a few other locations along the line of the growing motorway, under the dispensation allowed in the Construction and Use Regulations for a 'Works Truck' (more traditionally inserted to accommodate trucks where business premises straddled public roads). This dispensation did not, of course, allow for these wagons to travel any distance along the public highway. On occasions, however, drivers would, for as simple a reason as to go to the village for a packet of cigarettes, breach the dispensation. When we caught them on such errands the number of offences for which they would be reported was unbelievable as neither vehicle nor driver complied with normal road use legislation.

When we turned off the metaled road at St George, we had not travelled far before we realised that we were not going to make headway. Some distance from the A370, a temporary railway siding had been installed near Wick St Lawrence to allow for the unloading of 'fly ash' brought in vast quantities from the two steelworks in South Wales and, perhaps, further afield, and this was being used to form the under-platform upon which the motorway surface would be laid. We soon turned back to the main road and trundled the Land Rover up the A370 to Congresbury and then through Yatton to the north east of Clevedon where another traffic light controlled motorway crossing allowed access across the B3128. Here there was only a surface presence of the thick mud found at St George because the route north was being cut through the rock of the high hill behind Tickenham village.

Up the prevailingly gentle slope being created through the hill from the level land around Clevedon to the southern side of the Gordano valley there were still huge ridges and dips in the bare rock. Each dip had been the site of one of the many blasting sessions but, at that time, not too much effort had been made to even out the surface. Hence we started up the hill in a series of climbs and slightly lesser descents, gradually rising higher each time. When in these dips not much could be seen ahead and when climbing out to the next one the view in front of the Land Rover was often completely blocked by the spare wheel strapped to the bonnet. This 'switch-back' ride continued for quite a distance, until we were well above the B3128, with the high top of the original hill on either side.

Why I have no idea, because we had traversed so many of these dips and ridges and each looked much like the one we had just left, but, with the bonnet still revealing only the sky, I stopped. The Inspector asked why and I could not really tell him but I pulled on the handbrake as hard as I could, switched off the engine and left the vehicle in forward gear before opening the driver's door and making the long step to the solid ground beneath us. When I looked ahead of the Land Rover I was quite stunned for a second or two and invited the Inspector to get out and share my view. A couple of Land Rover lengths in front of us the succession of dips and ridges ran out and the next 'dip' was a several hundred feet drop into the Gordano valley, where now the elevated section of the M5 runs! With an Inspector on board I had not exploited our isolation to smoke my pipe but now he took a packet of cigarettes from his tunic pocket, handed me one and we sat on the front bumper of the Land Rover gazing into the gap that could have been our graves.

It was not uncommon for those of us patrolling near the Bristol boundary to be sent into the City to assist in various ways. There was, beneath part of the fly-over complex which carried the A370 south out of the City beside the Cumberland Basin, a transport type café which was, at evenings and weekends, frequented by gangs of youths who did not always get on well with one another. On a 6p.m. to 2a.m. shift, I was allocated to work the A370 and my crewmate for the shift was a Police Cadet on his attachment to learn what the Traffic Department was all about. These attachments were useful for the cadet but did not relieve the workload for the Constables to whom they were allocated. With probationary Constable attachments the Officer dealt with his own prosecutions and cautions but if a prosecution ensued while a Cadet was on board the driver ended up with the resulting paperwork, although we usually took the opportunity to show the cadet what was required.

This late evening, not too long after our 10p.m. till 10.45p.m. refreshment break taken in the canteen at Weston-super-Mare, we were slowly heading back up the A370 and were in Congresbury when we were called by Information Room. The cadet made a good job of handling our end of the radio exchange and we were instructed to go to the Cumberland Basin system to assist Bristol Officers with, yet another, disturbance at the café. In those days by after eleven o'clock at night the roads were already beginning to get quieter and we were able to make good progress through Cleeve, Backwell and Flax Bourton. We came out onto the, then relatively new but already accident notorious Long Ashton by-pass. As we entered the short dual carriageway section we were already up to about 100mph and the cadet was closely monitoring the calibrated speedometer in the middle of the MkII Triumph PI's dashboard. As we came out of the dual carriageway section and started the descent of the long two-way, three lane, carriageway section he shouted "A hundred and ten!" With the slope of the hill down towards Bristol in our favour, I did not try to accelerate any more but kept my right foot steady and let gravity do its bit. "A hundred and fifteen!" announced the cadet. As we reached the more level section, "A hundred and twenty!" he shouted. I then took my foot from the accelerator and started gentle braking as the level section turned into the slight incline and we entered across the City boundary at a more sedate mark-up as we entered the 40mph speed limit. As had happened on previous, but not all occasions, the Bristol Officers were there in such numbers that our small contribution was scarcely significant. Soon we were returning to our own area, with a satisfied Constable and seriously hyped up cadet on board!

That Triumph PI was no different to those others we had on the fleet. For their day they were probably the best performing car on the British car market. We also had Jaguars, which were lovely solid cars to drive but could not match the performance of the Triumph, although they were 900cc larger in capacity. The MkI Triumph PI, which I shared with my mild crewmate from early in 1970, had slightly better road holding than the MkII with which it was replaced. Both, unlike the Jaguars, came with all the up-market trim of walnut veneer and heaps of chrome, whereas the Jaguars were a 'police model' with mat black painted woodwork and rubber matting instead of carpets – more practical really. By that time the Jaguar XJ6 had been in production for a couple of years and we had the end of line Jaguar 240s but with the 3.4 litre XK engines. With the XJ6 model being significantly more expensive, it was not until the completion of the M5 loomed close that any were bought but the Triumph remained the mainstay of the Traffic Fleet for a few years.

The build-up of manpower through 1970/71, ready for the motorway opening scheduled for 1972, gave a significant increased availability of Traffic Officers at Weston-super-Mare. With all the conflict and mutual antagonism in the Middle East some intelligence was received to say that a Jordanian Princess was a potential target for a kidnap attempt. She, with quite a few children of other foreign dignitaries, was a pupil at Millfield School at Street, in central Somerset. The Special Branch Office at New Scotland Yard sent two Detective Sergeants down to assist the Force and quite significant arrangements were set in place to protect the teenage princess.

A small room sharing the landing with her sleeping accommodation was manned at night and she was escorted about the school complex during the daytime. Special Branch and other CID Officers from Headquarters supported the local personnel and the local Section Sergeant, who was to later reach Chief Superintendent rank, performed an admirable liaison role between school, police and the political powers that be. Our role was to man a MkI Triumph, one near the end of its days, which had been altered and additional radio equipment installed for local communications with the Officers in the School. This car was used, shift after shift, to patrol the roads forming the perimeter of the extensive school grounds. Even in those times, Millfield was building a reputation for sporting excellence and had large playing field areas. Each crew was allocated an hour for traveling either side of the normal eight hour basic shifts at Street. We drove across from Weston in another patrol car and swapped with the relieved crew somewhere on the levels near the small town.

Although much more 'ad hoc' in those days, there were occasions when Officers being equipped with firearms was considered appropriate. In this case all those involved in the protection roles were armed. We were each given a few minutes 'training', which really consisted of the essential knowledge of how to make the Walther PPK pistols safe. We were not given any opportunity to actually discover, at that time, what happened when you pulled the trigger! At that time many Officers had performed their two years National Service, I had only missed it by a couple of years, so familiarity with firearms was quite common among serving Constables.

We were all relieved, of course, when, after s few months, the risk assessment changed and we went back to normal patrolling without anything untoward having taken place. While patrolling around the school perimeter I occasionally surmised what we might be called upon to do in the worst event. Generally we saw ourselves as a political 'shield' against the Government being accused of not doing enough should all go wrong. In reality, we suspected that any genuine attempt at a kidnap would be 'mob handed', involve helicopter arrival and departure and be by 'insurgents' armed with something more sophisticated than a Walther PPK. The only plus side for us, was that the event was receiving Home Office funding support and had been declared a 'special occasion' by the Chief Constable so that we got paid the two hours each day overtime. At a time when my lunar monthly salary was still only between £80 and £90, the little bit of overtime was most welcome.

While talking of money my school friend, who sadly died in an accident in 2003, had transferred a couple of years earlier from Devon & Cornwall to the Metropolitan Police. He came to visit us with his young family just after the new Police Station opened at Weston in 1971. The new building held a bar on the top floor which we ran on a rota basis so I took him up to see it. Chatting with s few of my local colleagues we got to the topic of overtime. Prior to October 1972, only the Metropolitan Police paid overtime immediately after the month in which it had been worked, elsewhere we included it on a card with the theoretical procedure being for potential payment for time not taken off after three months - in fact we only ever got paid overtime where a 'special occasion' had been declared. Indeed, and born out when I visited the Met in 1974, overtime was administered there with a maximum of 99 hours claimed in a calendar month. Where appropriate hours worked were held over to produce a fairly steady 99 hour entitlement, even where the Officer had taken a bit of annual leave in a month. Because of that conversation, I remember clearly the contrast in pay, which made the London Allowance seem unnecessary. My lunar monthly salary seldom varied from £86 while that of my friend was consistently £225 per calendar month - well over two and a half times my income.

Another recollection that marked our financial status, or lack of it, in the 1970s was on Tanya's first outing after we bought the Cortina Estate car. With her not really knowing where she was spending the day with her mum and dad, Gill and I decided to take her out for the day somewhere other than the usually afforded trips to see her grandparents. I ensured there was plenty of petrol in the tank and had half a crown ready for the Severn Bridge crossing. We went over to Chepstow and up the Wye Valley to visit Tintern Abbey. It was a pleasant day and among the ruins of the old building we enjoyed the picnic Gill had prepared. With the more usual trip to Wellington using most of our petrol money, this was quite an extravagance and our 'holiday' for 1970.

The following summer, having worked a shift or two with a different colleague who informed me that he owned a static caravan at Shaldon, we did our sums and I paid him £8.00 to hire the accommodation for a week. By now Tanya was fully mobile and loved being able to run around near the caravan. Unlike more modern 'statics' there was only really one room with a small section which could be curtained off. Each evening, a little later than at home, we would curtain Tanya off to go to sleep and spend the evening, later by the light of a gas mantle, playing cards as quietly as possible. With no plumbing, the trip down the field for water and to use the toilets was quite regular but we had a lovely holiday, much of it in Shaldon to keep down our use of the car.

On the Friday, with the long journey back to Weston-super-Mare the following day, I realised that I needed more cash than was left in my pocket to ensure that we had enough petrol for the return. Knowing how much was in our bank account, I drove over to the National Westminster Bank at Teignmouth and handed over a cheque made out to 'Cash' for £10.00. The counter staff member took the cheque and went to a back room to telephone our branch at Weston to ensure that it was safe for them to cash the cheque. When the assistant returned, she gave me £9.75 (what I still saw as £9/15/-d so soon after decimalisation) in cash and explained that the 25p (five shilling) deduction was to cover the expense of clearing the cheque. Although I had not expected the process to cost so much, I knew that it would be alright as there was, before that cheque, just over £12.00 in our account – in August 1971 all the money we had!

Back to experiences on patrol. One winter evening the Sergeant briefed me and another Officer, with whom I only worked on odd occasions, to meet a man out at East Brent, on the A38 just south of the junction with the A370. It was only about 7p.m. when we met up with the man and his 15cwt van but at that time of year it was completely dark and this section was not, in those days, benefiting from street lights. Our man was from a Weston based company who specialised in producing folding signs and we already had some of their products in the boot of our patrol car. His wish was to try some new signs with, hopefully, improved reflective markings. He wanted to ensure that motorists would see them at night but could not do so unless there were police officers present when they were deployed. A successful trial and before we parted with him he enquired as to the registration numbers of our private vehicles. A few days later a package arrived at the Traffic Office addressed for each of us. Inside were new reflective number plates for each of our cars. I fitted mine, they were a sound safety measure, and I still have the old black and white number plates from that trusty old car in my possession.

There was another, more personal, benefit that I would derive from the temporarily excessive number of Constables in the Weston-super-Mare Traffic Department at that time. It made it quite easy for me to use up some of the time accumulated on my overtime record card to free up evenings when I would otherwise have been working. Having passed my Sergeants' and Inspectors' examinations before we returned to Weston, we discovered that, while we had been at Williton for that fifteen months, the new Technical College had opened. I got a copy of the prospectus, with a view to addressing the shortfall regarding 'A' levels that leaving school when I did had created and decided that Sociology was likely to be of most use to my police career. With time-off for attendance fairly confidently assured, we found the cash for the course and I attended on one evening each week through the winter and into the early summer of 1971.

With an 'A' level under my belt, I followed up with a further course in Psychology and, mistakenly, added one in Social and Economic History. I had, it seemed, bitten off a bit too much, although attendance on two evenings a week was usually possible thanks to the still increasing traffic patrol strength. I managed a pass at 'A' level in the Psychology and was awarded the consolation prize of an 'O' level pass in history, one I had not carried away from school. As I have earlier mentioned, throughout the time following my success at the Sergeants' examination in the autumn of 1968, I had presented myself, fruitlessly, before the promotion boards each year. The rules for admission to the accelerated promotion course at the Police College at Bramshill in Hampshire had recently changed. This course had been running since 1962 and was, unimaginatively, called the Special Course. No longer was it a requirement for candidates to have passed the promotion examination in the top 200 but all could apply. I had realised that my shortage of 'A' levels would not help my cause and applied in 1971 but without much confidence of success. With one 'A' level and studying for another, I tried again in 1972 with similar lack of success.

Another advantage from the excessive numbers of Traffic Officers at Weston at the time was my ability to be sure and attend practice sessions for the newly formed Somerset & Bath Constabulary Male Voice Choir. Having arrived not too long before on promotion from the Metropolitan Police, our new Deputy Chief Constable issued an invitation in General Orders for those who wished to join a choir. He obtained the services of a music teacher from Taunton School and rehearsals started with the accompaniment of a Sergeant with the gift of being an excellent pianist. The choir was to go on from strength to strength, being boosted in 1974 as the Force grew into the significantly bigger Avon and Somerset Constabulary.

In the autumn of 1972, Gill announced that she was expecting our second child and the Force announced that all Constables would, for the first time, undergo a Staff Appraisal. This staff appraisal brought for the first time since I had joined the Division, a scheduled interview with the Divisional Commander - not a process repeated when we returned to Weston from Williton. When I appeared, in best uniform, before the Chief Superintendent we had quite a long chat about my development thus far. He had not been the Divisional Commander at Weston when I started there early in 1966 but had taken over before we went off to Williton in late 1968. Inevitably he referred to my several appearances before the promotion boards and to my previous applications for the Special Course. His conclusion was that my field of operational experience was too narrow and that I should apply for a move to a Rural Section Station where it would be more varied and my opportunities for performing acting Sergeant's duties would be more frequent. I had performed as an acting Sergeant occasionally since we had returned from Williton but he was correct in seeing that as being limited experience compared with general police duties.

I thanked him for his advice and suggestion but pointed out that Gill had moved house from Williton back to Weston only two months before Tanya was born and that I did not feel that, in consideration for her, I could prompt another move of house while she was, again, pregnant. In typical mode for that time, he was quite dismissive of my concern for Gill and, as was the focus of that time, pointed out that my career should be the priority for her sake as much as mine! I left the room still thankful for his interest in my potential career but with no intention of provoking a move in the near future. About three weeks later, I was solo on patrol one afternoon on the A38 heading north towards Shute Shelve when the call came over the radio for me to return to Divisional Headquarters and see the Chief Superintendent.

On the journey, my mind was running through all my activities of the past few weeks. The most likely reason for the summons was some error on my part too dire for the attention of the Sergeants or Inspector. Waiting outside his office his secretary nor the Admin. Chief Inspector gave any clue but they did not seem to be looking upon someone just about to be executed! In his office, he did not speak but held out to me a buff envelope (the Police Service always called what others refer to as a brown envelope a 'buff' envelope). He signified that I should open it in his presence, which I did. It was an order from the Chief Constable directing that in two weeks and a couple of days I was to start duty on the Shepton Mallet Section and occupy one of the flats behind that police station.

Gill had enjoyed her time at Weston while Tanya was little and had made the good friend only a short distance from us, although they had decided to buy their own home a little further away on the new development across New Bristol Road. Not entirely happy, she saw the possible career development aspects clearly enough and, albeit with some understandable reluctance, agreed with the move. As usual, there was a sequel. Within a few days of the letter regarding the transfer I received another. Alongside the steady reduction in years of service required before we could apply to buy our own houses, a programme had started to equip all police houses with central heating and this second letter identified that our house in Milton Road was on the list for the pipework to be installed before we moved out. Gill had accepted the move but to have the disruption of heating engineers around us while we were packing all our worldly goods was a straw too many. The administration staff were less than helpful, identifying that a change of our date would also mess someone else about but the Superintendent Deputy Divisional Commander (he who ran the Hells Angels out of the county) just told me that it would not happen until after we had moved out.

Hence, two years and nine months after we had returned from our fifteen month stay in our first police house at Williton, we had another pantechnicon at the door and were off to another place I scarcely knew existed. Remarkably, Gill made the best of what was not much of a good job for her. She had liked living at Weston but was to find nothing to compensate the loss at Shepton Mallet.

Thankfully she would not have to bear it for too long and it has to be said we saw that small town in the middle of Somerset at its worst. The Showerings, of Babycham fame, invested a considerable amount of money in the market square centre of Shepton Mallet building a theatre but in the time we were there that area was a building site. Any way, we were on the move again.

9 Shepton Mallet

We arrived with all our furniture and found that the arrangement in the flats behind the police station at Shepton Mallet, although not as good as our house in Milton Road, had some advantages. It came with a garage in the station yard for our car and it was only a few yards walk from our door to the rear door of the police station. There were cost benefits, quite useful given that our pay continued all through the 1970s to fall behind the rise in the cost of living and in comparison to most others' pay.

The block of four flats, since they were built in the early 1960s, had suffered remarkably from damp. By the time of our arrival, in November, 1972, much remedial action had been taken. All four, three bedroomed, flats had been fitted with central heating pipes in the ceilings with metal tiles each drilled with hundreds of small holes for the heat to permeate down into the rooms. The floor of the upper flats had been cork tiled throughout to cope with the heat coming up from the ceiling pipes of the flat below. Not even this arrangement had been wholly successful and the two ground floor flats had been left empty and a small laundry built alongside the block as a shared facility with, for the time, a very modern washing machine. The heating was plumbed from the police station boiler and unlike the proposal we would have encountered at Minehead in 1970, the condition of the flats had determined that the occupants need make no contribution to the heating cost. There was a coin meter for the washing machine but Gill found that our new neighbour's assurance was correct in that it was very rare that another ten pence or two shilling coin (they were in joint use and the same size at that time) was required. Hence, there was quite a saving on the household budget and we were forced to spend most of that winter with windows open to enable us to live in the unregulated heat.

The Shepton Mallet Section was part of the Wells Sub Division, the City to the west, and of the Frome Division, the town to the east. With the quarry patrols still taking place across the Mendips and other hills in the county, checking those in our Section was part of the routine. Most of our patrol time was in the newly acquired Hillman, later Talbot, Avenger cars that had supplanted the Hillman Imps and were significantly larger. In the boroughs these cars were often two door 1250/1300cc versions but in rural sections we had the 1500/1600cc four door models. With one Sergeant, one receptionist/typist, a part-time cleaner handyman and eleven Constables we worked overlapping shifts. The car was manned throughout the 24 hours and three of the eleven Constables were on Beat Stations, at Oakhill, Pilton and Wanstrow. At that time the annual gathering, purportedly in support of the Campaign for Nuclear Disarmament (CND), at Worthy Farm was known as the Pilton Pop Festival. We 'policed' it, from a distance, with little support from outside the Section but it grew and acquired the name Glastonbury Festival, although still in the same place. The story goes that in the early days, with little prospect of getting planning consent any other way, the famous pyramid stage was a platform and superstructure on top of a new cow shed. The Festival had several reputation changes over the years before becoming the respectable, and expensive, gathering it is today.

Shepton Mallet Police Station (taken in 2015 but externally unchanged since 1973)

The early, late and night shifts were predominantly in the car, covering a huge area. The nearest other manned areas on a night shift were Bristol in the north,

Frome in the east, Yeovil in the south and Wells in the west, the latter being also only one officer. It is safe, the statute of limitations having long expired, to declare a daily trip undertaken on early shift. With another car, the small vans and motorcycles used by all of us, there was one of the row of garages which was actually a petrol and oil store, sensibly the one near the small covered car wash and farthest from the other buildings. Each morning, any empty petrol cans, all of which were marked for their appropriate vehicle, were loaded into the boot of the Avenger and taken over to Wells. There, either side of a seven o'clock cup of tea with the Wells early shift Constable and the civilian station clerk, the cans were filled and the petrol booked out to the respective vehicles. On the return journey the boot contained substantially more than the legal limit of two gallons of petrol.

Wells Police Station (taken in 2015 but externally unchanged since 1973)

When we not required to keep the car on the road we could use the Triumph 500cc motorcycle to undertake enquiries or perform foot patrols in Shepton Mallet. On a winter evening patrolling on foot was a bit of a lonely pursuit and felt most poignantly so around the narrow lanes beside the prison. The main employers in Shepton at that time were the prison, although we had surprisingly little to do with it or its staff, the Babycham factory alongside the main A37 road and the large furniture store of Haskins in the middle of the town. There was a market every Friday in the car park behind the police station and visible over our garden wall from our upstairs flat and Gill preferred going around there to the mud avoiding exercise of a trip down into the town. She soon made friends with our next door neighbour and she grew quite fond of Tanya. Gill sought out a play group but it was quite a walk from the flat. In the other direction, past Haskins store, was the park which was quite pleasant with a small lake and bandstand.

As had been the intention of the move, there was only one other Constable on the Section qualified by examination to Sergeant and he was quite long in service and did not really want the role. Hence, whenever the solitary Sergeant was absent, I performed the acting Sergeant role. With the amalgamation of April 1974 a future 'known', working parties had been set up to make the necessary plans for the linking and our Sergeant was away quite often as a member of one of those groups. At that time acting duties only brought a financial reward if they were carried out, unbroken, for a fortnight. It was only when the Sergeant was on annual leave that this was likely to occur. The compensation was that just before we arrived at Shepton Mallet, in the autumn of 1972, the pay regulations had changed to bring immediate payment for overtime. When performing the acting sergeant role, it was not uncommon to be called out after already performing a day's duty and to incur overtime as a result. At that time some officers, predominantly CID and lone supervisors, still worked 'split shifts'. This involved the eight hour day being divided into two, usually equal four hour segments. The system was rather exploited by managers in that a three quarter hour refreshment break only applied if at least five hours were worked continuously. By declaring the duty to be 0900 – 1300 and 1400 – 1800 the post, such as that of Section Sergeant, was spread over nine rather than eight hours and the refreshments taken in your own time. Not that you would not be called back to the station during the meal if there was some need.

The lady who was the Station Receptionist and typist dealt with most of the public visitors and only called upon one of the Constables where the nature of the caller's enquiry demanded. She was a dog lover and enjoyed seeking out 'foster' and 'adoptive' carers for any stray dogs that found their way into the two large cages opposite the rear door of the station. Unfortunately those kennels were directly underneath our bedroom window. This meant that any noisy dog could become a real nuisance when we were trying to get a night's sleep. The station was supplied with small orange sleeping tablets with the instructions stating one tablet for a small dog, two for a medium size and three for a big one. At the first hint that a dog was going to be noisy, I would get the tablets from the station and give the dog a double dose. The next morning, I would often be chastised by our dog lover as she had come in to work to find a dog fast asleep in its cage at nine o'clock. Because the dogs' home was near the University of Bath, the policy was to keep them at Shepton Mallet for a week, although they were sometimes 'farmed out' earlier. I successfully petitioned the Divisional Commander for this to be reduced to forty eight hours, much to our Station Clerk's annoyance.

I learned a good lesson one late evening while foot patrolling around the back streets in Shepton Mallet. With four years of Traffic Department experience, it was second nature for me to closely examine every car tax disc I encountered. Here was one on an insecure car in a small yard which had obviously been changed to show the registration number of the car on which it was displayed. I took it from the windscreen and to the door of the house, where I could see that downstairs lights were switched on. A large, tall and well built, man came to the door and I held up the disc and asked him if the vehicle parked in the yard was his. He said nothing but snatched the disc from my hand and slammed the door shut. Knocking on the door again achieved nothing. I returned to the police station and consulted with the Inspector at Wells, who happened to be on duty that evening. He asked me if I had made a note of the serial number of the disc before confronting the car owner. I had not. Truth is I simply did not expect the reaction I had received. On the Inspector's advice, I 'put this one down to experience'. His other comment, "He'll come again, they always do!" proved to be correct within a few weeks.

In my capacity as Acting Sergeant, I was called out one night because one of the Constables had stopped a car on Charlton Road, connecting the town to the A37, but the driver had locked himself in the car and was refusing to communicate. By the time that I got there, the Constable had reached the end of his tether and, equipped with half of a concrete breezeblock he had found in a nearby front garden was holding it above the windscreen of the car as I pulled up. Before I could utter my intended call for him to desist, he brought the lump of concrete down as heavily as he could. To both our amazement the windscreen did not shatter but there was just a deposit of concrete dust where the blow had struck the glass. At that time almost all cars were fitted with windscreens that characteristically shattered into small hexagonal fragments when struck hard. This was a Simca car and the first I had ever seen with a laminated windscreen. The shock of my colleague's action did not do the trick and the occupant seemed not even to have noticed what had happened. After some long period fiddling with the locks, we managed to open the boot and found that the rear bulkhead was nothing like as substantial as the windscreen. I was able to push the back of the rear seat forward and crawl through the gap to unlock the doors from the inside. Even now the occupant made no move to stop me. With still no communication, we called an ambulance and sent him off to be medically examined.

A priority for Gill was, of course, to register with a local doctor but she was less than complimentary as to his apparent capabilities. Through him, however, she was booked in to the local Maternity Hospital. The time arrived for her to go in but things did not go as smoothly as they had when Tanya was born. With the local unit having limitations, Gill was taken by ambulance, in the snow, to the Royal United Hospital (RUH) at Bath. My mother came up to look after Tanya and I made the journey up to Bath a few times but all worked out alright. On the day that the ambulance brought Gill and Cathryn back to the flat, its arrival coincided with the morning assembly for tea and everyone on the station spilled out the back door to see the new arrival. Although the labour had been too long, we had another lovely little baby girl. Unfortunately, Gill's view regarding the doctor did not alter when she attended his surgery for the usual checks. The same doctor was the local 'police surgeon' - in most areas the police identified a local General Practitioner (GP) for this role and paid them when they were called out.

Late one Sunday evening, I was again called out from the flat. As I went into the police station I saw a traffic patrol car in the yard beside the Section car. As I approached the interview room my local colleague quickly informed me that a man had been arrested by the traffic crew for quite extensive damage in Pilton Parish Church. When I looked into the room the man, who had been seated behind the scrubbed wooden table with the traffic officers standing either side behind him, leapt to his feet and thumped his fist on the table, splitting one of the planks of wood. The traffic men grabbed a shoulder each and forced him back into his seat. I went to the Sergeant's office and asked Information Room to contact the duty Police Surgeon. I then realised that there were three people in the public side of the front office and was introduced to them. One of the women was the man's wife and the other couple the people they had been visiting at Pilton. All were astounded at what had happened. He had said that he was going out for a bit of fresh air after they had eaten tea but had been gone so long that they went to try and find him. They had happened upon the traffic crew making their arrest following the call by the Church Verger on the 999 system.

The doctor soon arrived and received the same reaction from the man in the interview room as had I, but with the traffic officers somewhat more prepared this time. The doctor hastily retreated back into the corridor and asked to speak with the people in the front office. To my amazement, he asked the wife if she could drive and, when she confirmed that she could, started discussing the possibility of his sedating the man so that she could drive him back to their home in Taunton. I called him back into the corridor, where the three could not hear me, and told the doctor that the man was in police custody and it was, therefore, my decision as to what should happen next. I made it plain that I thought his suggestion held so many dangers for the man, his wife and other road users, that I was amazed as to how he had reached that possible way forward. I told him that I was going to seek a second medical opinion.

We contacted the large Mendip Psychiatric Hospital near Wells, and the duty Psychiatrist and a male nurse arrived in remarkably quick time. The local doctor took the Psychiatrist to one side and spoke briefly with him out of anyone else's earshot. The man from Mendip Hospital did not seem impressed with whatever he had been told and he too looked in at the prisoner. He immediately turned to the local doctor in the corridor and said "Temporary order, do you agree?" The local doctor simply nodded. The Mendip Psychiatrist had evidently anticipated his diagnosis as an ambulance arrived outside the front of the station and, after the traffic men had held him still long enough for an injection to be administered, the prisoner was taken off to the Mendip Hospital. The local doctor, having countersigned the form started by the Psychiatrist, got straight into his car and went home. The man's wife went back to stay with the friends at Pilton with a view to visiting her husband later in the day.

It was while stationed at Shepton Mallet that I for the first time appeared on local television, although it was extremely briefly. A group of 'hippy' type young people had taken over an unoccupied but substantial farm building near the link road between the A37 and Glastonbury. A Court Order had been obtained by the property owner and he had employed a group of bailiffs to remove the young 'squatters'. Our role was, as was usual for the police, to ensure fair play on each side and, as Acting Sergeant, I had been loaned a couple of Constables from each of the Frome and Wells stations to bolster our own numbers. The TV camera crew led the way but then cameramen were not as well equipped for such 'walking backward' filming and the piece that appeared on the local BBC News that evening was extremely brief. Knowing what was about to happen, most of the squatters had departed before the bailiffs arrived and those still present willingly left. A total failure for the TV people, who evidently had been hoping for a major disturbance to capture on film.

We received a call one morning from a demolition gang working on the old Territorial Army buildings just off Charlton Road, the road from the town centre to the A37 crossroads on the way out to Frome. The JCB they were using to clear the site had scooped off some concrete slabs that had formed part of the floor of the hut and exposed what looked like a large stock of half pint bottles still filled with 'milk' that had gone a rancid looking green colour. One of the workmen had picked up one of the bottles and thrown it against a wall, fortunately well across the site and away from the hole containing the rest of the bottles. Upon hitting the wall, the contents of the bottle had ignited and produced a large flash of flame and loud noise. All moved away to what they thought was a safe distance and were still sensibly sheltering from the hole when we arrived. After a quick look and in the light of the reaction that one bottle had caused, we simply reinforced the contractors' evacuation from the site and awaited the arrival of the Army Bomb Disposal Team.

The response came from somewhere in Wiltshire and did not take too long. The Captain in charge of the Team seemed to know, without looking, what it was he was confronting. He did take a look before directing his team's response to the matter and explained what the contractors had found. These bottles had been stored there either during the Second World War or early in the Cold War, probably the earlier period. They contained petrol and phosphor and, as had the one that was smashed, would ignite upon exposure to the air. The Captain went on to tell us, the site foreman and his crew just how fortunate they had been that things had panned out the way they did. Had the JCB dislodged just one top from a bottle the whole lot would likely have ignited and, in the confined space of the hole, caused a massive explosion right underneath the JCB.

Much preparation was required by the Bomb Disposal Team to open up the area around the bottles so that they could burn without being confined too tightly. The word had evidently spread and a television camera crew arrived in support of one of the local TV reporters. When the Captain gave us the information that his men were ready, we stopped the traffic on Charlton Road and made a quick double check that those householders close enough were away from danger. Fortunately what was left of the brick walls of the TA building would, so the Captain had calculated, safeguard the windows of the nearest properties. With all safety precautions in place and the TV film camera running, the stash of British 'Molotov Cocktails' were ignited. The sound of the explosion was not quiet but neither was it as loud as we had expected. What was noticeable was the cloud of smoke created by the flames which we could not see from behind the walls. The black cloud shot skywards with the heat and it put me in mind of the archetypal 'mushroom' clouds seen on televised recordings of the atomic bomb tests not many years earlier. With shaking of hands and a few salutes our Army friends got back into their Land Rovers and the contractors went on, now safely, with the task of clearing the site.

With Cathryn doing well and Tanya delighting in her little sister, Gill recovered from the enforced trip to the RUH. With my significantly increasing experience of supervision in this more varied environment, I applied once more to attend the Special Course. This time, I was called to the Central Interview Panel which in 1973 was held in the Police Federation Offices, then at Surbiton in Surrey. The interview panel was a Chief Officer and a Deputy Chief Officer accompanied by an Inspector from the Police Federation. I was duly informed that I had passed this filtering process and was being called to attend Bramshill House, The Police College in Hampshire, for an expended interview spread over three days. With my Cortina estate now eight years old, I arranged to stay overnight with my old school friend at Biggin Hill so that the morning journey to Bramshill would be only a relatively short trip.

As required, I arrived down that impressive drive well before the appointed afternoon start time and found my way to my accommodation for the next two nights. With loads of time to spare, I went for a walk around the large lake.

The Bramshill Lake

As I strolled, alone, along the footpath, my thoughts turned to wondering, after the couple of failed attempts, how I had suddenly reached this point. The thoughts were mainly of the absence the Special Course would create from Gill, Tanya and Cathryn and I began to question whether it was such a good idea. On the other side of the coin was the effort, sustained over quite a few years and always with Gill's full support. Passing both police promotion examinations, studying at Weston Technical College for the two 'A' levels and the commitment to the daily job both as Constable and Acting Sergeant. Besides the separation and strange environment, I even began to question myself as to whether a country boy from Somerset was suited to the 'high flyer' focus that this course, indeed the Police College, would demand. By the time I reached my starting point and having completed the full circuit of the lake I had, in a way, made up my mind. I could not throw away the effort already expended but made a very real decision that all I did and said over the next forty eight hours would be genuinely 'me', no false airs and graces and no pretence.

When we all met together, I saw that there were about thirty applicants, aspiring young people such as me, but they were a very mixed bunch. A surprisingly small proportion of our group, there were four such groups being interviewed over a two week period, were there under the Graduate Entry

Scheme. These people came into the police service from their university studies and were pre-destined for the Special Course provided that they could pass the Sergeants' examination at their first attempt. Some of those present were there because they had managed to come within the top 200 in the country and were very young in age and service but most, like me, had taken the opportunity to apply under the revised, more open, conditions announced a couple of years previously. The full group was divided up into sections of about six and each had a designated interview panel. Ours comprised the Commissioner of the City of London, Deputy Chief Constable of Derbyshire and a retired Civil Servant who had spent much of his time in the Colonial Service.

Away from our assessors I was somewhat surprised to discover that many in the group seemed almost paranoid about the process we were about to encounter. There were many concerns as to what would be the 'right' and 'wrong' approach and responses. Since my walk around the lake, I listened to what was said but knew that none of it would apply. I was going to be 'me' not some contrived conformity to a standard that none of the others knew to be correct anyway. We were required to sit a number of written tests and to have a group discussion of topics tossed in by one of the directing staff. If I had any sort of 'ploy' it applied in the group discussions. Whatever contribution I had made in the course of the discussion, I tried to gauge when was the appropriate time to attempt to summarise what we had all discussed, on a couple of occasions my timing was right and my summary was used by the directing staff 'facilitator' as the point at which to end that debate. We also had two interviews on our own, one with the two police interviewers and the other with the civilian assessor.

I discovered one unexpected benefit from the Psychology 'A' level course which I had taken in the evenings while at Weston-super-Mare. That course had required attendance on two evenings each week. One evening was where we were given lectures on the many academic theories and disparate areas of study and on the other evening we conducted 'practical experiments' usually on ourselves or on each other. Part of this was the study of the various test methods used and which were, in quite a few instances very similar to the tests used by commercials organisations and Mensa to determine Intelligence Quotients (IQ). My experience of this type of test and with some understanding of what they were designed to assess, must have produced an IQ result that reflected well.

When filing into a large classroom for a discussion group we were all shaken by the hand by a gentleman in plain clothes whom I did not know. He turned out to be the newly appointed Commissioner of the Metropolitan Police and it always impressed me that he would take the time to sit in on this selection process, quite a relevant exercise as there were a significant number of his Officers being assessed. My interview with the police assessors went, as was inevitable given my walk around the lake decision, in a rather non-standard manner. It was a hot August day and I was standing in the corridor in my suit when the door to the interview room opened and the previous candidate came out. He rolled his eyes as a silent indication that he thought he had been dragged through the hoop but could say nothing as the Commissioner of the City of London was close behind him, heading for the toilet with no jacket and braces showing.

He saw me standing there and told me to go in and make myself comfortable, commenting that the heat was too much to bear. Taking him at his word, I went through the door which he had left wide open and the Deputy Chief Constable was seated with his head bowed over the notes he was writing about my predecessor. I took off my jacket and folded it neatly on a table at the side of the room and moved the chair waiting for me closer to the desk. The Deputy glanced up once but said nothing. I had just sat down when the Commissioner returned and closed the door behind him as I stood up to acknowledge his entry. He waived for me to sit and I did. The Deputy had completed his notes and now started to examine me in what appeared to be fine detail, scarcely taking his eyes off me. The Commissioner started by asking me about Shepton Mallet and a few other aspects of my career to date. The Deputy then enquired as to why I was prepared to perform acting Sergeant duties on the few days at a time, for which I received no enhanced payment. His main focus appeared to be to entice me into being critical of the 'system' but my response was the importance that I placed upon gaining experience. The Commissioner then took back control of the conversation and introduced the 'pastime' I had included on my application of model railways. He informed me that his next door neighbour constructed working model steam engines and, to my complete amazement, the rest of the interview revolved around model railways.

When I recovered my jacket and left the room I could not make up my mind as to what among my earlier responses had prompted the Commissioner to 'waste' the rest of the time on a totally non-police topic. The quandary was whether my response to his early questions and the more challenging ones from the Deputy, had satisfied the Commissioner that I was a 'pass' or a 'fail'. Later I was interviewed by the Colonial type, a very gentle and quite elderly man. He started by identifying that as I was from Somerset I must be a cricket enthusiast but that did not go too far when I explained that I knew very little about the sport or our, then very successful, county side. From this uninspiring start, he resorted to the type of questions that our group had spent time talking about and expressing their views as to what were the desired responses.

First of these 'stock' questions was the enquiry as to what newspaper I regularly read. My response was the 'Western Daily Press' and, when his reaction demonstrated that he had never heard of the paper, I went on to offer a short explanation regarding its coverage of local and national events. He evidently looked upon this line of enquiry as being no more revealing than had been cricket. Next he asked what I liked watching on television. I explained that, in those days of very little day-time broadcasting, shift work limited what I was able to watch. I remained with my walk around the lake acquired way forward and told him that I tried to watch news bulletins and current affairs type programmes but that for entertainment I really enjoyed a good western. His expression and moment of silence confirmed that he had never received that answer before but he recovered quickly with the response, "Do you know what. So do I".

All in all, my thoughts on the return journey from Bramshill back to Shepton Mallet were fairly positive. I had, largely, come to the conclusion that my move to Shepton nine months previously and what I had been doing through that time and when I was performing acting duties at Weston, together with having reached the extended interviews would stand me in good stead regardless of whether I had been successful over the past three days. It was in the lap of fate. Either I would be selected or I would, hopefully, make career progress in the more conventional way. Either Gill and I and the little girls would have to manage most of a year in separation or we would not. In total honesty, I had no desperately strong preference.

Back to the routine of contributing to the policing the Shepton Mallet Section, one wet night I was alone in the 'panda' car on the A37 at Pylle when I thought that I saw a light in the timber yard behind the owner's bungalow. I skirted around the back lane and drove into the yard. I quickly realised that the illumination had been from a rear window of the bungalow but, having entered the yard drove around one of the large stacks of timber to return to the exit. As I rounded a 'tower' of pit prop shaped pieces of timber, there was a thud from the front nearside of the car. A quick flash of the torch revealed that one of the pieces of timber was protruding from near the base of the pile and I had struck it. There was a significant dent to the rear of the front nearside wheel arch. On return to the station, before going off duty, I completed a report to leave for the Sergeant when he came in for duty.

On a Sunday night, not really in keeping with it being in the height of summer, I was on 6p.m. till 2a.m. shift and patrolling with the night shift man. Although this 'doubling up' was legitimated by the need to visit our few quarry explosives stores, I was pleased not to be out in the pouring rain that night. We received a call that there had been an accident on the A37 north of Shepton Mallet and, as we had only just left the Station, it did not take us long to get to Long Hill, the section of the A37 which leads to the highest point at the cross roads with Old Frome Road.

Fortunately there were few vehicles on the road that awful night as we came up the hill to find that a small BMW car was on its roof in the middle of the road. The condition of the vehicle was a testament to German engineering and quality of metal used as the roof had not collapsed despite it having travelled a short distance in this inverted position. The occupants were somewhat shaken up but not physically injured and had ended up suspended by their seatbelts upside down in the car but had released themselves before our arrival. Miraculously, the rain stopped as we were approaching the upturned BMW but it was still quite easy to confirm what the male driver told us about not being able to differentiate the low kerb of the footpath from the rest of the width of the road. He had struck this 'invisible' raised section, the front wheel had been knocked to the right and the car had veered across the road, struck the low embankment of the opposite hedge and been 'flipped' over onto its roof.

My colleague spoke with the lady passenger in an effort to help her to return to normal after her considerable shock. Although the driver did not seem to have been drinking, I needed to be sure as there had been no other vehicle involved. I prepared the small glass file, mouthpiece and bag and invited him to provide the breath sample. This he did and, as expected, there was no trace of alcohol in the colouration of the crystals. I then started to fill out the standard form to record the administering of the breath test. I asked for his surname, which was unusual but familiar to me from the television. When I asked for his first name, it added to the media familiarity. When I enquired if he was who I now thought him to be he said, "I'm afraid so." He then went on to tell me that his accident was doubly inconvenient as he needed to get back to London for a television recording the next morning.

With the breakdown lorry sorting out the recovery of the car, we took our couple to Shepton Mallet police station. There, with a cup of hot tea, they began to show that the shock they had endured was wearing off. They were still better pleased when we called a local taxi driver from his bed with the prospect of a 'fare' all the way to Bath Spa railway station. Another call confirmed that a train was still available, one which the taxi driver confirmed when he arrived that he would be able to meet.

On the Thursday evening just prior to my long weekend rest days, the telephone in the flat rang and the Constable in the station told me that someone from Information Room wanted to speak with me. He was connected through and it was an officer I had known for quite some time, he having been on the coinciding shift in the Information Room for quite a lot of my time on Traffic at Weston-super-Mare. Although it was not that frequent that we would call in at Taunton for a chat with the Information Room staff we would do so occasionally on night shifts and were in much more frequent contact by telephone and, particularly, radio. He told me that a teleprinter message had been received from Bramshill House listing the names of the thirty Officers who had, nationally, been successful in obtaining a place on the 1973/74 Special Course. Realising that the message he was handling was really for the Chief Constable, and being careful, he was ringing from a telephone in a side office as some lines in the Information Room were recorded. He also used somewhat oblique language to avoid being open to having directly revealed the content. He said, "All I can tell you, Dave, is that your name does not fail to appear on the list!" I thanked him most sincerely for he did not have to tell me, perhaps should not have told me. The next question was, what was I to do with this 'secret' knowledge. The answer, of course, was to keep it to myself.

My long weekend had arrived, they came around every four weeks, and we set off on the Saturday to visit Gill's mother and my parents in Wellington. Not too late, with the children needing their sleep after a busy day being spoiled, we arrived back at the flat. Pinned to the door was a note from one of my colleagues telling me that I was to telephone the Chief Superintendent at Frome regardless as to what time I returned home. Having helped Gill into the flat with all the gear required with small children, I went down to the station to make the call. We had an extension telephone in the flat but it only operated if a connection had been made from the 'key and lamp' mini-exchange in the front office. A similar system applied at Frome between the larger switchboard and the home of the Divisional Commander, a police owned property adjacent to the Station.

When connected, he demanded to know where I had been all day. I explained, as tactfully as I could manage, that I had taken the opportunity of a weekend day off to take our children to see their grandparents. Not really accepting this as a good reason, he then told me that the Chief Constable had been looking for me, 'all day'! In, probably pretended bewilderment, he told me that the Chief Constable had directed that I was to transfer into CID at Frome from Tuesday morning. It would have been the Monday but that was the Bank Holiday upon which I had already been scheduled to work 6p.m. till 2a.m. My enquiry as to why the Chief had issued this direction met with a claim not to know the answer. I, of course, was able to make an educated guess as to the reason. Our Chief Constable was known to have a policy that he was not keen on promoting Officers who had not gained some experience in CID.

As is the case in a disciplined Service, I dutifully drove in my own car to the Divisional Headquarters at Frome on Monday morning and, in the absence of the Detective Inspector, reported to one of the Detective Sergeants. He had simply been told of my impending arrival earlier that morning when he had reported for duty. I was allocated to work with a very experienced Woman Detective Constable (WDC – a term later to be considered 'sexist' or 'discriminatory') and we just got on with enquiries which she already had in hand. Not to let me think that I was getting any preferential treatment, that first day in CID was a split shift of 9a.m. till 1p.m. and 7.30p.m. till 11.30p.m. With the knowledge of the teleprinter message received at Headquarters and my sudden transfer into CID, I could not contain myself any longer and, that afternoon between the shift segments, I went to speak with the Superintendent, Deputy Divisional Commander. I simply asked if he could find out if anything had been heard from the Extended Interview Panel. He, evidently genuinely, knew nothing but undertook to make enquiries of Headquarters Officers.

On the Thursday, I was sent with the WDC to try and apprehend those responsible for thefts from parked cars in the recreational areas on the Mendips. After checking a few likely locations we were directed to go to a telephone for me to make contact with the Superintendent at Frome. His enquiries had been persistent but the temporary absence for those few days of both the Chief Constable and Chief Superintendent, perhaps why the previous Saturday had seemed so urgent, had made everyone at Headquarters rather cautious about possibly stealing the Chief's prerogative to be the one to inform me. However, he had discovered that I had been selected to attend the 12th Special Course. The start date was to be Sunday, 16th September, 1973 and it was already now the 30th August.

The next few days were to be a mixture of CID duties at Frome and trying to sort out where we were going to live while I was on the course for the next twelve months. The Superintendent told me to add some of my annual leave entitlement to the three days we would be allocated for the move. Initially there was a debate with the Superintendent in Headquarters Personnel Department as to whether we would be best suited by living at Bath, nearest to Bramshill, or Taunton, nearest the support for Gill from our family in Wellington. Taunton won our vote and we had two houses offered. The first was at Somerset Avenue and was not in at all a good state of upkeep. Given that I would be absent and not available to decorate it, we declined that offer. The following day we travelled back to Taunton and looked at one of the row of eight police houses in Priorswood Road. This we agreed was suitable on 4th September and the furniture van was ordered for the 10th, less than a full week to go!

In the middle of all this, the Divisional Commander summoned me to his presence and told me, in no uncertain terms, of his displeasure at my selecting annual leave without his approval. I chose not to respond or to even say that his deputy had given his consent in the Chief Superintendent's absence. What was the worst aspect was that there was not one hint of congratulations in being one of so very few from the Somerset & Bath Constabulary to have achieved this selection. Two other, more satisfactory, sequels before we left Shepton Mallet. A letter arrived from the television personality whom I had breathalysed and then helped on his way, with comments from the Chief Constable that this was an influential man to have impressed. The other was the follow-up to my report of the Polac (police accident) in the timber yard at Pylle. This was dealt with the Chief Inspector at Wells, a charming man, who had the biggest grin on his face as he minuted the file on the accident and told me that he was "offering me suitable advice".

No time for a 'leaving do' but plenty of handshakes and best wishes to me and to Gill. We moved in to 74, Priorswood Road. Gill's most satisfying aspect, even though I was to be away so much, was that the house and location in Taunton was so much better than had been her experience at Shepton Mallet. More searching for play schools and, now, Tanya's first Infants' School but, as she had before and would again, Gill took all that in her stride. Having been listed in General Orders (the, then, weekly bulletin to keep everyone up to date) as transferring to CID, two weeks later another entry identified the promotion of DC Leach to Temporary Sergeant. I had, in fact, been in CID for six days. Over the following years, I often referred to my 'six' in CID, which everyone not in the know took to be six years and derived some amusement when immediately I enlightened them.

10 Bramshill

In 1973, and for some years afterwards, arrival on a course of any sort required that the Officers attending start at 9a.m. on the first morning. This meant spending at least half a rest day travelling to the venue for the course. Not wanting to take any chances in my already eight year old, but outstandingly dependable, Cortina estate, I set off from the new family home before mid-day to travel the 112 miles to Bramshill and get settled in before the real course started on Monday, 17th September. I would become extremely familiar with that journey across the county to pick up the A303 over the next eleven months.

With regard to the short weekends between 5p.m. Friday finishes and 9a.m. Monday starts, our course, the 12th Special Course, had an influence to the advantage of all Bramshill courses. Within weeks of starting, we got together with our course directing staff and made a suggestion which was accepted by the Commandant. Instead of the customary two hour lunch break, on a Friday this was severely curtailed and we then regained the time by leaving at 3.30p.m. on those days. The Sunday evening arrival could not be avoided for people, like me, with quite a journey to make from home.

With the amalgamation of Forces taking place on the 1st April of the following year, there were quite a few out of the thirty of us who would, before the end of the course, have joined up to be in the same Force. In my case, there were two members from the Bristol Constabulary, one under the graduate entry scheme and about my age, the other one of the people who had passed in the top 200 nationally and who was much younger. There was only one young woman on the course and no women amongst our few directing staff but this young lady seemed to cope admirably with her situation and appeared to be friendly with everyone without falling into the trap of becoming too friendly with any individual. A few months before the course started, I celebrated my twenty eight birthday and just after the start at Bramshill, eight years police service. Out of the thirty, only one had more service than me and only a couple were older. Like the younger member from Bristol, with whom I became good friends as our time together extended, a few had very little operational service.

It has to be said that some had so little practical experience that they had no counterbalance to their sound academic knowledge of police law and procedure. One young man from the City of London Police seemed, as our various discussion sessions developed, to have some knowledge of most aspects of policing. It transpired that the Commissioner of that Force, my principal interviewer on the extended interview session, had moved him about from one department to another and he had 'seen' quite a variety of policing activity. He had, however, been the 'officer dealing' on only quite rare occasions. The real essence of gaining police experience useful to carry on to higher and command rank, and one which looks in grave danger of being lost altogether within future police command structures, is to have taken full part in a wide variety of policing activity and have accepted personal responsibility for the outcome.

Front of Bramshill House Police College

Our Course of thirty were evenly split between the three Chief Inspectors who were the Syndicate Directors. In charge of the whole Course was a Chief Superintendent, from Sussex. All four of these Officers brought a sound operational policing background with them to the College, not necessarily a valid claim for all of those fulfilling these roles on other courses. I suspect that there was some secondary level selection for Special Course directing staff as there were many to choose from with a more than 120 strong Inspectors' Course, in each of the three 'terms', and smaller Intermediate Command Courses (two terms), Senior Command Course (summer term) and, probably a good 'earner' for the Home Office, the Overseas Command Courses (three terms).

Our Course was to start with the 'Police Studies Phase'. Given that everyone had passed the Sergeants' promotion examination in order to be considered for the course it seemed odd that we should spend quite a few weeks studying much the same material. The advantage for me, although it was a disadvantage in terms of comparison with the younger course members, was that I discovered something about the Theft Act. I had passed both Sergeant and Inspector examinations with the old Larceny Act still prevailing. Before the two week Christmas break we started on the Academic Phase, during which we studied Politics, Economics and Sociology. This phase included some limited, but welcome, trips away from the College. The final, Summer Term, Phase was tagged 'Operational' and involved quite a few excursions, which I will come to later.

In that first week, I discovered that I had been allocated as Duty Student from the following Monday. I found that the duties for this role were not onerous provided that nothing out of the ordinary occurred. What I did not find out, because we had started our course a few weeks after the beginning of the College term and had missed the bulletins for the first weeks, was that those involved were supposed to attend a briefing on the Friday prior to their allocated week. I was summoned to the Course Director's office during the Monday coffee break to be admonished by the Chief Superintendent for my failure. He went on to say that he had been compelled to apologise to the duty Directing Staff member, another Chief Superintendent, for my omission. Apparently the students from the Inspector's Course and Intermediate Command Course had attended. He told me that I should have read all the 'back copies' of the weekly bulletins to bring myself up to date upon my arrival the previous week. I was quite prepared to make a full apology and asked him for the name of the other Directing Staff member in order that I may personally apologise to him. This he told me was not necessary and I told him that I was not content that he had apologised on my behalf, telling him that if an apology was appropriate, I would make it myself. He dismissed this idea as he dismissed me from his office but I knew that I had made my point. Only he had taken this matter so seriously, wanting to ensure that I knew my place in the course hierarchical structure. I had shown him that I had enough character to deal with my own failures and that I did not want anyone making apologies on my behalf.

The bar at Bramshill House

There were a number of social 'clubs' which we could join. The most obvious for me was to substitute my enforced absences from the Force Choir by joining the College Choir. This, of necessity with the constant, every four months, massive change of personalities, was a very mixed ability group. The younger member within our course from Bristol was an extremely accomplished pianist and was immediately recruited as accompanist for that whole year. The Superintendent on the Directing Staff who 'managed' the choir soon recognised that I had some ability and I was to make my debut as a soloist while at Bramshill. We went out to a few old people's homes and junior schools to sing on the Wednesday afternoon recreation period. On one such visit, I gave a lift to a couple other 'choristers' and we were parking in the school playground when a Chief Inspector in the rear seat of the Cortina estate started giving directions. I thanked him, not very sincerely, and reminded him who was driving. About twelve years later, our paths would cross again, by which time he had risen to the rank of Commissioner of the Metropolitan Police!

The other 'club' which I and a few of my course colleagues joined was to learn Ballroom Dancing. Gill had taken lessons when in Wellington before we married and I had accompanied her on rare occasions when my visits home from Weston allowed, but I was no great shakes on the dance floor, still am not! The resident wives of the directing staff living in the married quarters behind the student accommodation blocks bravely turned up in response to the pleas from the lady instructor, so the gender balance was not too heavily skewed.

There was, on alternate Thursdays, a Dining In Night, when formal dress accompanied the dining hall being decked out with much silverware. I had been forced to the expense of a new suit for the extended interviews and, now, for the purchase of a dinner suit. The mass of silverware was mostly marked with the name of the course which had donated it, going back over many years. The barely hidden benefit from these evenings was to 'educate' students in the social graces and I soon recognised which item of cutlery was for which course and which glass was for what liquid. The other aspect of these evenings was that the entire assembly would repair to the main hall after the meal for an entertainment. Each course would be expected to provide at least one evening of entertainment and, because we were there for longer, we were allocated two. The Choir, of course, also provided one evening each term.

For what was probably the last Dining In Evening of the Autumn, our first, term we spent some considerable time in the long lunch breaks rehearsing. We had a few quite inventive course members who came up with some really funny ideas and I offered to sing Benny Hill's classic 'Pepys Diary'. I had a cassette tape recorder which I used for entertainment in the car on the journeys between Taunton and Bramshill and the Benny Hill record was recorded on to a cassette and played over and over until I had the words to perfection. Our whole show, and my small contribution, went very well. In the Spring term I sang a solo 'Little Liza Jane' with the Choir providing the chorus backing. On this occasion we understood why the Superintendent on the directing staff who was 'choirmaster' had found himself thus charged. His aunt was the guest of honour at that dinner and concert. She was a famous actress who had been made a Dame for her services to the theatre and she kindly spoke to me in the bar after the concert. Her enquiry was where had I received my voice training?

I explained that the only 'training' I had received was listening to my mother performing to perfectly throughout my formative years.

Later in the year, our course provided our second concert. This time, having been involved for so long since the previous September, our writers and ideas men became somewhat more adventurous. A small team constructed a whole set of new verses to the tune from the Benny Hill success of the December. On the lunchtime of the day of the show, we held a full rehearsal and the Course Directing Staff attended. I watched closely for reactions when I started singing as each verse singled out a directing staff member, starting with the Commandant. The Course Director was the least amused and took me to one side afterwards to insist that I should revert to the original words for the song. I explained that I would be letting the others down if I did so. On the evening, our Course Director was in the front row on one side of the central aisle and the Commandant on the other. Each was accompanied by one of the invited outside guests. When the music for my piece struck up the Chief Superintendent became more alert and, when he realised that I was singing the revised words, was frequently glancing across at the Commandant to gauge his reaction. It was, as the 'punchline' of that first verse was reached, one of uncontrolled laughter. Relieved, the Course Director had, of course, to show equal amusement as 'his' punchline arrived – with the Commandant watching him just as intently. I, just, got away with that one and, in fact, believe that it did me no harm whatsoever.

From January, as part of the Academic Phase, we went out from the College several times. On two consecutive days, I took some colleagues in my faithful old Cortina estate to visit Coldingley Prison and then Finnamore Wood Borstal, where we were given tours of the buildings and talks from the staff on their responsibilities and routines. In early February, a longer journey alone and direct from home brought me to a hotel where a group of course members were also staying in Leicester. This visit was billed as 'Social Administration' and other course members had gone to other areas for that same three days. Each group prepared a presentation for the rest of the course members to reveal what each visit had produced. At that time, February, 1974, Leicester was said to contain the highest concentration of immigrants from the Indian Sub-Continent. Visits had been organised for us to meet the leaders of various parts of that community and the local authority members involved with them. My most recent station, Shepton Mallet, was in an area almost entirely composed of a traditional white population, indeed the only person I recall in that town who was of West Indian extraction was one of the Special Constables on the Section.

On the evening of Monday, 1st April, 1974 one of the Directing Staff members and his wife invited a group of us to go around after dinner to their home, behind the student accommodation blocks. The group comprised all of the Officers on whatever courses who had, in the early hours of that morning, found themselves in the newly amalgamated Avon and Somerset Constabulary. On that day, the former Bristol Constabulary, Somerset & Bath Constabulary and the Staple Hill (southern) Division of the Gloucestershire Constabulary joined within the new Local Authority boundaries of Avon and, the redefined, Somerset.

The Directing Staff for our Course had evidently done quite a bit of advance preparation and, with the Course Director being a Chief Superintendent from the Sussex Police, received much assistance from that Force. The result of their efforts was a thirty six hour Crime Exercise which was held in the extensive buildings and grounds of a Church of England study centre at Battle. The exercise was set to run overnight and through both days with us split into shifts and cast in various roles, which were different on each shift. It started off as a missing child enquiry, with some very realistic role playing by some helpful local amateur actors. This developed into a hostage situation and a murder, with the local police providing realism with underwater search team, dog handlers, scenes of crime and firearms trained Officers. It was excellent and as near to reality as could be expected. The only 'plus' point I recall scoring was as the night Sergeant using the radio to direct officers not to rush in, a fortunate direction when we discovered that the hostage takers were armed.

We were taken by coach to visit the Fire Brigade National College at Morton in the Marsh, in Gloucestershire. Their Senior Officer training Course, somewhat similar to ours within the Police, entertained us for the day. They set up some very interesting exercises for us to witness and, with great care for our safety, in which to get slightly involved. My most lasting recollection was the section of a small ship fashioned out of concrete in which it was possible to simulate fires in the hold and train for rescues and fighting fires in such circumstances. It seemed that the visit was reciprocal on an alternate year basis but what Bramshill offered in the light of what Morton had to show must have been somewhat challenging. A similar, alternate year, arrangement had been established with the Royal Navy course for NCOs to be trained and selected for Commissioned Rank. In our year the Chief Petty Officers, all somewhat longer in service than most of us, came to Bramshill. Their day with us was unexceptional but the hospitality that we set up for them after dinner in the bar seemed to be well appreciated.

The other military connection was when we were warned to be up exceptionally early one morning for a coach journey to an RAF station. There we were given a briefing and each of our three syndicates had the use of a Puma helicopter with its well trained crew of Officer Pilot & co-pilot and Sergeant 'loadmaster'. Our early morning take off took us over Reading, where we were able to see the advantage of being able to observe the traffic flows (or lack of them) from the air. Upon entering the helicopter I had noticed that the seat backs were along the 'spine' of the fuselage, facing five to each side of the aircraft. On one side there was a pair of windows which gave a limited view while on the other there was a large sliding door. I positioned myself in the middle seat on the side facing the door and was pleased to see that we were to fly with the door left open. Each seat had a lap belt so I felt quite secure but the view of the ground was obstructed by the floor and, to compensate, the pilot maintained a slow manoeuvre of presenting the downward view by tilting the machine. Not all in our number appreciated this virtually constant and strange movement.

Sergeant 247 with RAF Puma helicopter in June, 1974

We flew in to the sports field at Bramshill for a late breakfast, which not everyone wanted. Another briefing and we were back in the helicopters for the second flight. This time it was a search exercise, with two of the Syndicate Directors in their cars, different coloured Renault 16s, driving around the Hampshire countryside. One was the target car and the other we could communicate with to try and direct it to intercept. Hampshire Police had set up a mobile communications facility at the side of the Bramshill sports field to facilitate the communications. Given that ground to air communications in the police was very much in its infancy, the Hampshire communications department did a good job. This experience of helicopter flight was, as things turned out, to be the first two of many but I think we all benefited from the experience, even those who had stomach upsets!

A few other memories from almost a year at Bramshill include the visit of Her Majesty Queen Elizabeth II. I was to be in quite close proximity to several members of the Royal Family during my police service but this was the only time I was that close to the Queen. On an occasion when we were having a discussion session, I had been 'cast' in the role of a Detective Sergeant at a simulated debriefing session. I received congratulations from staff and fellow students alike for the accuracy of my rather cynical comments throughout the session. We received a small amount of TV interview training, with my Syndicate Director as the interviewer. The idea was that our interview would be recorded and then we would, with the rest of our syndicate, watch it being played back and comment upon the performance. There were very many different ways in which we all reacted to the process but my main focus was not to get drawn into too much controversy, while the interviewer was seeking to make the whole interview controversial and succeeded with some of my colleagues.

Probably my favourite part of the course was the two week attachments that had been arranged for each of us. The principle had been to try and place each of us with as different as possible a Force area from that to which we belonged. From central Somerset, the small town of Shepton Mallet, the staff choice for me was, very appropriately, the Notting Hill Sub-Division of the Metropolitan Police. On a Sunday afternoon in late June, 1974, I drove the old Cortina to Paddington Green Police Station. Later, Paddington Green was to become the 'Central London Police Station' used as the top security holding centre for terrorist suspects. On my first morning I was collected by an Inspector from

Notting Hill, who hailed originally from Bristol, and with whom, coincidentally, I was to work at New Scotland Yard (NSY) nearly ten years later. He took me to NSY and Chelsea to meet the coordinating Chief Superintendent in A2 Department and Commander in charge of the Chelsea Division. The latter considered that, while I should spend time at Notting Hill, the smaller station at Notting Dale would offer some variety. I was also to meet an Officer, then with the soon to be abandoned rank of Station Sergeant, whom I would, again ten years later, encounter in connection with Public Order at the Metropolitan Training Centre at Hendon.

The rest of that first day was spent finding my way around that Sub Division and meeting so many people in so many offices that keeping track was impossible. I did encounter the divisional clerk, a Constable with many duties but principal among them being to maintain everyone's overtime records. He was fed by his colleagues with their information as to hours worked and balanced the returns submitted to maintain the monthly 99 hours claim that the Metropolitan accounting system would allow. This revealed the system behind what my old school friend had related a couple of years earlier in the police club at Weston-super-Mare and referred to in Chapter eight. While familiarising myself with the Notting Hill Sub-Division, I discovered that there were three distinct thirds to the area. One was very expensive property, with the Home Secretary's Official Residence included, another was quite mixed but predominantly white population, the third was a very highly concentrated population of West Indian background. What did surprise me was the geographic closeness of these very different areas.

On patrol one afternoon in the Area Car, we came across a black man looking under the bonnet of an Austin Cambridge car. We stopped to see if we could be of any help but, within a minute, found ourselves surrounded by people who evidently thought we had intentions to deal with him for some offence or another. What concerned me was the way in which all four of us, so quickly outnumbered, felt intimidated, when all we had genuinely wanted to do was to render the man some assistance.

One evening, later in that week, I was to witness something that would certainly not have happened in my own force. Quite a few of us attended a call to a fight inside a public house which had spilled out onto the road by the time we got there. With numerous Constables and more than one Sergeant in attendance, the Inspector with whom I had arrived immediately arrested one of the two men fighting in the street, the other was also detained. The reasoning was that the following morning, outside of the scheduled shift of 2p.m. till 10p.m., the Inspector would have to attend the local Magistrates Court to prosecute the prisoner and receive overtime payment. Although provincial forces had moved to immediate payment for overtime under the new Regulations eighteen months earlier, such payment was extremely restricted. In the Metropolitan Police, and for some many years later, it was really quite routine. As I commented earlier, on top of the London Weighting Allowances, the differential in pay between Metropolitan and Provincial Force Officers was, perhaps still is, massive.

My fairly recent time spent in the Traffic Department in Somerset had been picked up from the information on me sent to Notting Hill by the Police College and arrangements were made for me to spend the Friday of the first week in company with a Motor Patrol Sergeant based at the North West London Traffic Garage. After our lunch break, we went in his Rover 3.5 patrol car along the M40 heading for London Heathrow Airport but, just as we were approaching the entrance, we were diverted back to a 'bomb scare' at Middlesex House on the north side of the Thames in West London. It was, at that time, routine for a Traffic Supervisory Officer to attend all such calls. We travelled along the dual carriageway off the end of the M40 and the Sergeant used the full power of that V8 engine and its automatic gearbox to traverse each roundabout. Once the alert had been found to be another false alarm (there were many at that time), we returned more sedately to Heathrow. There we drove around the perimeter inside the fencing and all around that route there were military armoured vehicles and countless Army personnel, engaged in the security operation known in the mass media as the 'Ring of Steel'. This was in response to the strong concerns at the time over terrorist activity.

At the end of our traversing around the airfield, we entered a compound which was also overlooking the Heston M4 Motorway service area. This compound housed the motorway control facility for that route into London and was the first in which I had seen closed circuit television (CCTV) in operation. I was later returned to Notting Dale and invited, as I had already decided to stay until Saturday to visit the Portobello Road market particularly to witness the attempts to detect pick-pockets, to join the 'raid party' that evening. The arrangement within the Notting Hill Sub-Division was to form a plain clothes group each Friday evening on overtime from their 2p.m. till 10p.m. shift. The group was of an Inspector and a Sergeant, each with three Constables and they changed into casual civilian clothing at ten o'clock, took a refreshment break and were out to execute warrants obtained by the local CID office by eleven.

I attached myself to the group lead by the Sergeant. We had six warrants, known parochially as 'tickets', three for each team, and we set off to execute them. The first was a bit of a 'damp squib' as it was for a basement flat, which it turned out was occupied by an elderly couple. Next, just along the road, was a tall 'town house' type property which had been separated into bed-sits. The entrance was a small flight of steps up from the pavement and I was, intentionally, behind the four local Officers. The Constable beside the Sergeant, at the top of the stairs, was using a piece of plastic in an attempt to spring the 'Yale' type door lock but without much success. We, of course, wanted to get past this communal barrier to be able to visit each bed-sit with some level of surprise on our side. From my distant viewpoint, I realised that I could see no reflection of the street lighting from the large window panel in the upper half of the front door. I threaded my way up the steps to the front and, as I had expected, put my hand through the glassless window and released the door catch. There was much mirth, directed mainly at the young man with the piece of plastic but quickly silenced by the Sergeant. We visited all seven of the bed-sits but found nothing to signify that the information laid to get the warrant was accurate.

Back in the street, we met up with the Inspector and his small team. They had one 'ticket' left, for a substantial building with quite an imposing front door through which access would not be gained discretely. Although not a rarity, the door looked remarkably like one shown in the much later film named after this area of London. We all prepared for a quick entry if the Inspector's loud knock on the door brought someone to investigate. It did, the door was soon pushed wider than the small gap for the respondent to the knock to see who was the late caller. This building had a large hallway with, what once must have been an impressive staircase. Now everything looked dowdy and the living arrangement seemed more communal than separated into bed-sits. A couple of the Constables dashed up the stairs to an open door into what looked like a toilet but the disgustingly dirty toilet pan had been flushed before they reached it and a 'hippy' looking young man stood beside the door with a huge grin on his face. A thorough search, but avoiding some of the worst areas of unwashed clothing and unfinished food was looking like another failure until one young man was seen to drop something from the landing to the feet of another in the hallway. The latter made the instinctive mistake of picking up the small package of cannabis resin so both were arrested.

After a few hours' sleep back at Paddington Green, I joined up with the Chief Inspector Operations for the Division and, in plain clothes, we spent the morning in the Portobello Road and a few of the side roads around that area. The crush of people was remarkable and it was easy to see how simple would be the operation of pick-pocketing that my guide hoped I may see. A pair of plain clothed Constables did manage to witness a 'dip' in action, but that was the only arrest that morning. Having surrendered this half of my day off, I left London in the early afternoon to arrive home in Taunton by teatime. To compensate a little, I followed the Sunday rest day with a late start back to Notting Hill, allowing me to spend most of that Monday at home. I then spent an interesting 8p.m. till 4a.m. out and around the Sub-Division, where even Monday nights were constantly busy.

To catch up on a bit of the lost sleep of the latter part of the previous week, I again reported at lunchtime on Tuesday, this time to Notting Dale but spent much of that shift seeing the station procedures at Notting Hill. As I have mentioned, the Home Secretary's Official Residence was on this Sub-Division and warranted a full-time armed police presence outside the front door. The firearms trained Officers who carried out this, what must have been pretty tedious, task collected and returned the revolvers they used to the front office at Notting Hill. The Metropolitan Police had reverted to revolvers as they had, quite recently, experienced the attack in the Mall on Princess Ann, where the Walther PPK automatic pistol carried by her Personal Protection Officer (PPO) had been found to jam. At that time, in the new Avon and Somerset Force we had only a very limited number of firearms trained Officers and I was amazed at the apparently relatively casual way in which these weapons were handled. With a little overtime built in to allow for the exchange at the residence, the relieving Officer came on duty and went into the front office at Notting Hill. This 'office' was a large room with the public counter in one corner from which callers could see the entire room. The Constable opened the drawer in the desk used most often by the Station Sergeant (as earlier referred to, still a distinct rank in the Metropolitan Police at that time and signified by a crown above the 'V' of the sergeants' chevrons) took out the revolver and the hand full of rounds of ammunition and put his jacket on over the shoulder holster. A while later, the man he had relieved, came to the office and deposited the other revolver and ammunition in the drawer before going off duty. What the members of the public who witnessed this, what I will loosely describe as a, procedure thought I can only imagine!

Before leaving late that night, I experienced a quite furious ride in the back of the Area Car to a pizza café on one of the major roads through the Sub-Division (still often referred to as it had been in the old Dixon and Dock Green programmes as 'the manor'). Upon arrival, along with every other mobile unit from some miles around, the small building was surrounded but the two young men inside, whom the 999 call had identified as 'robbers' were holding aloft their Police Warrant Cards. They were from the drugs team of a neighbouring Division acting on what they thought was good information but had omitted to tell anyone local of their intended action. Back to Paddington Green to sleep on what that day had brought.

After the Metropolitan Police attachment, the next few weeks back at the College seemed to be a bit of a wind-down. My performance throughout that eleven months had, I think, been as good as I could have managed. With the 'walk around the lake' defined attitude that I am sure had brought me to the Special Course, I had continued through my time at Bramshill with no artificial or contrived approach. I had been what I was and, somehow – much to my own surprise, that seemed to have been enough. My significant investment while at Weston-super-Mare between 1970 and 1972 and the acquisition of those Social Science 'A' levels made my passage through the Academic Phase reasonable secure. It had, I was told, produced the recommendation from the civilian directing staff that I should be considered by the Home Office for a Bramshill Scholarship. At the inception of the Graduate Entry Scheme and with its more certain entry to the Special Course, the Police Federation had negotiated, in a time when degree level education was much more rare, that serving officers thought to be suitable while attending courses at the Police College should be given the opportunity to also achieve a graduate level education.

Our year was to be the subject of some sort of mix-up as the projection that a Bramshill Scholarship would commence the year after completing the Special Course did not materialise. We were not told what had happened to our application forms, I presume that I was not the only one, but did receive notification, too late for 1975, that we were to be supported for a degree course to start in October, 1976. More of that in Chapter Twelve. Of more immediate concern as the end of the course drew ever nearer, was where would I be going when I left Bramshill? My fellow, ex-Bristol, Force members on the course were equally concerned and the copies of General Orders which arrived each week told us nothing. In early August, our Chief Constable visited the College and took us to one side in the bar area during an afternoon when there was no one else there. He dealt with the two from Bristol first, both of whom were living in their own houses, and they were relieved when he told them that they were to stay in the City. I suspected that I would not be allowed to stay at Taunton, although having not worked there it would have breached none of the old taboos of knowing your subordinates too intimately that County Forces seemed to take so seriously. He informed me that my move was to become one of the Borough Sergeants at Bridgwater. He must have seen my concerned expression as he immediately informed me that I could remain living at Taunton. The condition was that I would make the eleven mile journey at my own expense, at a time when seven miles was the normal maximum travel expectation for Officers living in Police accommodation. I, of course, accepted and Gill, having enjoyed her year at Taunton with me largely absent, was also pleased to be getting another year without a further move of home.

Last day at Bramshill

11 Bridgwater

Having returned from Bramshill on the previous Friday, I enjoyed an uninterrupted weekend and made my first of many journeys to report for duty at Bridgwater Police Station on Monday, 12th August, 1974. I met for the first time the Borough Chief Inspector, a former Bath City man who was a no nonsense but very fair manager. I also, of course, had to parade in front of the Chief Superintendent, Divisional Commander, for his welcome (back) to the Division. It had only been four and a half years since I had 'crossed' his intentions by refusing the flat above the police station at Minehead and I was not at all sure how he would react to my being returned to work within his command. At that time, and before and since, too many Supervisory Officers in the Police Service could hold grudges for an unbelievably long time. The Chief Superintendent at Bridgwater from the late 1960s and throughout the 1970s was much more enlightened. That interview was a genuine welcome back to the Division and there was no hint that we had not seen eye-to-eye those few years earlier. Neither was that earlier time ever mentioned or form any part of his assessment of me through that year as a Sergeant under his command.

After the first few days at Bridgwater, I was required to visit Headquarters, now in Old Bridewell in the middle of Bristol, to be shown what I needed to know regarding various aspects of administration peculiar to the Sergeant role. While there, I was to have an interview with the Chief Constable. It transpired that the interview was regarding my success in being recommended for a Bramshill Scholarship to attend University. Neither of us knew at that time that the scholarship would be delayed. For me, the big advantage of a Bramshill Scholarship was that, subject to College approval, I could make my own application to whatever University I wished and to study whatever subject or combination of subjects. I had not thought too much about the University, being aware that it would mean either another separation from Gill and the girls or another house move for the two years and eight months of the secondment

(Bramshill were capable of arranging accommodation with Forces in which a University was located).

Bridgwater Police Station

The interview with the Chief Constable did not run at all as I had expected. He immediately told me that he was not convinced that studying Sociology, my declared choice identified while at Bramshill, was appropriate for a Police Officer. I explained that I saw most of what came within the subject heading as closely related to policing. He went further and offered to guarantee me a place in 1975 on a Force Scholarship. At that time the Force had a standing arrangement with the University of Bristol, I think originated by the Bristol Constabulary, for two Officers each year to attend the Law Faculty to read for an LLB. Although I knew a few colleagues who had been and were on these secondments, I did not see the relevance of most of what a law degree course offered and stuck to my guns. At the time, I was unsure whether the Chief was testing my resolve but I was to understand, later, he was quite against anyone studying Sociology.

There was a reason for the Chief Constable's concerns, not known to me in 1974. A former award of a Bramshill Scholarship had taken one of the Officers from the Force to the London School of Economics to study Sociology. Upon his return his senior officers were concerned, rightly or wrongly, that his attitudes had been too heavily influenced by his time at the LSE. I remained, still do, convinced that studying Sociology was far more beneficial to my continued service as a Police Officer but nothing was going to convince the Chief. Perhaps I was somewhat foolhardy, given the clearer perspective of looking back, but I stuck with my choice, supported by the Police College academics.

I soon established quite a good working relationship with the small Section for whom I had assumed responsibility. They were, as may be expected, a mixed bunch, some quite bright others well blessed with 'common sense' but all were committed to the Service and held in common the values which I, too, saw as important. We got on with the job, whatever that was on each shift. The attitude of the Constables on the Section helped immensely my grounding in managing others. Although I recognised that supervisors had to keep a slight distance I think that I soon acquired the right balance between retaining authority while maintaining personal relationships. I had never espoused the idea that being a supervisory Officer meant that I was no longer a Constable in the policing sense of the word. Whatever rank in the Police Service, with the one-time exception of the Commissioner and Deputy Commissioners of the Metropolitan Police, with their origins in the Magistracy from 1829, every Officer still is a Constable in the eye of the Law. Because of the way they seemed to enjoy total impunity for non-agricultural use, my former Traffic experience made me focus some attention on the unlawful use of agricultural tractors within the Borough. This became a bit of a standing source of amusement on the Section but it demonstrated that I remained a practical 'copper'.

One of the duties I enjoyed much more than I anticipated was that allocated on days when the Magistrates Court, next to the police station, was in session. While an Inspector, sometimes a solicitor engaged for the session, would prosecute what the public would view as criminal matters, the early turn Sergeant prosecuted the traffic offences short of Driving Without Due Care & Attention. I soon got into the swing of the way the court operated and became quite adept at presenting the cases, introducing the prosecution witnesses and challenging by cross-examination defence witnesses and defendants. A few years later this small amount of experience would stand me in good stead but more of this in Chapter fourteen.

One of the striking aspects of policing Bridgwater was the frequency with which we were called to domestic disputes. At that time the main streets of the town had lost a few such premises but still had more than its share of Public Houses. Whether the access to alcohol had any relationship to the number of domestic arguments could not be scientifically proven but there was ample room for supposition. The 2p.m. till 10p.m. shift, usually one upon which it is possible to catch up with some non-urgent paperwork, always seemed busier at Bridgwater than elsewhere I had worked. There was always something, often not just domestic disputes.

Bridgwater Magistrates' Court (taken in 2015 but as it looked in 1975)

One Sunday afternoon a small corner shop not far from the police station and near the old wharfs suffered an explosion. The emersion heated water tank in an airing cupboard in the first floor living quarters blew up and there was a minor fire. One fire tender was in attendance when we arrived and had backed up the service yard at the side of the building to facilitate placing the hoses through the back door. After we arrived, another fire engine arrived and stopped in the road directly in front of the first machine. The crew got out and looked through the shop windows, where their colleagues were easily visible. A fireman (they were not called 'firefighters' in 1975) took out his axe and proceeded to smash down the shop door! The Fire Service has a proud tradition and many dedicated, even brave, people but it was my, too frequent, experience that many loved breaking things!

Another Sunday, 2p.m. till 10p.m. shift produced a much sadder incident and brought us to a residential street on one of the estates. The middle aged widow occupier had returned from her local Church Service to find her adult son hanging in the hallway. She answered the door with him hanging behind her so we quickly took her in to the living room and were fortunate that there was a police woman who had just finished duty and was quickly called back to sit with the lady. The mother was remarkably calm about the horror she had seen, not always a good longer-term emotional signal. The young man did not appear to have really intended to take his own life but had used an old webbing army belt around the pillar at the top of the stairs to reduce his air flow. The local doctor who was on call as our police surgeon attended and explained that such action can, in some people, prove to be sexually stimulating. On this occasion it had brought a young life to a very premature end.

On a Monday morning, before the 9a.m. till 5p.m. Bridgwater County Section Constable reported for duty, we received a call that a bull was feeding off of what was left of the roses in people's gardens in a road of bungalows in Cannington, a village a few miles west of Bridgwater. I was conferring with one of the Constables when the call came in and was using the supervisory car, so he got in and off we went. On arrival, we soon found the bull and he was, indeed, feasting well on the previously attractive flowers. O.K., we had arrived but, what now? We thought better of getting out of the car immediately but realised that the eyes of many would be upon us from the bungalows. Before we had formulated a plan (to be honest we did not really come up with one) a man approached from behind the police car with his newspaper under his arm. "Not out again, is he?" We watched, somewhat in embarrassment, as the man hooked his finger through the ring in the bull's nose and lead it a short distance to a gateway that was only slightly open. The bull followed the man into the field and he returned to the road, shutting the gate securely behind him. We were, now, out of the vehicle and thanked him for his assistance. He was obviously amused but made no comment. Why, we thought, did the caller not know what this neighbour evidently knew?

That incident at Cannington was on our early turn Monday and that week of duties was, as usual, followed by the, four-weekly intervalled, 'long weekend' and then back to night shift. We started back on nights on a Monday and our second night shift that week was to prove something quite different from the routine. At 5.27a.m. on Wednesday morning, 23rd October, 1974, just as we were thinking that we would soon be handing over to our early turn colleagues, two goods trains collided on the main south-bound line just north of Bridgwater Railway Station. I attended with one of the Constables and found a deserted train engine just short of the station platform with all its lights on and the doors hanging open. We, correctly, assumed that the crew had walked along the line ahead of them to place detonators on the northbound track to warn any trains coming in that direction and to confer with the signalman.

Scene of the crash near Bridgwater Railway Station on 23rd October, 1974

We separated and walked at level pace one each side of the large box-van trucks behind the abandoned engine. Having passed innumerable box-vans the street lighting from the over bridge on the Weston Zoyland road disappeared from view but their glow made an outline of a huge mound from the front of which half of another engine was visible. The two men in the front of the diesel were barely conscious but remarkably lightly injured as the front of their engine was imbedded in the rearmost box-van of the leading train. The mound, by which the back half of the engine was buried was a huge heap of coal with trucks sticking out of it at all angles. Funny how your mind works, I had a flash-back to my Dandy comic of childhood days where sausages and mash were always depicted as a heap of mashed potato with sausages sticking out of it! I immediately reported on my personal radio and the control room at Bridgwater police station started notifying all and sundry.

Soon ambulances and fire tenders started arriving in too great a number, following a pre-set routine that took account of the potential for passengers to be involved. This was soon rectified and the two from the crashed engine were taken to hospital. There was no fire, although that was extremely fortunate as the rear box-vans, only one of which had actually been split open, contained paper sacks of artificial fertiliser, a potentially very dangerous ingredient around fire. Underneath the edge of the heap of coal, in the rear cab of the crashed engine, was the train's guard but it was some time later in the day before his body was recovered. It transpired that the engine crew had missed a couple of signals indicating that the first train was blocking the southbound line and had not seen the leading train until too late. Their braking, it seemed, had prevented extensive damage to the leading train's trucks and had probably saved their lives but the concertina action of the long train of coal trucks shunting up against each other into that mound had taken the life of the guard. There was, some time later, a prosecution for manslaughter against the inattentive crew. We members of the night shift were soon sent off to our beds, with much left to be done by our own colleagues and British Transport Police but the Borough Chief Inspector did not forget my initial organising actions when he finalised our police report.

Although dealing with death is, too often, part and parcel of policing responsibilities, one I shall not forget came our way one afternoon. The headmaster of a local junior school had called an ambulance and then telephoned the police station as a ten year old boy had collapsed during the afternoon playtime. Before taking the child off to the local hospital, the ambulance crew had informed the headmaster that the little lad was already dead. In those days before paramedics this had to be an opinion rather than a diagnosis but we all knew that they must be correct and it was soon confirmed from the hospital.

When we arrived at the school all the children were back in their classrooms and the headmaster, supported by another teacher and the school secretary, was in a pretty bad state of shock. We brought him some relief when I told him that the Constable with me and I would deliver the awful news to his home.

We arrived on the doorstep of a tidily cared for home on one of the council estates, at just about the same time as the poor dead boy would have normally been bounding through the front door to tell of all he had done at school that day. Instead, his mother opened the door to two police uniforms. Some of the most difficult part of delivering bad news is eased by the fact that people, seeing an unexpected police attendance at their door, half anticipate that it will not be good news. We invited ourselves in, sat mum down and told her probably the worst news she could ever have imagined she would receive. Her husband, she told us in a peculiarly unemotional way, worked for the then huge British Cellophane factory north of Bridgwater and he was soon on his way home. Indeed, much of the extended family arrived in very short time as they all lived quite local to the address.

I was, again, as much concerned about the mother's apparent lack of outpouring of emotions as I was about any other aspect of this sudden death. How she coped in later years I never found out but would hope that her large family would have gone on supporting her. Following a family discussion in which we took no part, the mother's brother was nominated to carry out the formal identification. When we revealed the small body in the hospital mortuary chapel he confirmed the identity and it was some considerable time before he was prepared to stop hugging his beloved but lifeless nephew. It transpired that the boy had a heart which was twice its appropriate size and that his premature death was almost inevitable as medical science stood in the 1970s. His enthusiastic engagement in all aspects of school sporting activities had supported the lie as to his apparently high level of fitness.

Christmas and New Year were not particularly spectacular although the, then thriving, Bridgwater Police Club put on even more activities under the guidance of the County Section Sergeants and Constables. Now long-since folded, the police club at Bridgwater was second to none, with some form of special activity taking place alongside the bar being open on almost every evening of the week. Not alone in the demise of social activities among police officers and support staff, Bridgwater club seemed, then, as though it would be 'there' forever. That it and its counterparts have been allowed to fall by the wayside has served no good for the police service as it now exists.

At 2.05a.m. on Wednesday, 15th January, 1975, we received an unusual call to Dunball Wharf, a couple miles north of Bridgwater and where small ships still called regularly to load and unload cargo. In what must have been an act of some desperation on his part, the call came from the Master of an Italian registered ship but plying between the UK and Norway. It was not usual for foreign ships' captains to involve local authority in any dispute on what they considered to be their territory. To safeguard ourselves, I ensured that he was requesting that we go aboard his vessel and he could not usher us fast enough up the gangplank. With not the best of English and me nor the Constable with me having any Italian or Norwegian, we managed to identify that one of the crew was supposed to have attempted to cut his wrists and then resisted the captain's attempts to put him in a single small room to keep him away from the crew. In the course of that resistance, we were told, he had thrown a knife at the captain which had missed him and become embedded in a wooden locker door.

Not quite sure what we were about to meet and having ensured that we had notified both the Divisional Control Room and Force Information Room of our being invited to go aboard, we were even less sure of our legal status when confronting whatever awaited us. When we entered the crews' quarters we found the errant seaman sitting chatting with his crewmates. He willingly let us examine his wrists and he had not cut himself recently, although there was a scar which indicated that he may have made a serious attempt at self-injury some considerable time in the past. There was every reason to believe that the Master of the ship had requested our attendance for no better reason than to prove to his crew that he was prepared to take such a course of action. With everyone seemingly getting on well, at least while we were present, we returned to the wharf and our car, thanking the Traffic crew who were awaiting any further instructions having been told by Information Room to provide us any support we may need. Back at the police station, I reported to a very relieved duty Inspector, who had been called from his bed, that no 'international incident' need be declared.

The Special Course 'promise' was that the successful completion of a year in the rank of Sergeant would 'automatically' bring promotion to Inspector. Having completed the course at Bramshill on 10th August, 1974, my target date was that same date in 1975. Just over three months earlier, on the night of 5th May, 1975 what started out as a routine incident was to cause me considerable disquiet. With two Constables, following a disturbance near a fish and chip shop in Taunton Road, we arrested two youths under the Public Order Act for their efforts to cause a breach of the peace. In the course of the arrest, because they resisted our efforts, both of them were handcuffed. Charged later that night shift, there seemed nothing unusual about the procedure. One of the youths had continued to struggle with the ratchet handcuffs on and had caused a slight abrasion to one of his wrists but, other than noting the matter, there was no medical attention required.

A short while later, after they had consulted with a 'legal aid' provided solicitor, the two Constables and I received summonses for assault in the name of the youth with the small abrasions from the handcuffs. The summonses we received accused us of Assault Occasioning Actual Bodily Hard (ABH). We were told that the Force would pay for our legal representation and the Police Federation and Headquarters recommended a solicitor who practiced in Yeovil. After taking his advice, we agreed that the alleged offences should be heard by the Magistrates. It seemed sensible (if anything about this saga made any sense) to see the matter through alongside the charges against the youths for the public order offences.

None of the three of us had any cause to feel comfortable. These youths were evidently not averse to lying and would, we were sure, do so in court. The ABH charges against the three of us could have led to a significant prison sentence. Beside the financial support for a defending solicitor and the continued direct support of my colleagues in my Section, there was not a lot of other moral support. Not suspended from duty, the Constables and I had to carry on as though this 'sword' was not hanging over us and I was left with the impression that, beyond my immediate colleagues, everyone else was keeping a distance lest I should be found guilty. I made as light of it as possible at home. The girls were too young to really understand and there was no point in burdening Gill with any more than her natural appreciation that I was inevitably apprehensive about what was to come.

The designated date for my promotion to Inspector arrived the day before the joint hearing in Bridgwater Magistrates Court. I presumed that the two colleagues, formerly from the Bristol Force, with whom I had ended the Special Course that year earlier had received their promotions on the 10th, even though it was a Sunday. I had not. The Magistrates Court had been allocated for two days for the joint hearings of the charges and the unusual situation prevailed, with all five of us being subject of charges, that we were all in the court throughout. For some reason, probably for the convenience of one or more of the Magistrates, the cases were to be heard on 11th and 13th August, with a day's break on the Tuesday in between.

The two solicitors acted as both defence and prosecution lawyers in this unusual cross-summons situation. We concurred with our excellent solicitor's submission and the Magistrates agreed to hear the cases together. The Court Clerk, rightly, pointed out that a finding of guilt against us could be referred by the Justices to a Higher Court for a more severe sentence to be applied than was within the power of the Magistrates' Court. That really brought home to me what an awful day this was in my life and career, thus far. As expected, the youths exaggerated our actions and stood before the Court with every effort to appear to be steady young men who had been attacked by the police.

The middle day, 12th, was fortunately a weekly rest day. I did not want to be at Bridgwater, less still about the police station. I cannot recall what I did with the day but the children were a natural distraction from my thoughts of what could be the outcome of what was to be the closure of the hearing the following day. After further submissions being heard on Wednesday, the Magistrates retired to their chambers and there was the wait, apparently much longer than it was in reality. They returned and announced that they had a finding of guilty against the two youths and then one of not guilty against we three police officers. No one can describe the relief. None of the three of us felt any inclination to celebration, we were, simply, glad to be free from that career ending and life changing threat.

Back in the police station there were many of those who had kept some distance who wanted to congratulate us and we, all three, silently accepted their assurances that 'there was never any doubt about the outcome.' I had the further approach made by a Detective Inspector, that the solicitor for the two youths and our prosecutor (more than likely he who had suggested the cross-summonsing as a significant 'smoke screen' for his clients) wanted to meet with me and shake my hand to show that there were no hard feelings. My message, I never knew whether the DI delivered it faithfully, was that there were, indeed, hard feelings and that my best possible future was never to set eyes upon that solicitor again. My view of too many solicitors acting within criminal law was, still is, that they, too often, hide behind the importance of defendants being represented to totally abdicate any responsibility they should have for the pursuit of Justice.

The pressure of potential total disaster for me and my family had passed but it was nearly another week, Tuesday, 19th August, that I was called to see the Chief Constable in Old Bridewell. His opening comment was one with which I did not totally agree but I simply remained mute at the time. He told me that he regretted that he could not promote me to Inspector on the 10th August with the 'unfortunate business' still pending. It was my view then, although perhaps softened with time, that nothing would have done my case more good than for the Force to show its support by promoting me before the two dates upon which I appeared before the Bridgwater Justices. He went on to tell me that he was back-dating my promotion to the 10th, so that I would not lose 'seniority' with my fellow Special Course members. He also offered the benefit of returning to my much-loved Traffic Department, albeit requiring another move - to Gill's much-unloved Bristol.

Reluctant though she was to leave Taunton for the big city, Gill was as supportive as ever for my pursuit of my career and we went to view a house in Reedley Road, Bristol. It was soon to be vacated by a Superintendent and his wife, who were buying a house not far away towards Westbury on Trym. As may have been expected, we accepted the house, the resident couple moved out but we could not move in. A new Assistant Chief Constable (ACC) had been appointed to the Force and it was not known whether he would require a police house while he was resettling. Just in case he did, we had to wait. With my promotion being back-dated, the Chief insisted that I get my change of uniform immediately and the stores had evidently been pre-warned of my impending arrival.

Fully equipped with my new uniform, the transition from Constable to Sergeant only required the addition of the chevrons but to Inspector necessitated a whole new uniform, I returned to Bridgwater. With a few surprised expressions as I moved through the building, I went directly to the first floor and reported to the Divisional Commander. Although I knew that the move to Bristol would not be welcome at home, indeed was not of my best choosing, I thanked the Chief Superintendent for his support in respect of my return to the Traffic Department. His major concern was that I must move my equipment from the Sergeants' Office to the Inspectors' Office forthwith. There were only two Inspectors so, with the help of a few others, I moved my locker temporarily to a small vacant area of floor in the Inspectors' Office.

A couple of days later, on a scheduled weekly rest day, I went to Bridgwater to see the Chief Superintendent and to wish farewell to those about the station. I had a few days off but, with the temporary block on the house at Reedley Road, started at Headquarters Traffic in New Bridewell, Bristol, travelling from Taunton to Bristol in a patrol car which I left in the rear yard at Taunton between journeys. There had been no further reference to the Bramshill Scholarship, which would normally have started with the upcoming College year but the ball would get rolling on that score later in that year and through 1976. I had very much enjoyed my time at Bridgwater, despite the trauma of the court appearance and Gill really did like living in Priorswood Road. She was, at least, to get a couple of extra months there thanks to the vacant house in Reedley Road.

Fully equipped with my new uniform, the transition from Constable to Sergeant only required the addition of the chevrons but to Inspector necessitated a whole new uniform, I returned to Bridgwater. With a few surprised expressions as I moved through the building, I went directly to the first floor and reported to the Divisional Commander. Although I knew that the move to Bristol would not be welcome at home, indeed was not of my best choosing, I thanked the Chief Superintendent for his support in respect of my return to the Traffic Department. His major concern was that I must move my equipment from the Sergeants' Office to the Inspectors' Office forthwith. There were only two Inspectors so, with the help of a few others, I moved my locker temporarily to a small vacant area of floor in the Inspectors' Office.

A couple of days later, on a scheduled weekly rest day, I went to Bridgwater to see the Chief Superintendent and to wish farewell to those about the station. I had a few days off but, with the temporary block on the house at Reedley Road, started at Headquarters Traffic in New Bridewell, Bristol, travelling from Taunton to Bristol in a patrol car which I left in the rear yard at Taunton between journeys. There had been no further reference to the Bramshill Scholarship, which would normally have started with the upcoming College year but the ball would get rolling on that score later in that year and through 1976. I had very much enjoyed my time at Bridgwater, despite the trauma of the court appearance and Gill really did like living in Priorswood Road. She was, at least, to get a couple of extra months there thanks to the vacant house in Reedley Road.

12   Headquarters Traffic

Without the need for an immediate move of house, I had a few days off, one interrupted to bid farewell to the Bridgwater Divisional Commander, before setting off, on Tuesday, 26th August, 1975, to Bristol for my first day as a Traffic Inspector based on the first floor of New Bridewell in the centre of the City. The amalgamation had scarcely affected places like Bridgwater but, even twenty months into the combined Forces, there was much bad feeling among those I encountered in Bristol. In reality, the amalgamation had had no greater affect upon Bristol Divisions than had it in Somerset, indeed the South Gloucester people had the greater cause to feel aggrieved as they could look north and see their former colleagues untouched by this politically driven boundary change. The irony is, at this distance in time, that the contrived county of Avon had only a life-span of 22 years. I suppose it should not be a surprise that it took the politicians that long to recognise how much of an expensive failure were the changes wrought in 1974. If only that realisation could have caused their successors to recognise that political dabbling with no real understanding does untold, sometimes, irredeemable damage to structures developed over decades.

I have already referred to it earlier but must reiterate what a shame it was that so many, mainly those from the former Bristol Constabulary, would not adapt to what we all had to get used to some way or another. I think that part of the reluctance stemmed from the new name for the Force having no reference to Bristol and another that the Chief Constable from Somerset & Bath was appointed by the combined Police Authority to command the new Force. Quite why the excellent relationships at all levels when we were neighbours prior to 1st April, 1974 became so strongly opposed on the day of the amalgamation I still find incredible. It remains sad that so many of those, now long retired, who served in Bristol prior to that date remain unrelentingly angry that their beloved Bristol Constabulary ceased to stand alone.

My arrival as a shift Traffic Inspector at New Bridewell was viewed by many as another 'county man' ('man' was often replaced by one offensive term or another) was imposed upon the largely ex-Bristol contingent in the department. At that stage, Headquarters Traffic had Force-wide responsibilities but the group Sergeants and Constables remained mainly dedicated to patrolling the, then still four, Bristol Divisions. The concept of Groups and Group Inspectors was entirely inherited from Bristol (I had only elsewhere seen it in London) and, in my previous experience, had witnessed two significant affects upon the rank structure. It made Constables and Sergeants much more familiar with their Group Inspector, working directly alongside each other almost all of the time. It also significantly reduced the individual 'autonomy' of the Sergeants, none of whom experienced in Bristol, or later throughout the new Force, the level of responsibility of Sergeants without an Inspector to whom to easily refer.

I like to think that my fairly easy going nature helped me to 'fit in' reasonably well and that was aided by the fact that I came with a 'Traffic Man' pedigree and, unlike several of my fellow Group Inspectors, I had achieved Advanced Driver status. Indeed, I was surprised when I first paraded with the Group that the Sergeant, who was also an 'import' from Gloucestershire but had been there much earlier after the amalgamation, asked me which Constable I wanted to be my 'driver'. I invited him to choose and then vary the Constable with whom I would be 'crewed' for each successive shift. If it was possible for there to be a more concentrated Bristol sensitivity it was to be found among the strong contingent of Traffic Motorcyclists based at New Bridewell. The long-established Sergeant looked upon by all, even many of the Bristolian public, as the leader of the motorcycle pack, was given the task, after his early morning involvement with the 'rush hour' traffic (of which more later) of driving me around in a patrol, car for a few days to try and familiarise me with the city's roads and areas.

For some unaccountable reason, we seemed to 'hit it off' very quickly. His knowledge of the city and most of what went on in it was second to none. My difficulty was trying to assimilate all that he was so willingly imparting to me. That we visited all the many police stations then still operating in Bristol had a dual benefit. Not only did I find out where they were and what areas they covered but I was introduced to many of the Officers working from those stations. That I was given a reasonably positive introduction by this long-respected Traffic Sergeant did no harm for my potential credibility. At an early stage, I adapted to being referred to as 'Guv', a term I had heard as commonplace when on the attachment to Chelsea Division, but one day one of the younger Constables, not much different in age to me, enquired regarding my reaction to the familiarity towards me by him and his colleagues, supposing that it would not have been like that in 'the county'. My reaction seemed to be amusingly accepted, as I told him that in the county the familiarity would be much more subtle.

The large contingent of Traffic Motorcyclists based at New Bridewell had been built up over many years of the City Force. There were still 'pointsmen' provided by the Divisions or Traffic Wardens' Department, administered by a lady Traffic Warden Controller who was, at once, formidable and very supportive of the wider traffic policing effort within the City. The number of points to be covered had reduced, not least because the senior officers brought in from either side of the City found it to be a rather manpower sapping demand. While the number of points along the major routes were less, the objective of keeping traffic flowing was still important. It was largely achieved by the Traffic Motorcyclists patrolling those routes and dismounting to direct traffic where bottlenecks had developed.

It was the role of the shift Inspector, on early and late shifts, to man the Traffic Console in the Bristol Control Room during the peak inbound and outbound traffic times. There had been, since 1st April, 1974, a new Force Control, which stood on the same floor as the former Bristol Information Room, now known as Bristol Control. The former Chief Constable of the Bristol City Constabulary, was a radio enthusiast and had ensured that there had been a significant investment in up to date communications technology. The consoles in the Bristol Control Room had been designed with light codes for the current status of all the units on the air and some cars had been fitted with 'Mufax' an early 'over air' system by which printed messages and photographs could be sent to those vehicles. I can only surmise that this was an expensive commodity because it did not last long after the amalgamation.

As a slight aside, the expenditure on communications equipment was not matched elsewhere. The patrol cars were mainly relatively cheap Ford Cortina MkIIIs, with the only 'extra' being an automatic gearbox for their intended use within the built up area. The equipment carried in the cars was sparse compared with those with which I had been familiar when at Williton and Weston-super-Mare. This was thought appropriate because further equipment could be deployed over the short distances involved if that from one car would not suffice.

The role of the Inspector, who occupied one of the Bristol consoles for the two hours, or so, each rush hour, was twofold. He was there to 'direct' the motorcyclists, who in turn gave directions to those on the manned traffic points. He was also the point of contact for the researchers for the local radio presenters who passed out regular updates for listeners in their cars. Later on, the contact would get the Traffic Console Inspector much more involved, as the presenters contacted the Traffic Console 'live' and the Inspector would be heard on the public radio. Several of those who came to the role after I had left became very adept at this process and became well known 'personalities' across the Radio Bristol transmission area.

It has to be said that the motorcyclists, particularly the Sergeants, really considered themselves to be 'running' the process and to a large extent they were, with the Inspector simply monitoring and relaying messages where required. On one morning, fairly early in my involvement, the Sergeant who had been my guide in my first few days, came up on the air with a suggestion for a course of action along one of the routes. I had already picked up from other sources, the media contacts and local divisional personnel, that the real cause was one that the Sergeant could not, yet, have seen. I, therefore, directed him not to do what he intended but to take a different course of action. The reaction of the other console operators and Inspector in charge of the Control Room said much and that of the Constables in the tea room after we had closed the Traffic Console was even more indicative. All were waiting to see what would be the Sergeant's reaction to my 'countermanding' his intended course of action. The hubbub within the tea room as the Sergeant's voice could be heard, as he mounted the stairs from the yard, fell silent and every face was directed towards the door or to me, or alternating between the two. The Sergeant walked in and simply said, "Alright Sir?" The hubbub resumed and I think there was some disappointment on the part of many.

There were two other, debatably Traffic, responsibilities that fell to the Bristol Traffic Unit and, hence, were the responsibility of the duty Inspector. Both have, long since, ceased to be a policing function. One in which I received only the most modest of training was the Rocks Rescue facility. This involved a specially adapted breakdown truck with two jibs instead of the regular one. With an extension set of pullies where required, the vehicle was placed as close as was safely possible to the edge of the Avon Gorge cliff top, accessible in this way for quite a large area from the Downs. Two cables were slowly paid out and a Traffic Officer attached to each with a stretcher suspended between them. They were lowered down the cliff face to any climber or faller who was trapped on the side of the cliff and then hauled back up with the casualty. When the Avon Fire Brigade, along with many others, rebranded themselves as a Fire & Rescue Service, they successfully petitioned for the rocks rescue responsibility and the Chief Constable of the day thought it such a good idea that he gave them the two-jibbed truck! We will return to this rescue requirement in Chapter 21.

The other, long defunct but at the time seen as very important, responsibility with only a peripheral Traffic connection was to support the Metropolitan Police escorts provided from London to the Bank of England building on Castle Green in Bristol. The Met had a team of firearms trained Officers with two Rover 3.5 patrol cars who escorted the deliveries and returns from the Bank of England in London to the several Regional Bank of England buildings. Local Forces provided supporting escorts with two cars, each with a firearms trained man on board and the Traffic shift Inspector was in charge of the Force element of this escort. I believe that these escorts had been established in the wake of the 'Great Train Robbery'. We picked up the escort from the Wiltshire Force at junction eighteen of the M4 and it was a matter of the top speed of the bullion van determining how quickly we reached Castle Green.

Although 1975 marked my, albeit belated, elevation to senior officer rank it was certainly not the happiest year of my service. On top of my feelings of guilt at the fact I knew Gill did not want the move to Bristol, my court trauma in August was soon to be followed by another. Still awaiting the decision regarding when we may be able to occupy the house in Stoke Bishop, I remained on the daily trek between the Traffic Offices in Taunton and at New Bridewell. On 17th October, I made the trip up to perform a night shift and, late in the night, was involved in the arrest of a violently resisting man my Constable crewmate and I had stopped near the, then, Wills tobacco factory at Hartcliffe. When we arrived at Broadbury Road police station, to make things worse, as we were struggling to get the man out of the patrol car, my hand was caught in the door as it was slammed on my fingers. Knowing I was in pain but somewhat preoccupied by our prisoner, I managed to partially ignore the discomfort and it eased as the night went on, signifying no permanent injury.

Come the end of the shift, I set off with the intention of getting back to the Taunton yard at about 6a.m. The drive down the M5 terminated at that time near North Petherton where I picked up the A38 and drove into Taunton. On the way up through East Reach the rigours of the night must have overcome me. The next thing I knew was that the patrol car had come to a shuddering halt with its front end embracing a large concrete lamppost. I was to discover that I had suffered a further minor injury by way of a jolt to my neck but my only concern at that time was that I had become involved in a 'polac' (police vehicle accident) - as a Traffic Inspector not something to wish to contemplate. Before I had summoned my thoughts and tried to radio the Control Room, a police vehicle arrived with two Constables, following a call from a member of the public.

They, rightly, checked that I was alright and that there had been no one else involved and soon a Chief Inspector had been raised early on that Saturday morning to attend and deal with the 'polac'. I had no explanation for what had happened other than to agree with his 'lead' that I must have fallen asleep at the wheel. His subsequent report signified that I had admitted that fact. In retrospect, my Chief Inspector colleague could have identified the underlying cause of my tiredness and may have, by doing so, avoided for me the further court appearance. More importantly, I have been eternally grateful that there was not some innocent person on their way to work that morning for me to collide with, at least I was spared such an outcome on my conscience.

Ironically, as I was speaking with the Chief Inspector after the accident, he asked me how much service I had and I realised that it was ten years, that morning! My minor 'whiplash' injury required me to be off sick for the uncertificated three days and these ran directly in to the three moving days. I did go on one of them to see the Chief Inspector at Taunton Police Station but then, on 24th October, we were in Reedley Road, Bristol. Just after the removal van men had departed there was a knock on the door and the Constable with whom I had been working on the night of the accident was there to enquire what it was that he and the others on the group should be saying to assist me in my difficulty. I told him that I was not making any attempt to avoid whatever was to be the outcome but thanked him and the others for their loyalty. I would not have wanted any contrived support but the reaction of my newfound colleagues was reassuring as to my level of acceptance.

I was suspended from driving police vehicles, not the most auspicious status for a Traffic Officer, and allocated to work alongside the ex-Birmingham Officer, with whom I had shared earlier experiences (related in chapters seven and eight) and now promoted to Chief Inspector Traffic Administration. The exercise of discovering all about the running of a Headquarters Department was important but, at the time not valued. One interesting little project was to assist the Fleet Manager, a civilian who had been a time-served police officer in another Force, to evaluate and report upon the use of low pressure gas (LPG) fuel. At that time the conclusion had to be that the 'dry' fuel was likely to cause damage to the valve gear of the cars used for Traffic patrol work, a problem to become more widespread in the late 1990s with the introduction of unleaded petrol.

In anticipation, and with the legal payment support of the Police Federation, I was ferried down to Yeovil to meet once again with my earlier defending solicitor. We agreed that there was not much point in fighting the summons for Driving Without Due Care and Attention (for which falling asleep at the wheel was the usual charge). Instead, he would plead mitigation on my behalf. To minimise the publicity and with not an entire absence of irony, the matter was scheduled to be heard at Wellington Magistrates Court on Monday, 1st December, 1975, perhaps not an inappropriate start to the closing month of a year not best remembered! I appeared in civilian clothes and the case was simply listed in the court agenda as against 'Mr D. E. Leach'. Immediately the case was called, two of the three magistrates declared 'an interest', in that they were members of the Police Authority. A quick consultation with the solicitor brought from us no objection to them hearing the case, although they may have been, to my disadvantage, interested in the amount of damage I had done to a Police Authority owned vehicle.

The case was outlined and, in view of my registering a plea of guilty, no evidence was called. There were no press representatives in court, they being prepared to simply pick up the result from the Clerk later. The Yeovil solicitor then came into his own. His plea on my behalf fully outlined the events that had led up to my unfortunate accident and all three retired to return quite soon with the imposition of a fine of £25, a very small sum for a 'Without Due Care' offence even in 1975. The solicitor then responded positively to the enquiry as to whether there were any 'special reasons' why my driving licence should not be endorsed. They retired again for a brief spell and came back with the decision that there should be no endorsement placed upon my licence. Gill and the two girls had stayed with my parents at Tonedale in Wellington while I was at the court and my mother insisted on refunding me the £25 when I returned to them with the report on my day.

On the home front, Gill had made hasty arrangements for Tanya's education to continue. We were told by many in Bristol that the local primary school to Stoke Bishop had the reputation of being the best in Bristol. Gill's acceptance of the unwanted move to the City was not enhanced by what we found by placing Tanya there. In Taunton, she had started out in an infants' school on the council estate opposite our police house and we had seen her blossom under the teaching she received. In, supposedly the best, such school in Bristol, she simply 'marked time'. When Gill enquired of the teachers, they simply said that she was too far ahead of the others and they had no initiatives available to carry her forward until her classmates had caught her up. Although there are claims of improvement more recently, Bristol seems to have had a long-term problem with its education provision. It certainly did nothing towards Tanya eventually achieving her Masters' degree.

Back in the Traffic Department, there was a further spell in the Administration Office pending the decision as to whether I should receive any disciplinary action. This was cleared and I was re-authorised to drive patrol cars on the 18th December, exactly two months of standing under another 1975 cloud. From that day I was back to the Group and felt to be welcomed. On night shifts, now that they were without that long haul at either end, I took to occasionally taking the unmarked Jaguar XJ6 and visiting the Traffic crews elsewhere in the Force area. The car was equipped with a flap on the rear parcel shelf which was operated by a solenoid and showed 'Police Stop' in the back window when required. It also had a rotating blue beacon on a magnetic base with a power lead to a small plug socked under the dashboard. With the similarity to the item used in the television series of the day with Telly Savalas, we all called these items 'Kojak Lamps'.

My City colleagues were to identify some added respect when, at 1.20am on 7th February, 1976 one of the crews identified a Ferrari on the roundabout in the centre of Bristol which failed to stop and had been stolen from London. We joined the chase, we were allowed to call them that in 1976, and followed the

Ferrari across the Cumberland system, witnessing its sheer power advantage as it shot away from us up the strait of the A370 Long Ashton by-pass. The crew that had first seen the car followed us and both patrol cars kept on the A370 with occasional glimpses of the rear of the Ferrari. The former city man driving the other car found he was having difficulty on the bends down the A370 through Backwell and Cleeve, a road which at that time I knew like the proverbial 'back of my hand'. In Congresbury we came around the bend over the river to find the Ferrari in the middle of the road with steam and smoke coming from the rear engine compartment. The thieves had evidently driven the car to its destruction and abandoned it. A dog handler had come from Weston-super-Mare to meet us and was instrumental with his dog in bringing the thieves back to the road.

That was a busy weekend as the following night, at 4a.m.on Sunday 8th a Traffic Sergeant based at the motorway centre at Almondsbury found himself on the centre of a roundabout at Filton. As the only Traffic Officer his senior, I relieved a Divisional Inspector of the responsibility and took over the investigation. The, normally bright, street lighting on the roundabout had failed that night and he had simply misjudged his entry to the roundabout while responding to an emergency call. My own, all too recent, 'polac' brought me no intention of pointlessly making this Sergeant go through the same hoops as I had experienced.

On a night later in the year, when the weather was enticing people to use the then popular Severn Beach, we were made aware of a car stuck in the sand and in danger of being overtaken by the incoming tide. From the railway line embankment we could see the car. It was not far away but was below the high tide line. I called one of the remaining early Range Rovers from the M5 and they were able to drive up the railway embankment. With our knowledge that there would be no trains until the commuter run much later that morning confirmed by a call to Temple Meads railway station, the Range Rover lodged its front wheels against the rails and the crew deployed the winch wire then fitted to those vehicles and hauled the car clear of the later high tide. The climbing ability of those early Range Rovers, not the luxury vehicles they were to become, was nothing short of astounding.

As 1976 progressed, the promise of the Bramshill Scholarship came back. This time it was processed through the centralised selection system but having moved, albeit reluctantly, to Bristol and having had six addresses in our less than nine years of marriage, the prospect of either another separation or family move did not look very welcoming. With my mind still set on a Sociology course, despite the Chief Constable's obvious opposition, I made contact with the Sociology Department at the University of Bristol. My call was, fortunately, picked up by a Lecturer whom I would get to know quite well over the coming three years. He suggested that I did not do what the UCCA form suggested but fill out all five options for Bristol, with the lead one being single honours Sociology followed by four combined honours in which Sociology featured. He explained to me that the University offered the option at the end of the first year of study to vary the degree option chosen, so whichever I was initially offered I could move to the single honours course later.

I followed his advice and the form was accepted and processed in the unusual way in which I had completed it. Some time later, I was called for interview in the Woodland Road offices of the Social Sciences Faculty. I had been offered an interview for four out of my five options, fortunately one of them was the single honours Sociology I really wanted. The interviews were combined, so I was confronted in a very small office, by four Lecturers, one for each option, and they took turns to ask questions. This could have been quite daunting for the more average eighteen year old but after the old system of police promotion boards and at thirty one, was not a concern to me. I only remember one of the questions posed, "Are you concerned, as a serving police officer, that attending this Department may fundamentally change your attitudes?" The very concern of my Chief Constable. My response seemed to go down well, "Are you not concerned that I may change some of yours?" I was offered places on all four courses and remained faithful to my original intention by accepting that for single honours Sociology.

The only other incident of real note as the day for my secondment to the University drew nearer was on Friday 3rd September, 1976. When reporting for duty the Superintendent spoke with me and we assembled a group for a quick briefing before setting off to collect and escort prisoners from Leicester back to Horfield Prison. Over the previous few days there had been an internal riot in Hull Prison and, having quelled the situation, Leicester Prison was being used to hold those brought from Hull, pending their distribution across the country. We had two patrol cars and a Regional Crime Squad car. Each patrol car had a crew of three, Constable driver, Constable firearms trained and armed officer and either an Inspector or Sergeant. The RCS car, a relatively diminutive Austin Maxi 1750, was included as it was equipped with radio that could access any Force system all along the route and the RCS provided hand-held car-to-car radios so that the crews of all three vehicles would remain in contact. They also brought a hand-portable 'local area' radio for the HMP Service coach commander to use on the return run. The coach was already on its way to Leicester and we set off after the briefing.

On the upward run, I drove our car and the Sergeant drove the other, so that we would be free from the driving responsibility on the way back. It was a brisk run up using the motorway system as much as was possible. The somewhat surprising aspect was the capacity for the little Maxi to set quite a good pace and we made Leicester prison in good time. There were dozens of coaches and police vehicles around the prison and Her Majesty's Prison Service had excelled themselves in providing food for everyone before the return trip. On the way back we had only one minor difficulty as the petrol tank on the Maxi was running low. We had temporarily lost sight of the RCS car as we ran through the traffic into Leiscester and they had not seen us filling up at a local petrol station. The small convoy kept going at a slower pace until the Maxi re-joined us and we travelled together directly back to Horfield Prison. The coach driver, local to Bristol as were the Prison Warders, seemed to really enjoy this assignment. Never before would he have had the opportunity for such a high-speed run and with police encouragement! Without untoward event, all were safely delivered.

We had not been in the house in Reedley Road for many weeks before Gill announced that Tanya and Cathryn were to become three. Her labour was to take her into one of the hottest summers most of us can remember, with Emma arriving in July, and it was not at all comfortable for her. For some reason, having not taken any interest in religion since leaving Wellington in 1965, I decided to take the two girls to the local chapel. At Reedley Road that was the Baptist Church on the same road but the other side of Parry's Lane. Although not in the tradition of the Baptist Church, having been a Congregationalist while growing up, we were made very welcome and the girls started to gain from the benefits of the church fellowship.

With the administrative aspects set in train, I was to receive a 'plain clothes' allowance, be enabled to reclaim the cost of books and, even, have my Students' Union charges covered, I was ready for the start of a whole new phase of my life.

As well as this financial support, I was of course still a serving Police Inspector and my salary continued to be paid. Although the time at the University of Bristol Sociology Department proved to be as rewarding as I had hoped, it really only warrants the specific chapter which I am about to devote to it because of what else I did during that period of two years and eight months. The return to Traffic in the rank of Inspector had lasted only just over the year, albeit somewhat too eventful at the start, but while seconded to the University I was still shown as 'supernumerary' in the Traffic Department. This produced a vain hope that I may return to Traffic at the end of my secondment but that was not to be the outcome.

13 University of Bristol

That first morning at Woodland Road brought me to a strange environment in which my near eleven years as a police officer seemed, already, somehow distant. I was not inclined to hide my status as a still-serving Police Inspector but neither did I intend to advertise the fact. As it turned out it was some weeks before the truth was 'out' and by that time I had become established enough for there to be just a short spell of surprise among my fellow students. The only aspect on the first day that made me wonder how long my police 'identity' would be kept quiet was passing the lecturer who had interviewed me for this subject on the stairs. With most of my fellow students, new and more seasoned, in very casual clothing, I was not unique but in a small minority wearing a jacket and tie. The Lecturer simply said, "We shall watch with interest your sartorial deterioration." That did not happen, although jacket and tie became more 'optional' during the hotter months.

The first year was to include such matters as statistical analysis and we all had to follow a variety of disciplines to facilitate any change of direction we may want to consider as we were to move from first into second year. I did Politics, Economics and History. In retrospect, much later after I graduated, my role as a police officer may well have been better suited to have opted for Psychology and even for me to have pursued a joint honours Sociology and Psychology course in the second and third years. At the time my focus on a full single honours course was too strong for that to happen. With Emma only three months old, Cathryn at playschool and only Tanya at school all day, Gill had her time cut out in keeping me isolated in the dining room to enable me to study at home. I did spend quite a bit of time in the college common room and library but she had to contend with me being in need of quiet a fair bit of the time.

At Weston, in the early 1970s, I had bought an old Raleigh Runabout moped to save on car petrol and my legs with the push bike (which I left at Weston). After a few weeks at Reedley Road, I had tried another such moped for the trip from Stoke Bishop into New Bridewell but found that the hills in Bristol were too much for its rather primitive belt drive system. I had, instead, found a similarly old Honda 50 and that, with its automatic clutch and four gears, was much better suited to the terrain.

Later, in early 1978, I was to be knocked from that machine by an errant driver on the Bath Road and to sustain injuries for which I have suffered renewed acquaintance as the years have started to catch up with me. It wrote off the Honda 50 but my Bramshill colleague who had moved to nearby Westbury on Trym sold me his Honda 90, which I kept for quite a few years and must have saved me many pounds in petrol costs.

With the course administration aspects came the notification that there was an expectation on the part of the Chief Constable that I would spend at least two weeks of my long Summer vacation, June through till October, in Headquarters, where a programme of visits to Departments would be set out for me. Having spent the most recent period of my service in Headquarters Traffic, with the enforced spell in the Administration Department while suspended from driving and a couple of later short spells as acting Chief Inspector to cover for the ex-Birmingham man's annual leave, two weeks of Headquarters attachments did not appeal. I knew from experience that people on attachment were always made welcome out of politeness but were, in reality, a bit 'in the way' of everyday office activities. Instead, I asked the consent of the Chief Superintendent Administration to make my own arrangements and offered four weeks back in the Force. This she accepted.

One aspect that appealed greatly, despite my 'six' in CID, was to work with the Regional Crime Squad (RCS) and the opportunity to arrange such an attachment came along at the Seconded Officers' Lunch. Our Chief Constable, at that time my only Chief Constable, hosted a lunch at Canonsgrove early each summer for all Officers currently on secondment and working outside the Force. There were quite a number of such Officers and they were from such secondments as the Regional Driving School at Devizes, Wiltshire, regional initial training at Chantmarle, Home Office activity and the Regional Crime Squad. I had met the RCS Coordinator, when he was our force Detective Chief Superintendent and visited Shepton Mallet one day when the Detective Constable was absent, and he evidently remembered that encounter. He readily agreed to me being attached to the Squad for four weeks, indeed seemed to welcome the idea.

After the somewhat traumatic end of first year examinations, taken in very strict format in The Assembly Rooms at the bottom of Whiteladies Road, I was informed that I had 'passed' that hurdle. With no desire at that time to diversify, I went off on that long vacation with the expectation of resuming the single honours course in October. In discussion with the Chief Superintendent Administration, I had established for myself how the three months of each of the two long vacations would run. I would spend the first four weeks with the Force, in some fashion or another, the school holiday weeks with the family and the final few weeks studying ready for the next university session. Hence, on Monday, 27th June, 1977, I reported to the RCS Offices in New Bridewell. Incorporated in the day of finding out how things ran and who people were, I saw the D/C/Superintendent who asked if I was a registered car casual user. There were three levels of private car reimbursement for duty commitments at that time, Permanent User & Casual User, with a much lower public transport rate normally used for longer out of Force journeys. Permanent Users received a smaller mileage element but a monthly lump sum, Casual Users no lump sum but a higher mileage rate, in both cases registration included an inspection of the insurance cover that indemnified the Force. I told him I was registered Casual User and he told me to travel up to Reading in Berkshire early the following morning.

I set off in the faithful old Cortina estate at 5.30a.m. on the Tuesday, 28th and arrived at Reading Police Station for the briefing. The security man at the police station car park readily accepted that I was with the RCS, presuming my old car to be one of those used for more covert operations. The joint operation with the South West and South East Regional Crime Squads was to follow a man who it was correctly anticipated was setting up to break into a safe but it was not known where and which safe. I was totally amazed at the efficiency of the teams that had combined to attempt to catch this man and his associates in the act of perpetrating their crime. Only scheduled to stay in the single quarters at the police station for one night, it was wise on one occasion for me to be the 'strange face' in the bar of the Coopers Wine Vaults public house that the man had entered. By swapping personalities frequently and despite the man, later men, being said to be highly 'surveillance conscious' they had no idea that they were under constant observation.

Late in the day, with our focus man having spent time in various parts of Reading, he was near the railway station. Suddenly, he and the sole other man then with him jumped up on to a lorry loading stage, ran across the platform and got into the train waiting to pull out towards London. There were a couple of RCS Officers on the platform who immediately also got on to the train just before it pulled away. We all rushed back to the cars and there was a mad dash out of Reading. The Detective Inspector from Reading knew that there was greyhound racing at Slough that evening and it was decided to trust to good fortune that this was where the 'target' was heading. His profile had shown a proclivity for gambling and his visits to licensed betting shops during the day had born that out. The train was pulling away towards London as we in the cars screamed into the station concourse, being careful to spread out around the area. The two RCS personnel, a man and a woman DCs (detective constables), were some distance behind the two men we had been following and, sure enough, they headed for the greyhound stadium.

We left our man and his friend to their evening at the dogs and returned for a meal, a drink and a night's sleep. We started back outside the 'target's home next morning and a similar pattern of changing places with each other while someone always had 'eyeball' on the man ensued. It looked as if it was going to go on for some days before the man made his move and there was a woman Detective Constable who needed to get back to the Bristol office so, late on Wednesday evening, she travelled with me back the M4. The annoying aspect was that the very next day the man in Reading made his move and the RCS people saw him break into a service garage and start to use their oxy-acetylene equipment to attack their safe!

The following three weeks were spent on various observations of a number of criminals and their vehicles. One of the more memorable of these started with a 'follow' out to the rural area near Winterbourne. We sat in our cars, spread around a remote farm premises to which a couple of the pairs of RCS Officers in their cars had followed the 'targets'. The situation was such that to actually see what they were doing was impossible without 'showing out' but the time they were taking indicated that they were committing the burglary. The really difficult bit, without being able to keep them in view, was at which point to move in when they had actually done something criminal and could not claim their innocence. With the DI in charge just calling around the units in preparation for our combined descent upon the farm house, the 'targets' car came away from the farm at speed.

The nearest car carefully came out of its side lane to follow the 'target' but just a little too soon. The already fast moving car accelerated even more and headed in towards Filton. At one point, it was baulked by traffic on a junction with a petrol filling station on the corner. The driver took to the filling station forecourt and drove maniacally between the pumps, with the innocents filling their cars having to dive out of his way. Among our car crews the party included an RCS motorcyclist and he was the only one who was able to get through the chaos, but not before the culprits had cleared onto the road and sped off toward the A38 and south towards Bristol. The end story was that the RCS Officers knew who it was they were dealing with and quickly set up observations close to the home of their suspected 'fence' (dealer in stolen goods). Sure enough, the car having been swapped for another, they arrived there a couple of hours later and, after a further few minutes of delay to allow for the 'fence' to be fully involved, the arrests were carried out.

At the end of my very enjoyable and informative four weeks with the RCS, the Regional Coordinator asked me if there was anything I had seen while I was with them that I thought could be improved upon. In truth, I had found the crews and what they were being asked to do most impressive but there was one aspect that caused me a little concern. I told him that the requirement, on occasions, to drive at high speeds without even the safety factor of police markings brought me to the conclusion that all RCS drivers should have some form of special driver training. I am not sure whether this was acted upon and realised that those being seconded to the RCS were there, primarily, for their detective abilities. The comforting aspect was that the RCS actually had quite a good record in respect of driving accidents.

The other very interesting visit brought my way because of the RCS attachment was to Swindon. There the gymnasium at the quite modern police station had been taken over as the exhibits store for one of the biggest operations of its kind mounted by the police in this country. The information had been coming in of drugs on the streets being manufactured in the more remote areas just north of the valleys in South Wales. Led by the Detective Superintendent, Deputy Coordinator, of the South West Region and in conjunction with Officers from the Welsh RCS, a very remote farm was kept under observation for a long time. Officers even had to 'dig in' in fields around the property and endure quite severe conditions to obtain the evidence needed. The effort was named

'Operation Julie' and became quite a celebrated event once the arrests had been made and the court hearings commenced. The gymnasium was packed with all manner of items of equipment from the farm and other addresses.

The school holidays started and for the next five weeks I was able to spend all of my time with the girls. Emma had her first birthday in the first week of Tanya's holiday and there was no playschool for Cathryn. Although we went out all together much of the time, it was also good that Gill could find a few minutes all to herself and I spent many an enjoyable hour with the girls, quite a few of them on the downs just above Reedley Road. I am eternally thankful that I managed to find the money at that time for a Super 8 cine camera. Many years later I had these four minute reels combined together on VHS, later DVD, format and watching the girls having fun all those years ago is a perfect way for me to spend forty minutes whenever I wish.

During that first long vacation, Gill and I did our sums and decided to take the big leap into house purchase. With the calculations done, we were in no position to buy in the area of Reedley Road, not that we wanted to stay in Bristol longer than necessary anyway. We looked around in the, rapidly expanding, Yate area north of Bristol and the, also developing, estates behind the older part of Clevedon, to the south of the city. We even put a, thankfully returnable, deposit on a house still being built at Clevedon. Finally, we settled on Keynsham, as being our size of town and well placed for the hope that we may be able to avoid subsequent moves. The house was available to us late in the autumn and we moved in to the smallest accommodation we had occupied since the flat in Weston-super-Mare which we had left nine years earlier.

With the house purchase well in the planning, it was back to school and playschool, and I got down to some serious preparation for the forthcoming second year of my secondment. I had not found the first year easy and really did try to prepare myself for 'phase two'. The most obvious difficulty was that, although there were other mature students, the vast majority of my colleagues were much younger than the thirty one years that I was in 1976. They had the younger person's ability to assimilate information more readily and, dare I say, were more inclined to simply absorb what they were told. There were occasions when the lecturers projected images with which I could not easily agree and, as tactfully as I could, I brought some of these aspects to notice. The main difficulty for the lecturers was that, even those who thought they were left wing, were predominantly from educated parents and lived in middle class surroundings. Their involvement with the working class about whom Sociologists like to show empathy was almost entirely from reading books. The classic such reference that I recall most clearly was when a lecturer came out with the message that "Bristol is a middle class city!" I invited him to come on a tour around the city with me so that I could show him how narrow was his interpretation but he declined the offer.

Another eight months in the University and the advantage as the end of the session came close that there were, unlike the end of the first year, no second year examinations. I had acquired the ability to express myself reasonable well in the many essays and, low-level, research papers that were required of me. My main stumbling block, one I was to comment upon probably too often, was that too many of the lecturers were nowhere near as objective as their social science credentials would make it reasonable to expect. On more than one occasion essays I had submitted were 'marked down' with comments such as, 'a well-reasoned document but I cannot agree your conclusions.'

Although it had been easily possible to fill the whole of my four week return to policing with the attachment to the RCS, that was not really repeatable in the Summer of 1978. Instead, by various contacts and with the support of the Chief Superintendent Administration, I negotiated three separate attachments. They comprised, one week with Special Branch, one week with the Community Relations Office and two weeks with the Press Office. I also attended with the Chief Inspector from the Press Office, a one day seminar within the locally run National CID Course at Kingsweston House.

I had determined, with the support of one of the Lecturers who was working towards publishing his doctorate thesis in book form, that my undergraduate dissertation topic would be the Television Image of the Police. The Lecturer went on to become Professor in one of the London School of Economics social science faculties and actually quoted my 'unpublished paper' as a reference in one of his books. The assembling of the questionnaire and the assistance I received from about one hundred of my serving colleagues, produced an interesting reflection of what police officers thought of the way they were presented. I supported this with as objective an analysis as I could manage from watching a wide range of fictional and news items on television relating to police and policing. With so much effort concentrated into that dissertation, I suppose it was unsurprising that it achieved a better result than my overall degree.

I reported to the Special Branch office in New Bridewell on 26th June, 1978 and was given a quick briefing on what it was they saw as their role and had a visit to the post at Lulsgate (later Bristol) Airport to see what was the task for the Officers based there, dealing with people entering and leaving the country. I had, to some extent, been encouraged to seek this, probably unique, opportunity to see inside SB by some of the comments of other mature students at the University. One of these had a bit of a fixation that SB were synonymous with the 'secret service' (note, not security service), He was such a committed Marxist that he even wore the beard and was always trying to encourage other students to join him on demonstrations, with coaches organised locally to attend rallies in London and elsewhere.

I found the work of the SB office at times interesting but at others quite boring. The boring bits were only made bearable by the humour with which they were injected by the Officers. An example was our requirement to 'pick up' and follow two Russian diplomats on holiday from their Embassy and staying in Bristol. We 'tailed' them all day and watched them visiting all the places of interest in Bristol. They were all too aware of our presence and at one time invited us to catch up with them so that we could give them directions! The process was well established and would, of course, be repeated across the world, although I am sure that some of our diplomats would not have felt as comfortable as did these two as they strolled around the City.

A more interesting day was the visit of the Prince of Wales to Wells. Because I was an addition to the SB contingent and no-one had thought of it in advance, I was deputed to act as the landing authority for the Wessex helicopter of the Queen's Flight when it arrived on the large school playing field. All the dignitaries were lined up at the side of the field to be introduced to the Prince and I, having checked the wind direction, stood in the middle of the field. The helicopter came in, circled around and approached me, landing a few yards in front of me. I thought that was my job done and had not been warned that the RAF Sergeant 'load master' would get out of the aircraft, march smartly up to me, offer a salute and ask permission for HRH to disembark. Without really thinking what I was saying and with not a glimmer of reaction from his facial expression, I said, "Carry on, Sergeant". In the reception for the Prince, after he had inspected the extensive work taking place on the outside of the

Cathedral, we mingled with the invited dignitaries. That was the first of a very few occasions upon which I tasted caviar and I still cannot understand quite what the fuss is about in respect of that expensive foodstuff.

In the previous February and referred to earlier, I had been knocked from my Honda 50 while on my way to the University one morning. With the claim for damages to me and the bike well in progress, I was advised by colleagues in the SB Office that I could get legal cost support from the Police Federation to pursue my claim. This I did, but wished I had not. The Federation provided a solicitor and he appointed a local surgeon in private practice in Clifton to examine my injuries. Whereas the surgeon for the insurance company had described my knee injuries (I had a mended collar bone fracture as well) as likely to be a life-time problem the Federation funded doctor's report, wrongly, minimised the long-term prognosis.

In the Community Involvement Department I was given a real insight into the important work that took place in this small unit. The relationships that had been built up with the ethnic minority communities in Bristol were a credit to the Officers in the Unit. I was intrigued to visit a club in the St Pauls area where those of West Indian origin, at that time many first-generation immigrants, seemed so enthusiastic about the game of dominos. All of the people to whom I was introduced made me feel welcome. How sad that much less than two years after this visit, and only the day after that team had organised a five-a-side football tournament for local youngsters, St Pauls was to erupt into a full-scale riot following a perfectly normal visit by police officers to regulate activities at a local café. At that time, I found it much more disconcerting when I visited the Offices on Colston Street, Bristol of the local arm of the Commission for Racial Equality. After a long, one to one, discussion with the deputy head at the office, I was somewhat dismayed at his response to one of my questions. It seemed to me rather incongruous that the deputy head of a government funded organisation purporting to be there to foster equality saw it as his main mission in life to 'develop black consciousness'.

The attachment to the Press Office was made even better for me in that the Chief Inspector in charge of the Unit was well known to me. He hailed from Wellington and had attended the same school, albeit a few years ahead of me, and had been an Inspector on 'C' Division, based at Redland Police Station, on the same shift cycle as me when I spent my year as Traffic Inspector before going to the University. Probably the most interesting day of that attachment was the visit to the, then HTV, studios in Bath Road, Bristol. The Chief Inspector was interviewed every Wednesday on the local version of 'Police Five' and I was intrigued to find just how basic was the set furnishings compared with its glossy impression of the TV screen. That programme went out as part of the teatime independent television news bulletin and appeared to be a live broadcast but was actually recorded a couple of hours before the scheduled transmission time.

The other interesting day was when I was with the Press Office team at the 'topping out' ceremony on the new Trinity Road Police Station. With not a little ironic foresight, this building, the first designed and built in the city for some years and first of the combined Avon and Somerset Constabulary, had very few window actually directly next to the public roads. The face of the building was of several stories high plain red brick and that wall continued around a sizeable yard. All office window looked out toward the yard. The architects of the 1970s either thought, or were encouraged to think, that police stations were more vulnerable to attack than had previous generations of police station builders. Only less than two years later, whether or not because of its imposing outward appearance the building did not suffer following the disturbances such a short distance away.

Following those attachments and with only the odd day or two of following up the dissertation research, another school summer holiday of much time with the children. I really count myself fortunate, more in later years than I realised in 1977 and 1978, at those extended holidays with the girls when they were so young. The house purchase and our move in to Glebe Walk at Keynsham late in 1977 brought a whole new area for us to explore locally between the two long university and school vacation periods. The Downs and Blaise Castle featured most strongly in Bristol and the area near the top road at Lansdowne and the newly developed picnic area at Chew Valley were most popular when at Keynsham. The move from the large four bedroom police owned house in Reedley Road to the much smaller three bedroom one we could just afford at Glebe Walk in Keynsham forced room sharing for Cathryn and Emma, with Tanya in by far the smallest bedroom above the front door. The chest freezer we had owned since Shepton Mallet days had to go in the dining room, as did I when trying to tackle the study required. It was not ideal but the house was ours! A bonus was that ours was the middle house of a terrace of three and we found that we got on well with our neighbours.

The final examinations came and, thankfully, went. Although the honours attached to my Batchelor of Science degree looked as though they may turn out as a two-one, I was awarded a two-two, right in the middle of that hierarchy, so not too much to fret over. The graduation award ceremony took place a few weeks after I had returned to policing and I was entitled to have two people with me on the day. This arrangement probably brought about by the presumption of a pair of parents for the more normally aged student. Gill and my mother attended. The award ceremony took place in the main hall of the Wills Building at the top of Park Street in Bristol and this was followed by a gathering in the grounds of Senate House, with the weather keeping in tune with the summer dresses of the ladies.

Although the Police Service was to do little to capitalise on the significant investment of sending me, and quite a few others, to study at degree level for thirty two months, I never regretted taking up that opportunity. Although, as we will see in the next chapter, there was a penalty to pay, the ability to study a topic for which I had acquired a real interest brought a lasting personal reward. On top of that, we had more time together as a family, especially through those two summer long-vacations and, through the several summer attachments, I found opportunities for developing my police knowledge that would not, otherwise, have been accessible.

14 'A' Division

Remaining on Traffic was much more than I could have expected, despite my keeping in touch and the kind assistance from one of the typists in writing up my undergraduate dissertation. Instead, a few days before the end of my attachment to the University of Bristol, I was told to report to the Deputy Divisional Commander at Old Bridewell. No gentle breaking in but an immediate start on Group Two on early turn on Monday, 25th June, 1979. The compensation was that we had very recently been informed by all the daily newspapers that the Edmund Davies Report pay settlement from 1978, of which the Labour Government who had commissioned it would only pay one half, had been fully implemented by the new Conservative Government under our first lady Prime Minister, Margaret Thatcher.

I simply knuckled down to picking up the ropes which had been relaxed for so long and soon got to grips with what 'A' Division required. After the wide variety of experience I had assembled and very soon after my arrival, I found 'A' Division far too restrictive. It was, with very little exception, shoplifters by day and public disorder by night. Getting to know the names of all the others on the Group was the first priority and not easily accomplished. The Group, as did the other three on the Central Sub-Division, consisted of me, five Sergeants and thirty five Constables. A Sergeant each in the Charge Office and Divisional Control Room and three on patrol. A senior Constable on the radio console, assisted by one other who was taken from the street strength and a middle service Constable to assist in the Charge Office. There were two response cars, then the earliest models of the Vauxhall Cavalier, and all the other Constables were on foot patrol. More senior Constables were used to regularly provide cover around the higher area near the Bristol Royal Infirmary, along Hotwells and the opposite side of the former docks area and around Redcliffe.

Of the five Sergeants, on average two would be in their probationary year in that rank and someone would move on soon enough to keep that fairly standard.

Of the thirty five Constables, sustained again by Officers moving on not long afterwards, an average of eighteen were in their two year probationary period. The Senior Officers saw 'A' Division as so busy that it both demanded these high numbers but also that it made a good training ground for young officers. It was my view that it did not offer anything like enough variety for young Constables to acquire what they would need to see them through their later service. I was also still quite new to the Group Inspector system, having first encountered it in Headquarters Traffic, and still thought that the presence of an Inspector at all times denied the Sergeants the real individual responsibility that I had experienced and enjoyed at Bridgwater.

I, of course, 'inherited' a number of traditions that, even five years after the amalgamation, were largely drawn from the former Bristol Constabulary days. The first that I felt I had to change, even though it was to do me no favours the following year, was to stop the early and night shift tea breaks, respectively at 7a.m. and 4a.m. being taken in the cell passage. Although there was always the cover by the response cars maintained during these tea breaks and they were more justified than 'imported' more Senior Officers would understand because there were not the abundance of 'tea stops' found in smaller communities, I was not prepared to be party to these gatherings taking place with prisoners just a door's thickness away. On two counts this seemed to me to be ridiculous. Firstly it signified to any regular visitor to the cells at what time the streets would contain less Constables but secondly and more importantly, the prisoners in the cells were privy to whatever conversations were taking place. Anyway, on Group Two these gatherings moved to the large report writing room near the front door of the police station.

All of these aspects of getting settled in on 'A' Division were, of course, very visible. What was not, and grew in my suspicion over my first year there but was not really confirmed until much later, was the repercussions of my persistence upon taking up the Bramshill Scholarship benefit of selecting what subject I wanted to study. The Chief Constable had not forgotten and his concern had evidently been impressed upon the Divisional Commander. In the early 1990s the then Chief Inspector who in 1979 was the senior Sergeant in the Charge Office on Group Two confided that he was 'taken to one side' by the Chief Superintendent a few days before I arrived on the Group. The Sergeant was told that the new Inspector was arriving fresh from attending a Sociology degree course at the University and that the Chief Superintendent wanted the Sergeant to watch me closely and report back personally on anything the Sergeant thought worthy of report. As I have said, my start back on normal policing was a matter of 'in at the deep end' on early turn and no-one had thought that they should interview me to test out whether I had 'changed' while at the University. It appeared, on later reflection but unbeknown to me at the time, that conclusions had been drawn without any evidence.

One of the compensations of working shifts in the way we did on the former Bristol Group system was that it seldom brought extended tours of duty with everything being handed on to the next shift. Hours were, certainly more so than through much of my earlier service, very predictable. Much of that first winter was of the most routine nature. One exception was my arrival on early shift one Saturday morning to find the very experienced night shift Inspector in somewhat of a state of panic. The previous evening a woman from America had stepped off the pavement on the city centre and the assumption was that she must have looked in the wrong direction for the oncoming traffic and been knocked down by a passing car. It appeared that the incidence of a fatal road accident in the city, still less on 'A' Division, was such that no one on duty, not even the night traffic crew, had previously dealt with one. I sent him off to his bed, comforted that my time on Traffic would enable me to cope but then found that the greatest complication was the poor lady's relatives all being thousands of miles away and with quite a few hours' time zones displaced.

The spring of 1980 was to bring something that no serving officer of the time could remember and was only recorded in the much earlier history of the City. Two things had happened on 1st April, 1980. All bar five of the smallest Sub-Divisions had seen their Chief Inspector Sub-Divisional Commanders elevated to the rank of Superintendent and the Force had taken the decision, in the light of the annual cost, to cease the insurance premium for damage to fleet cars. Central Sub-Division, together with Weston-super-Mare and Bath had been commanded by 'scale two' Superintendents for some time and the deputy Divisional Commanders had been full Superintendent for a number of years. The arrangement from 1st April seemed to do no more than regularise the situation, albeit with a significant increase in superintending ranks in the Force. The Superintendent at Trinity Road, while still a Chief Inspector, had planned what, it has to be said, was a long overdue raid on a café in Grosvenor

Road in the heart of St Pauls. The plan was for observations to indicate the best time and that had been declared to be mid-afternoon.

Two of the aspect of being an Inspector on 'A' Division were the number of complaints against the police that came my way (people would travel in from all over the city to make complaints about local matters at the Central Police Station) and the familiarity I acquired with dealing with Identification Parades. Not really too concerned about what was taking place over on the Trinity Road Sub-Division, I was busy from the start of my 2p.m. till 10p.m. shift getting an ID parade sorted out. Although no-one recognised it in advance, the raid on the 'Black & White Café' could scarcely have been at a worse time. The raid was not the quick in and out, with the necessary evidence of the suspected drugs and alcohol dealing secured, but dragged on so long that the young people from the local senior schools started assembling in the area.

Surprisingly, at the time, the heated activity around the café became infectious and large crowds of people in their teens and a bit older started throwing items at the police officers. It quickly escalated into a very ugly confrontation in which the police officers already there and those who went from the two sub-divisions of 'A' Division to join them were hopelessly outnumbered. The Divisional Commander went to the Control Room and the Central Sub-Division Superintendent went with as many men as could be mustered to assist his beleaguered Trinity Road counterpart. Eventually, I was forced to abandon all hope of mounting the ID parade and was directed by the Chief Superintendent to gather together the few riot shield from the store in Old Bridewell yard and take them to City Road. With the assistance of the cell reserve Constable, we loaded the thirty shields, at that time the full complement held by the force and used only for training up until this time, into the 15cwt van which had recently been parked after its daily post run around the Force area.

With the Constable and the shields, I drove to City Road. There the Officers had deployed across the road facing a large crowd of stone throwing youths and I was surprised to see that the Chief Constable, his Deputy and a crowd of television crew members were standing close behind the line of police officers. Those in the line had seized whatever they could find, such as dustbin lids and milk crates, to ward off the stones and bricks coming their way. That there was a building site at the Ashley Road end of City Road meant that there was ample reserves of 'ammunition' for the rioters. The Officers soon dragged the shields from the back of the van and now had a more effective defence. I saw a brick fly over the line of Officers and it struck one of the TV people directly on the head. A police woman Sergeant, with whom I was to work closely a few years later and who went on to very senior rank, got into the back of the van with the injured man and I took them to the Bristol Royal Infirmary (BRI).

Riot Protection Equipped Officers in the 1980s

I immediately returned to City Road and found that the line of shields had been effective as a defence, with the rioters having fallen back towards Ashley Road. Later we would discover that they had turned their attention on a bank and business premises in that area. The Deputy Chief Constable was trying to get things organised and instructed that we should deploy in the van, followed by a Task Force Unit Land Rover, down City Road as two patrol cars, unfortunately operating on the different vehicle radio system, had just gone across the end of City Road and towards the horde in Ashley Road. With about a half a dozen Officers with riot shields in each vehicle, we reached the junction of City Road. The crowd had enveloped the two patrol cars, both of which were severely damaged and set alight, and the crews were running ahead of the mass towards us. I turned left into Ashley Road and the Land Rover reversed back returning along City Road.

The Officers from my van deployed and managed to filter down side roads and alleys with no real affect upon such a mass of advancing people. The cell reserve Constable had remained in the rear of the van and shouted that a Traffic Inspector running behind us had fallen and the crowd were rapidly gaining on him. I stopped and, unable to think of anything better to do, reversed back at the crowd. This action served a purpose, in that the Inspector regained his feet and ran past the van to relative safety. I went to get the van into forward gear but was now surrounded and found that a half brick that had come through the smashed windscreen was lodged under the clutch pedal. In the time it took to kick it away, the van was totally surrounded. There were stones and bricks coming from all directions. The saving aspect for the Constable in the back was that a shield had remained and he lay down with his back against the seats and the shield in front of him. I had no such protection and, at one time, my right arm was being pulled out of the broken driver's window.

I, later, discovered that the Task Force Unit Land Rover had used side roads to get to the upper end of Ashley Road but their Inspector instructed that the men around him should not join in the melee in which our van was trapped. Fortunately for me and the Constable in the rear of the van, a Sergeant from our Group at Central led a band of our own Constables to our rescue. By now the crowd were rocking the van in an effort to turn it over and, given what we later knew had happened to the patrol cars, may well have set it alight. The rush of Constables led by the Sergeant distracted those around the front of the van and I was able to get into forward gear and accelerate up Ashley Road with our rescuers running beside me. We stopped long enough for them to crowd into the van, the Land Rover already heading away, and we drove out into Stokes Croft. As we were doing so I heard the instruction over one of the radios for all units to return to Trinity Road Police Station.

At Trinity Road, conscious that my hand and face were hurting quite badly but not aware just how badly damaged my face was from the broken windscreen glass, I reported to the Deputy Chief Constable who had taken up occupation of the Sub-Divisional Superintendent's office. Having told him briefly what we had encountered since leaving him in City Road, he directed that I be taken to the BRI. At the hospital, with quite a few others, my facial wounds were cleaned up a bit and my right hand was X Rayed. Unfortunately, the swelling to the area around my right knuckle was such that the x ray image was not clear. Not until the pain remained after some days had passed did I get back to the BRI. Now, with a clearer image, it was found that joints in my first finger had been broken and now were mending crooked. It was decided that a further, medical, fracture would not bring an affective return to the joint and I would have to live with the injured finger.

I was returned to Central Police Station and had to go through the crowd of mass media people thronging the steps and front office. They had seen the state of my face as I passed through them and the, relatively newly appointed, ACC who was dealing with their enquiries spoke with me in the Inspectors' office. The media men wanted to interview me but the ACC left it to me as to whether I would agree to meet them. I was, of course, in a state of shock through my injuries and what had caused them and was not at all sure that I would say the right things in any interview at that time. I declined and was taken home by a policewoman. At home, of course, Gill had seen the teatime news coverage and knew that it would have been unlikely that I had avoided involvement in what was going on. Over the years, I had never telephoned her with any updates as to what I was doing while on duty. She operated on the assumption that she would hear soon enough if there was anything seriously wrong. This was, perhaps, a borderline instance but it was probably better that she see I was, roughly, in one piece when I arrived home.

Quite a bit, several months, later I went to the then DHSS offices at Flowers Hill, Brislington, for an assessment of my 'industrial' injury. Two retired doctors interviewed me and tut-tutted as I explained what had happened on 2nd April. They concluded that I would be disabled for life to the degree of 6%. I received about a thousand pounds and the Criminal Injuries Compensation Board (CICB) decided that their interim payment of £500, when added to the DHSS award, was sufficient.

After the couple of days immediately after the injuries, I returned to the Group. I had found that the camaraderie with which members of the Group had become familiar was holding things together. There was, however, a very real sense that we, the police, had lost the day on the 2nd April and over the couple of days of continuing strife that followed. After much legal debate, given that the Police Authority had a responsibility in law to compensate for riot damages, it was finally decided that what had occurred that day was, at law, a 'riot'. On the day and in the follow-up there had been about half a dozen people arrested for their involvement, only a tiny minority of the hundreds participating. There were many attempts to make the day's happenings into a 'race riot' but we knew that there were all colours and creeds involved that day.

Some weeks later, with the day of the appearance in Bristol Magistrates Court set for those charged, we were on 6a.m. till 2p.m. shift. I had received a note to say that all of the Group were to be around the Magistrates Court building before 9a.m. Realising that this would prevent the Officers from taking their normal mid-shift refreshment breaks, I arranged for the usual 7a.m. tea break to be enhanced by the collection of doughnuts from the bakery. Keeping the two response cars on the road, pretty well the whole Group gathered in the report writing room and were in good humour, given the fact that we would later be 'looking after' some of the horde that had 'thrown us out' of St Pauls a few weeks earlier. None of us wanted a re-run of 2nd April, least of all right in the middle of the city.

Probably because he could not sleep with the thought of what the day could bring, we were all surprised by the early arrival of the Divisional Commander. When he saw the crowd in the station, he ordered them all out and came along to the Inspectors' office to tell me, "Mr. Leach, his is not supervision." My attempts at the obvious explanation were summarily dismissed and he stormed off up to his office on the first floor, not to be seen again by us that day. I suppose it has to be admitted that what he saw that day was no more, to him, than confirmation of what he had discussed with the Charge Sergeant before my arrival. At a more normal time, the Sub-Divisional Superintendent arrived and it was his, Chief Inspector, deputy who was visible after 9a.m. as our Group were spread around the elevated area where the front doors of the Court building were accessed. All those charged had been bailed so they all arrived, with various legal and more casual supporters, with a smaller than expected mass media presence to see what was happening. Thankfully, all went off quite peaceably.

Throughout this saga, from the day it all erupted and well past the court hearings, there was no visible appreciation above Group level of the sheer negative impact upon those who had been directly involved. Worse, those involved saw how little their more senior officers understood the affect upon proud police officers of being delivered the sort of ignominy that those at Group level still felt. It was as though there was a simple expectation that it would 'all wash over' and everything would quickly return to normal. In fact, the effect was to last a long time. In early 1981, before the disturbances to be experienced in many other parts of the country, a few of the Group commissioned a jumper with an embroidered badge of a candle and the 'motto' reading 'Who cares who wins'. That was a year later and still the sores had not really healed and still those at the higher levels in the organisation had not adequately recognised that fact.

Despite the background observation I felt under even at the time and to be confirmed much later, I did whatever was asked of me and that was pretty well everything. I was taken off the Group on many occasions to stand in for those in the Administration Office, Process Office (court administration and traffic offence prosecutions), Courts Office (dealing with the prisoners being arraigned in the court), Licensing (administering and court presentations for the many licensed premises in the city centre area) and several switches across to the Trinity Road and back to Central Sub Divisions. While it appears I had shown aptitude for all these aspects of what it took to run such a busy Division and at my Staff Appraisal interviews I was being told nothing detrimental, what was being written on reports about me to Headquarters was very different. Much later, near the end of my service, I had the unusual opportunity to actually see my personal file. At that time I found that in 1980 it had included the comment, "He has lost control of his Group!" It would be difficult to think of a more damaging comment so my appearances on promotion boards were, unbeknown to me in the early 1980s, a total waste of time.

Within the Group and in the offices where I often stood in for the regular managers, all went well. The boredom of the routine was made up for by the great feeling on the Group. The five Sergeants were very different but all committed to getting things done in an efficient manner and the Constables, probationary and more mature in service were, in the main, enthusiastic. On one Sunday late shift, I came on duty to be told that the personal radio system had 'gone down'. I instructed the Sergeants to devise telephone kiosk 'points' for the Constables in the pre-personal radio way of doing things. It has to be said that this brought home to the Constables what working without instant communication was all about but they all seemed to quite enjoy the experience – provided it was only for one afternoon and evening.

At that time the River Station, now a restaurant which has kept that name, still contained two police launches. One was small and each Group had a couple of Constables who were authorised to navigate it. The other was larger and much more powerful, for use in the tidal races out in the Severn Estuary, and was the responsibility of specially trained Traffic Officers. One day we were informed by someone heading in to work early that the hull of a boat upon which the owner was still yet to fabricate the superstructure, was riding free in the reach of the floating harbour near the Lightship. This hull was, unusually, made of concrete and was of significant proportions. By the way, the Lightship had received internal modifications to be used as a nightclub and was to become quite famous as a backdrop to the television series, 'Shoestring'.

I went with the authorised Constable who was on duty to take out the small launch to recover the hull, which had obviously been untied by some revellers in the early hours. When we reached the River Station a patrol car drew up and the Traffic Sergeant insisted that we should use the larger launch in view of the weight of the hull. Not at the time seeing anything with which to argue, we got on to the larger launch and went out around the corner to where the hull was across the reach. Officers on the quay had got a hold of one ends before we intervened but our Traffic Sergeant started nudging the side of the hull to push it back level with the harbour wall. Suddenly there was a horrendous noise from beneath our boat and we came to an abrupt stop. The Officers on the quay managed to complete the securing of the hull but we were stuck in the middle of the channel. It transpired that a little below the surface there was a wire-rope hawser extending all along the reach by which the mooring buoys were held in position. One of our propeller shafts had become entangled with this wire.

The problem was that our dilemma was not private. There were by now, fast approaching eight o'clock in the morning, a steady flow of people who walked in or parked in the, then restriction free, Redcliffe area. Their 'flow' had eased as many had stopped on Bristol Bridge to see what the police launch was doing. The irony was that the smaller launch that we had left back in the boathouse was propelled by water jets and had no visible propellers, so could not have been fouled by the submarine cable. The ignominy was that the Divisional Control room staff had mobilised the Harbourmaster who arrived in a diminutive little motor boat and ferried me and the Constable who had started out with me back to some steps in the harbour wall. We left the Traffic Sergeant on board to supervise the recovery of his craft.

In the early 1980s the Floating Harbour was taken over for a few days each summer for a round in the Power Boat equivalent of Formula One. The Bristol Grand Prix was very different from others in the annual series. It was much more accessible for close-up viewing by spectators, who lined both sides of the harbour all the way down from St Augustin's Reach to the Cumberland Basin. Unfortunately, and probably the reason it did not continue for very long, it was also extremely dangerous. At the other GP venues there was a marked out course on a large expanse of open water and boat drivers who miscalculated simply slid off the correct line. In Bristol there were high and very unforgiving stone walls to mark the route. Many accidents led to grave injury and far too many to fatalities.

Each Inspector at Central Police Station was allocated specific responsibilities by the Sub-Divisional Commander. I had two principle such duties. One was quite a headache, being responsible for ensuring the maintenance of our substantial stock of 'no waiting' cones. These were of the shape now still in manufacture but had, in the distant past, been preceded by small 'A' board type items and the former Bristol Officers always referred to the cones as 'boards'. It was fortunate that we usually took a delivery of 200 new cones each summer, just before the Power Boat Racing, because there were significant routes along which these and the remnants of our older stock had to be placed. It seems difficult to explain, I really cannot, how we always seemed to manage to 'lose' the equivalent number to our annual new allocation in the course of each twelve months. On quiet nights, Officers would enhance the stock levels by mounting 'recovery' missions on to neighbouring Divisions. On one such occasion, a cone appeared with 'Metropolitan Police' moulded above the 'No Waiting' wording. It had to be that 'recovery' missions taking place in Forces all across the south of England had 'liberated' this cone on many occasions for it to have made the 120 mile journey from London to Bristol. We did not bother the Met with the logistical problem of recovering their cone! Another No Waiting cone recovery device was to encourage the Underwater Search Unit to seek them out when they were doing their practice dives in the Floating Harbour,

The other regular responsibility was, for me and several of the others on the Group, far more pleasant. In the basement of Old Bridewell and, we believed, probably installed when the building was being constructed in the 1930s, there was a diesel engine driving a generator. The machine had a huge single cylinder and a brass ball centrifugal mechanism to determine the strokes upon which it fired. The piston drove a huge, probably about eight foot diameter, flywheel which was of iron spokes and a massive brass rim. The centrifugal mechanism opened the inlet port as the speed slackened and cut it off as a firing stroke sent the huge wheel spinning again. It probably only fired about once every six to eight revolutions, which must have significantly aided the lowering of the fuel consumption. My duty was to check it once a month to ensure that it worked. To start it there were two possible methods. Alongside the machine were large tanks containing compressed air. The compressed air was released into the cylinder to start it rotating the flywheel and the knack was to turn it over to the inlet of fuel at the right time for it to start firing. The stock of compressed air was not adequate for too many failed attempts but we had got it off to a fine art after a few attempts and did not encounter the problem of running out of air. The purpose of the engine was to substitute generator power in the event of a mains failure and when others sometimes had to start it the compressed air could become exhausted. A local lorry tyre replacement van would arrive to replenish the tanks with their on-board compressor. Once the flywheel was revolving the power from the generator was brought to the emergency circuit within the building by throwing a double lever which always put me in mind of a scene from a Hammer Frankenstein film. In the 1990s the machine was, with great difficulty, extricated from the basement and taken to a museum and the power back-up brought by cables form the massive generator in New Bridewell.

One of the 'standing in' jobs that regularly came my way was to relieve the female Process Inspector for her holidays or course attendances. Process, in this context, meant the processing of summons offences through the decision making to the prosecution of offenders before the Magistrates Courts, all then still in the hands of the police. The small team in the Office were a combination of police officers and support clerks and typists and all were very well conversant with what it was they had to do. My main role was to mark up the papers for prosecution and, on each Wednesday, attend the 'traffic court' and act as prosecutor. Having experienced this in smaller numbers as a Sergeant at Bridgwater, I really did enjoy the role of prosecuting advocate. Where the defendants were represented by solicitors I soon realised that none of them knew the law relating to the type of offences we were dealing with anywhere near as well as did I, or any other experienced police officer.

On one day the Solicitor employed by the Bristol City Council, who had been frequently involved in many aspects of legal advice to the Force, telephoned me and then came to the office to discuss what he had been told was to be his new role. The door had been opened for the start of the Crown Prosecution Service.

When I showed him the typical prosecution files, one sheet of paper with the charges and brief statement of supporting evidence, attached to the result of the records search to determine any driving licence endorsements, he was very concerned. His view was that his new, most yet to be recruited, band of mainly inexperienced solicitors could not work from so slender a brief. My response at the time, but soon to be overruled, was that this was all that we were using and would have to suffice for his purposes.

To give the upcoming system a full trial and with the assistance of the Chief Magistrates Clerk, we split the court into two benches on the following Wednesday. The normal case load included about a dozen where the defendant was pleading not guilty and a further dozen where the defendant was pleading guilty but appearing usually to plead special reasons for his endorsed licence not to lead to him being disqualified from driving. There were a further two to three hundred cases in which there was no appearance by the defendant and a written plea of guilty, these we referred to as 'read offs' as they could be dealt with very quickly. Normally, I would prosecute the guilty plea appearances first, then the not guilty plea defendants and end the session with the 'read-offs'. The first two parts of this day were, of course, very formal and would normally be completed by just before or just after the lunch recess. The 'read-offs' were usually with the Magistrates and their Clerk and me without any observers, press reporters being quite content to rely upon the court results list but usually showing no interest in these offenders. This latter section of the day was more relaxed, with the Magistrates inviting me to be seated as I recited the lists of offences. There was such a routine in terms of penalty that I had to resist writing the result on each sheet before it was announced.

On this unusual Wednesday, it was agreed that the split between the two benches of Magistrates would be for me to deal with the guilty appearances and read-offs while the advocate appointed by the Force Solicitor would deal with the not guilty plea defendants. I ploughed on in my customary fashion and then, with the court now clear, whistled through the read-offs in the usual more relaxed manner. This brought us to within half an hour of the usual time of the lunch recess and, not having heard anything from the other court, I asked the Clerk to not release the Magistrates until I had checked. In the other court the young solicitor was just sitting down after addressing the Justices toward the end of his second case. In discussion with the more senior solicitor, soon to become Crown Prosecutor, we further split the remaining list of defendants. Back in session in both courts in the afternoon, I dealt with my cases, took a further one from the other list and was complete soon enough to go back to the other court to watch the final half of the last case.

This early example of how the new process looked likely to slow things down considerably did nothing to hamper the 'progress' towards the increased bureaucracy and certainly no greater effectiveness of the introduction of the Crown Prosecutions Office system. My brother-in-law had, in the early 1980s, been a Magistrate in the Wellington Court for about ten years. On a family visit to them some time after the introduction of the Crown Prosecutors, he said to me, "We all wish we could bring back the prosecuting Sergeants." As we know from experience before and after the introduction of the Crown Prosecutions system, politically engineered solutions are never acknowledged to have failed and it is very seldom that there is any attempt to revert.

I enjoyed a few stints as acting Chief Inspector, deputy to the sub-Divisional Commander and similar 'acting up' duties over in the Courts Department, mainly dealing with the reception and handling of prisoners arriving and departing on remand or after sentencing. These spells of acting were, unbeknown to me at the time, not really doing what I then hoped. I was still under suspicious observation despite my capacity to handle all these jobs, a sign of just how serious can be a bias born of a totally unrelated situation involving a completely different person and set of circumstances.

In the early part of 1981, Gill and I had spent months cogitating over an issue which was extremely important to us as a family. Tanya was coming up to eleven and was due to start at senior school in the September of that year. We seriously considered, now that it was going fully co-educational, funding her education at Wellington School as a day pupil and exploiting the spare room which my parents had in Wellington. I am sure that they would have been delighted to have had her with them so much and she was already a holiday visitor with Gill's mother in Wellington so knew her way around a bit. What prevented that course of action was the recognition that there could be at least one year when all three girls, with their average three year age spacing, would be in secondary education together. While my Inspector's salary could, only just, have stretched to funding Tanya, there was no sensible prospect of being able to do the same for all three of them together.

Hence the notion was abandoned and we struck out on an alternative approach. At that time the school covering the western side of Keynsham had not the best of reputations for academic excellence while that on the east side certainly did. The solution, and one that served the further purpose of separate bedrooms for Cathryn and Emma, was to move across town and find a four bedroom house. Another addressing of the regular finances and realisation that our little house at Glebe Walk had exactly doubled in value between 1977 and 1981, brought the decision that we could make the move. The house-hunt brought us to a few yards from the rear access to all three schools and only a short distance from the local shops and post office - to Cherwell Road.

While the occasional office hour's attachments had been great for spending more time as a family at weekends I did not welcome the lengthy spell in the Divisional Administration Office to cover for the regular incumbent attending a course at Bramshill. It started the Monday after we moved to Cherwell Road, when I could have done with the free time offered by shift work to sort out the decorating and more serious alterations we had decided were required in our new home. Somehow we fitted everything in and soon settled. With a few weeks of the final term at junior school remaining, Tanya cycled and her violin got a lift on appropriate days with the headmaster at Kelston Road School, who lived not too far from Cherwell Road. Cathryn moved schools and, in the September, Emma started at the infants at Chandag as Tanya began at Wellsway School.

Not far from the first anniversary of the riot in St Paul's similar disturbances brewed up in quite a few other parts of the country. The different tactic employed by the hooligans elsewhere and, thankfully, not seen in Bristol in 1980, was the throwing of petrol bombs. Although the preparations we had made in terms of training and equipment were not to be seriously rested in 1981 we could not ignore the potential for petrol bombs to be used against the old Central Police Station building. The more sensitive area of Trinity Road Sub-Division had the new police station with its solid brick walls but Old Bridewell had masses of ordinary windows directly overlooking public thoroughfares. While I was doing another stint as 'spare' Inspector we liaised with the local Fire Service and they delivered a portable Coventry Climax pump unit.

The rear yard between the headquarters buildings had been the old fire brigade training area, the tower and underground water tank were still there (as too was the pole from the first floor to the former garage). The water in the underground tank was pumped out by a fire tender and replenished with somewhat fresher water and I spent some hours training a few Officers from each Group on how to use the portable pump. Thankfully, this precaution never had to be brought into use.

The Chief Superintendent's post on 'A' Division saw a series of changes in 1981, following the transfer to Taunton of the Officer in place since my return from University. Over the forthcoming eighteen months there were to be four men moving into the role. One was there so briefly that I cannot recall his name, another saw out his brief time to retirement and the third came on promotion from deputy in another Bristol Division but had started his police career elsewhere and joined the force around the time of the 1974 amalgamation. His arrival coincided with another new venture for me. The 'powers that be' had decided that the mass of licensed premises in the central part of Bristol and their frequent applications to the Licensing Justices necessitated a dedicated Inspector role to deal with them.

Once again, and just as strangely given the on-going suspicions I had unwittingly engendered, I seemed to fit the bill and was posted from the Group, not simply temporarily detached, to become the first Licensing Inspector for the Division, with some responsibilities for files coming from other city divisions. Although my total lack of any support brought the more boring aspects of maintaining a significant filing system, never one of my most enjoyed occupations, I enjoyed this role immensely. The difference in terms of court appearance was that the Licensing Justices held the responsibility for adequately supervising the activities of licensees and I was seen more as their front line support than as the prosecution advocate I had been in the ordinary Court. Much of what was applied for was dealt with by a telephone call. If we, the police, were going to object to an application it would, most often, be altered to suit us or be withdrawn.

Only occasionally was it necessary for me to appear in Court to object and, far more often than not, the Magistrates would find in our favour. On one significant occasion a nationally renowned chamber of solicitors involved in licensing law pursued all day an application for a special hours certificate for successive Sundays at the, then, Exhibition Centre. Our objection had been only to the Sundays, knowing that the small entry fee to the exhibitions would bring some to the Centre just to drink while all the usual outlets were closed. After the long, and I suspect for the Magistrates somewhat tedious, application and my cross-examination of the several witnesses that were called, they retired to make their decision. When they returned I was as surprised as the esteemed solicitors, but not nearly as cross, that the Magistrates had decided to find against all the applications for extended hours, not just the Sundays. The senior partner of the firm, who had been sitting behind his junior and offering him advice throughout the session, came over and asked me how much longer I had before I could retire. With at least another twelve years to go, his suggestion that he could 'find me a job' was unrealistic, but the approach none the less satisfying.

One of the most interesting diversions form the Group at Central, the only good part of which was the people with whom I worked, was when the Special Events Inspector was on annual leave as short notice came in of an 'Animal Aid' demonstration in Bristol. At that time, late 1982, the animal aid support groups were particularly active and had an on-going campaign directed against the laboratory use of animals and the sale of animal furs. Their plan was to start a protest march on the Downs and parade down through Whiteladies Road, past the BBC studios, along Park Row, near the University, and down to the Broadmead shopping centre. There were along the way and in Broadmead several fur shops and, of course, at the University there were laboratories where their assumption was that animals were being experimented upon.

My task was, in liaison with the Assistant Chief Constable and Senior Officers on 'C' and 'A' Divisions, to prepare an Operational Order and arrange the logistical elements and briefings for the policing of the event. The outcome was to be just about the largest pre-planned event for the Force in terms of the variety of areas to be covered and, consequently, number of Officers engaged. With the Traffic Department and other specialists supporting the mainly uniformed presence, drawn from all parts of the Force to spread the load, there were over 600 involved on the day, Saturday, 23rd October. Just to provide some further variety, I also got involved in the entirely separate security arrangements at Castlemead, a new building on the edge of Broadmead, regarding the display of presents and regalia from the wedding of HRH Prince Charles to Lady Dianna Spencer eighteen months earlier.

In respect of the Animal Aid March, there were a number of vulnerable properties to protect, all of which were either on the demonstration route or near to it and could become targets for unwanted attention. The route was of between two and three miles in length and passed many shop areas with their large glass windows. Saturday was always a busy shopping day in the City and one of our objectives had to be to minimise the inevitable disruption to the normal activity that this brought. The support of prison vans was included, so that we could cut down the time taken for arresting officers to be committed with their prisoners. With not very much advance warning, the uniformed Officers were drawn from all Divisions and there was a need to arrange for their briefing and feeding. The Bristol Grammar School became our base and was well placed and cooperatively made available to us on that Saturday.

With so many Officers coming from other parts of the Force area, we recognised that many would not be familiar with the area along which the demonstration was to pass. We engaged the help of the relatively new Video Unit within the Force Training Department, a 'unit' of two young men. They made an excellent job of producing a video for the briefing which contained the whole of the route, with commentary of places of interest within the operation, and a recorded briefing by the ACC. On the day at the large assembly hall of the Grammar School and with several of the largest televisions then available spread around the room, the Video briefing started. Fortunately, the tape ran through the route identification section before someone moving around at the front of the room tripped over the electric cable and dragged the video tape machine off the table. The machine was not going to show any more video that day but the ACC was present and did his bit direct to the assembled audience. It simply demonstrated just how easily vulnerable can be any innovative move to involve technological solutions. With as few arrests and as little disruption and damage as we could have hoped for, the march went on that day and, afterwards, we all breathed a sigh of relief.

After the personality changes in the role of Chief Superintendent on 'A' Division the Superintendent formerly from Central Sub Division came to that position. The Chief Superintendent from not long before had been promoted to ACC and, in early July, 1983, I was summoned to his office in the Headquarters part of Old Bridewell. He told me that the Force had been asked to support a team assembled in the autumn of 1982 by the Association of Chief Police Officers (ACPO) and based at New Scotland Yard (NSY). The requirement was for an Officer of Inspector rank who had both practical experience of public order situations and the ability to produce good written reports. The ACC, based largely upon what he had seen of me while he was my Divisional Commander, told me that he could not think of another candidate who would represent the Force better than me. Had I, at last, slid out from under that unwarranted cloud?

15 Public Order Forward Planning Unit

My immediate response to the ACC was that I needed to know a little more than he was able to tell me and, more importantly, to discuss the proposed nine month attachment with Gill. He seemed somewhat surprised that I had not immediately grasped the opportunity. I telephoned the Unit Chief Superintendent, a Metropolitan Officer with significant experience particularly in relation to hostage negotiation and who would later rise to become Deputy Chief Constable of the West Midlands Police Force. His immediate response to my call was that I should travel up to London to see what they were doing before I made my decision. Reluctantly, the ACC agreed to the cost of the trip! At home, I wondered what Gill's reaction would be but was not to be disappointed. She had known, more than I had realised, just how frustrating I had found my situation on 'A' Division and firmly identified her approval for me to take up such a rare opportunity.

Next day, by train from Bath Spa, I spent several hours in New Scotland Yard meeting the members of the ACPO Public Order Forward Planning Unit (POFPU). I spoke at length with the Inspector from Merseyside who was nearing the end of his nine month attachment and whose place in the Unit I was to be filling. It gave an excellent opportunity for me to have a brief hand-over of a couple of projects upon which he had been working. I also met others within the Unit, particularly the Met. Chief Inspector, who was to reach Commander Rank before he retired, with whom, theoretically, I was to be teamed up. The structure was the Chief Superintendent (Met.) a Superintendent (provincial – at that time from the West Midlands Police), two teams each of a Chief Inspector and Inspector (one of each from the Met and a provincial force – in July, 1983 the provincial C/Insp. was from the Cleveland Force). These 'project officers' were supported by a small administrative team, all of whom were Metropolitan personnel - a Sergeant, Higher Executive Officer (civil service grades applied to civilian staff in the Metropolitan Police) and a typist. In practice, the 'pairing' of

Met/Provincial Inspecting ranks was not applied as there were too many topics to be examined and we each became tied in with our individual projects.

The formation of the Public Order Forward Planning Unit had been somewhat slow. In 1980, when we were confronting the rioters in Bristol, many larger Forces, those where such actions held the greatest likelihood to be repeated, simply thought they could have done better than did Avon and Somerset. A very few Forces took measures to try and prepare for such an eventuality, ironically not those who were really at the greatest risk, probably best prepared were Norfolk.

The full realisation hit home to the ACPO General Purposes Committee, responsible to ACPO Council for Public Order Policing matters, that it was not a one-off problem when, in April and again in July 1981, rioting took place in areas such as Brixton (London), Handsworth (Birmingham) and Toxteth (Manchester), with some smaller, copy-cat, actions elsewhere. If Forces like the Metropolitan, West Midlands and Greater Manchester were not really coping with this phenomenon, ACPO had to do something. In forming the Public Order Sub-Committee of ACPO General Purposes Committee it was recognised that to make adequate progress they would need an 'executive arm', hence the formation of POFPU.

With more time available, this may have been passed through the Home Office and have become another of the many Central Service secondments then available in a wide range of specialist areas but that time was not available. So, the 'grace and favour' within the structure of ACPO as it then existed came into play and suitable Officers had been 'volunteered' by those on the Sub-Committee to work with the Metropolitan personnel from the offices on the 12th floor made available by the Commissioner.

The first task set for the Unit by the Sub-Committee was to generate a Public Order Tactical Options Manual for all Forces to have available the 'best practice' examples of the tactics and manoeuvres to be deployed under large scale public disorder situations. Upon my arrival at NSY, nine months after the formation of the Unit, the first edition, an already sizeable version, of this Tactical Options Manual had been completed and was in the process of being distributed. I delivered the copies for Wiltshire and Avon and Somerset on my way home for the August Bank Holiday weekend. It has to be said that this production was a testament to the industry and devotion of that first POFPU team. There was much more to be done to make the Manual fully comprehensive but that first version was being distributed to all ACPO Rank Officers throughout the country and a 'Force' copy went to the Senior Officer in the Operations Department of every Force.

I must issue a short apology at this stage as to present this chapter in either a wholly chronological fashion is not feasible. Projects ran very much in parallel and reached critical and completion stages at differing times. It will also unavoidable to completely separate topics as much as would be desirable. I can only hope that the reader can bear with me and will find the matters discussed of interest.

The main project that I inherited from the Inspector from Merseyside was one which he had advanced quite a long way already and involved the markings on police riot helmets to identify officers. Much of his time had been spent in liaison with the Home Office Scientific Branch at Sandridge, near St Albans to ensure that adhesive used for the markings would not degrade the fabric of the helmets. My role was really only to promulgate what he had researched to the Forces and with the manufacturers. I also had a lasting input to the map in the front of the Police Almanac, issued annually from a metropolitan Police Office at the opposite end of Caxton Street from NSY. The Provincial Forces on the map had been numbered, but not the Met or City of London. After my visit to the appropriate office, all 43 Forces in England and Wales were numbered in alphabetical order. Avon and Somerset remained Force number one; the City of London became number five and the Metropolitan number 25.

Somewhat incidental to the markings on riot helmets, at that time the only vehicles with regular roof markings were the bullion vans used by the Bank of England. There were already thoughts on such markings being applied to police vehicles but they had not, yet, been implemented. The distant relationship between roof markings on vehicles and those on helmets formed a pretty lame excuse for me to accompany the provincial Superintendent, from West Midlands, on a trip out to the Metropolitan Air Support Unit at Lippitts Hill on the edge of Epping Forest. At that time the Met had three Bell 222 helicopters and one of these took us up and over to the Bank of England depot where the roof markings on the vans could be clearly seen from the air. While over north east London, with the call-sign 'India 99' we received a call to a robbery at a Gateway. Initially we thought this to be a supermarket but it was, in fact, a

Gateway building society. The speed with which we traversed central London at the peak of the morning rush hour was impressive. The way in which the culprits were easily spotted was even more so. We were able to observe one of the culprits enter an arch under a long railway viaduct and to direct the officers responding on the ground to be able to affect an arrest.

It was recognised by the ACPO Sub-Committee that there was a need for Forces across the country to make full use of the Forward Planning Unit when considering how to confront large scale public order issues. To this end a series of Regional Seminars were planned from early after I joined the Unit. One of the earliest was in my 'home territory' and was held at Kingsweston House, the Avon and Somerset Training School, in mid-September, 1983. The others in which I was involved were at Guildford in October and Glasgow in December. I was with the recently replaced Chief Superintendent (Met.) and soon to be replaced Superintendent (West Midlands) on the visit to Scotland. We flew up but used the return journey to make a visit to the National Police Training, Central Planning Unit at Pannel Ash, Harrogate. These regional visits and presentations were to be supported in February 1984 by a presentation to the ACPO Carousel Course at Bramshill.

The trip to Scotland produced a few amusing asides. We were transported out to Heathrow by the Unit Sergeant and, as the junior rank on the flight, the bag of equipment we were taking to show at the seminar was allocated to me. We handed over our bags and, without a second thought, went to the coffee lounge to await our flight. An announcement was made for me to go to one of the reception counters. When I arrived there I was conscious that there was a man standing immediately on each side of me and they reinforced the counter clerks request that I go to a room which she indicated. In the room a man was standing behind a desk with two other men standing behind him and the holdall containing the exhibits was on the desk in front of him. He confirmed that I was responsible for the holdall and, at last, I realised what was the problem. I went to reach for my wallet from my back trouser pocket to show them my police warrant card but my arm was grasped by one of my escorts. When I explained, he let me show them the warrant card and the man behind the desk, quite correctly, told me that we should have known better. The bag contained side handled batons and small canisters that were individual fire extinguishers. On the X-Ray machine these looked suspiciously like a broken down gun and hand grenades. The man was right, we should have known better.

While presenting the seminar, in the middle of our two night stay in the former Gorbals Police Station, then used as a training school, we were told of a football match at Celtic Park between the home team and Nottingham Forest. We expressed an interest in spending our evening observing the policing arrangements at the ground. This was of particular interest as the Sports Ground (Scotland) Act had only recently come into force and we wanted to see the impact of its more rigorous restrictions. The Training Chief Superintendent could not really get hold of the notion that we wanted to observe the policing and was at pains to point out that getting us tickets to watch the match at this juncture may be difficult.

Eventually we got the message across and one of the Chief Inspectors from the Operations Department was deputed to be our guide for the evening. We arrived at the local police station, only a few hundred yards from the ground, to be shown the local control room with its communications to the stadium. We were told that all was quite orderly on this evening and walked, with the fans, up the road to the entrance to the ground. We made for the main doors of the larger grandstand but our guide experienced some difficulty in persuading the doorman that we should be allowed to enter. While we were waiting for him to negotiate, two mounted officers appeared and saw us beside the front doors. They moved in and one pinned the West Midlands Superintendent against the wall with the rump-end of his horse. Unable to reach for his warrant card or to be heard above the general hubbub of those entering through the turnstiles, I waved my warrant card in front of the Constable on the horse and, eventually, he got the message. The Superintendent had nothing more than his pride damaged and we all three saw the comical side.

Unable to gain access through the doors we were sent to the 'tradesman's entrance', the access route to the police facility. As we approached those doors, they flew open and two young men were unceremoniously thrown out into the puddle in front of us. We walked around them and followed our guide through the door, all four waving our warrant cards. Inside, our Chief Superintendent enquired of the Inspector who was running the facility as to why the two young men were being ejected when the new legislation indicated that all of those causing problems would be arrested rather than ejected from sports grounds. The Inspector, in his Glaswegian accent, evidently saw no humour in his reply,

"They were not being ejected, they were just being chucked out!" We were then shown the observation area on top of one of the stands in which the one police officer with a pair of binoculars and a personal radio was squeezed to one side by a large number of representatives from the press. In truth there was not much unusual to see but the legislation regarding drinking and restricting items, such as bottles, were having some obvious impact.

The ACPO Public Order Sub-Committee met at NSY at two to three month intervals although the members did occasionally call in on the Unit if in London for some other reason. Dependent upon the stages reached with each project, we made presentations to the Sub-Committee and I pleasantly surprised myself at my lack of self-consciousness regarding my Somerset accent. From that time, I realised that even the most senior officers seldom had special knowledge and were keen to pick up information from those who, because of their intimate involvement with a topic, knew more than did they. After these presentations and the more casual involvement with many of very senior rank and others from such hallowed halls as the Home Office and Palace of Westminster, I never again felt the least bit concerned in whatever company I found myself.

As well as the occasional visit from members of the ACPO Sub-Committee, we had liaison Officers for the Unit in each Force and some took the opportunity to come to London and see who we were and what we were doing. One visit, from our liaison Officer in Northern Ireland, necessitated our warning the housekeeper (whom I only met once) that the fourth bedroom in our maisonette at Swiss Cottage would need to have the bed made up. In the late afternoon I collected the Superintendent from Heathrow in the Branch car and we went directly to the accommodation. The others, the Superintendent from West Midlands and Chief Inspector from Cleveland, joined us and we went to our usual watering hole at the nearby Holiday Inn. Next morning, we went out to the car park and I got into the Branch car and started the engine. My passenger stood back for a while but then joined me in the car. He explained that this was the first time in years that he had got into a car that had been parked outside overnight without performing a thorough search around and beneath the vehicle. He also described how he had chosen his home near Belfast to ensure it had bay windows so that the door could be checked before responding to the doorbell.

The one project with which I did share some involvement with my 'paired'

Chief Inspector was in relation to the considerations as to whether the Police Service in England and Wales should establish equipment holding centres to 'pool' resources of items such as CS gas, baton rounds (known in the media as 'rubber bullets') and their dischargers. Some significant effort was expended on this topic, with visits to a number of potential sites around and distant from London. The concern was driven by the additional aspect of the disturbances in 1981, not seen in Bristol in 1980, of petrol bombs being produced and thrown. In the event such stores were not called for and most Forces determined their own needs and held what they thought to be appropriate.

Because of my Traffic background, although it was growing ever more distant by 1983, I was involved with the Metropolitan Police Protected Vehicle Committee and we had a meeting at the training facility at Greenwich in July. I had little on-going involvement with this Met. Group until much later, as it turned out in my last few days with POFPU. Following a much earlier attack on a coach taking aircrew between Heathrow and central London the Military Vehicle Research establishment at Chertsey had been given the task of developing a coach which would be proof against such an attack. In March, 1984 I accompanied the Chief Superintendent from the Unit on a visit, with other invited interested people, for a demonstration of the coach which they had produced. The demonstration was fairly convincing but was very much focused upon what had happened during the earlier attack. We pointed out quite a few aspects which left the vehicle potentially vulnerable - largely because the research had not been widened to encompass other scenarios.

One of the real likelihoods for centralised equipment was the consideration then being given to the deployment of water cannon. These machines were in common usage on the continent of Europe and farther afield and a pair from Belgium were borrowed. The early trials showed that the Belgian machines had two main defects. Firstly the respect with which these machines seemed to be received on the continent was unlikely to be repeated here and there was real potential for them to become a targeted focus of demonstrators' attentions. Secondly, the Belgian machines relied upon a power take-off from the main driving engine for propulsion of the water jets and this often meant clutch slipping when making slow progress and using the jets at the same time. With this in mind, the Home Office commissioned the two major Fire Engine manufacturers to each create a prototype machine. At significant cost, the two machines were produced. They both had separate engines for running the, extremely powerful, jet nozzles and minor differences in the ways in which those nozzles were controlled from inside the vehicle.

I believe that other than on the old gasworks site at Greenwich then being used by the Metropolitan Police for public order training, while the facility at Hounslow was being constructed, the only demonstration of these machines was at RAF Locking near Weston-super-Mare. This took place in the November, when I had been with the Unit for four months and made one weekend journey home a little shorter. The full evaluation of these machines included a report from Porton Down which identified that their use could be 'excessively' dangerous to demonstrators against whom they may be deployed. The project was shelved and I believe the machines were returned to the respective manufacturers for conversion to more conventional firefighting appliances.

One project which I shared with several others in the Unit was to research how best Officers should deal with women and children who were involved in demonstrations. This was, of course, quite a delicate matter as the 'bad press' potential from getting it wrong could be significant. It has to be recognised as beneficial that the only real such confrontations, even thirty years on, have been largely within peaceful demonstrations. Loosely linked to this topic was the assessment of the Mini-Baton, which held some potential for issue to Women Officers and was capable of being deployed alongside the growing focus on self-defence and restraint hold Aikido training. There were two other bodies interested in these small batons, about four inches (10cm) long by half and inch (1.25cm) in diameter, HM Prison Service and the Royal Military Police. I was privileged to visit both, at Chichester (RMP) and Morton Hall, Lincolnshire (HMP) in August and October, 1983. As an interesting aside, at that time serious consideration of the much larger, side handled, baton was eliminated from our consideration as this item was seen as likely to be too provocative.

In the several months through to the autumn of 1983, there had been a long-standing demonstration, which varied in intensity, at the Greenham Common Airbase where it was commonly thought that nuclear missiles were stored. Many of these demonstrators were women, some with their children and they were camped out all around the sizeable acreage of the base. In October there was a sizeable Campaign for Nuclear Disarmament (CND) demonstration from Parliament Square, along Whitehall and to Trafalgar Square. One of the few

Saturdays that I remained in London during my attachment to POFPU. In November, we were invited to visit the base and taken up for a reconnaissance flight in the police helicopter which the local Force used on such occasions. To see the extent of the campsites was quite something and I had to feel quite unusually sorry for the well-heeled residents surrounded by these encampments. Several had lost extensive garden fences to the campfires around the area.

One item that we were sent for evaluation, an indication that the existence of the Unit was become better known, was an ultraviolet liquid spray aerosol can. The idea was that trouble makers at football matches and elsewhere in situations where immediate arrest was not feasible, should be sprayed and later identified by the use of UV lamps. The manufacturer's proposal was that large UV lamps be positioned near the exits so that those who had been sprayed during a football match could be 'picked off' as they left the ground. We set up a trial near the manufacturers with the assistance of the Kent Force at Maidstone. The practicality of UV lamps capable of revealing sprayed items of clothing in open conditions just did not prove to exist.

A more interesting and, although not taken into wide use, feasible project with which I was involved was to find a way in which police officers could be safely trained to confront petrol bombs. Early in 1984, I visited several potential manufacturers for a simulated petrol bomb. One, where the regular products were for the cinema and TV industries, was quite spectacular but did not really fit in with open-ground police public order training. A more satisfactory item came from a firework and military 'thunderflash' manufacturer based near Derby. The production facility was in wooden huts and everyone, mostly women, wearing clothing, including footwear, with low spark or static potential. My being there brought a huge spread of food on a covered snooker table in the old building that housed the offices. I asked my host who else was visiting that day to be told that there was only me. All the staff had been forewarned that there was a visitor that day and all had ensured that they did not bring their sandwiches but came in to help themselves.

The simulated item this company had produced was a one litre plastic bottle with a third-size thunderflash in the neck and a waterproof fuse of a few seconds duration. The firm had experimented until the length of the fuse was just right for it to be thrown and to ignite just as it was hitting the ground and the bottle was filled with the right amount of non-perfumed talcum powder to give a spread similar to what would be presented by a real petrol bomb. The idea being that there was a high degree of safety but any officer in training with talcum powder on his clothing would know that he would have been affected by petrol. More importantly, anyone not finding talcum powder would know that his shield would have kept him safe from fire.

Armed with a test consignment of the these simulated petrol bombs, I went with the Metropolitan Inspector from the Unit a couple of weeks after the demonstration in Derbyshire to a Public Order Training Session run by the Norfolk Constabulary at Caister Holiday Camp. The exercise was over two days, starting on the Thursday until late, overnight at the Holiday Camp and resumed the following morning. This gave a slightly more realistic session for those taking part as few real instances of large scale public disorder end in one shift. The simulated petrol bomb brought some amusement but actually did what was required, not that the product went into wide acceptance or production. On our arrival at Caister we were told how to find our chalet and took our kit bags there ready for the end of that day. In late February the whole Camp was within the heavy 'chill factor' impact from the adjacent North Sea and inside the chalet it was as cold as outside. We opened the doors of the kitchen and two bedrooms and left the gas cooker on a low oven setting. The following morning, at breakfast before the second training session, we were the only two not complaining at what an awful night they had endured. Well, we were from the Forward Planning Unit!

A new innovation which was in its infancy as I was in what should have been my final few months on the Unit was a video equipped protected van for the purpose of recording disorderly activity with a view to retrospective arresting. The media got to hear of it being taken out on trial in London and christened it the 'hooley van'. I was not to see the vehicle in use until in 1986 when it was brought down to Shepton Mallet for the 'travellers' gatherings that were common in the 1980s, usually on the build up to the, then Pilton, now more gentrified Glastonbury, Festival and the Summer Solstice gathering at Stonehenge over in Wiltshire.

Early in the New Year of 1984, members of the Unit became involved with two Chief Inspectors at Hendon in the preparation for and training of those who would deliver Command Band Public Order training around the Regions. One of these Chief Inspectors had been the Station Sergeant at Notting Hill to whom I referred in chapter ten. Command Band training was for those in the ranks from Chief Inspector up to Chief Superintendent and who would be taking command at serious public disorder situations. There would, later, be an application of a 'gold, silver & bronze' structure but we will return to that later. This small team trained those who would, in regional centres, train the appropriate officers.

A few days before the arrival of a Superintendent from the South Wales Police to replace the man from West Midlands, I visited the Public Order Training with which he was involved at RAF St Athen near Bridgend. I then met up with him at the motorway services on the M4 so that I could show him the best route from Hammersmith to Swiss Cottage. Neither of us knew at that time how important it was that we found we were well suited. We were very different in character and he was more the normal, tall, stature for police provincial officers of the day but, thankfully and in so many ways, we complimented one-another exceptionally well. A former course colleague of his from the Inspectors' Course at Bramshill was working at Shepherds Bush police station and invited us to the Queens Park Rangers football ground at Loftus Road to see their policing arrangements for an evening match.

There had been another unproductive visit to a promotion board during my time on the Public Order Forward Planning Unit. With a few weeks remaining in London, my expectation was that I would reach the end of the nine month attachment and return to the less-than-appealing prospect of resuming where I had left off. The time spent at New Scotland Yard had been rewarding in so many ways that I was not relishing the idea of going back to 'A' Division. The only positive thought about the end of the attachment was to be back more with my family. A compensation available to we provincial officers was that the maisonette at Swiss Cottage was empty at weekends and, with a bit of discussion between us, we could bring our families to stay in it. I did this three times during the period of my attachment and we enjoyed visits to London attractions as well as to old school friends from my youth who lived north and south of the metropolis. I have already mentioned my old friend who had joined the Metropolitan Police from Devon & Cornwall many years earlier and he was working in the side block of NSY so we met quite often while I was based in the main building.

Through the winter of 1983/84 we had been aware, but no more, of the renewed activities of the National Union of Mineworkers (NUM) under their relatively new leader. There had been an overtime ban since the autumn which it was apparent to everyone, particularly the NUM members, was having no tangible affect. By this time the Conservative Government elected four years earlier had presented and passed through Parliament legislation to seek to avoid the disruption caused by trades unions through the 1970s. This legislation, among other aspects, made it obligatory for strike action to follow only after a proper ballot of a union's membership. Without such a ballot, the NUM executive declared a strike on Monday 12th March, 1984.

With only a few weeks to go before the scheduled end of my attachment, my circumstances were about to change significantly.

16 National Reporting Centre

Before I draw an, inevitably abbreviated, picture of the operations within the National Reporting Centre throughout the National Union of Mineworkers (NUM) Dispute from March 1984 till March 1985, I must try and dispel some misconceptions, often purposefully created, regarding the policing operation during those fifty one weeks. There were people at the time who saw real capital to be achieved by trying to politicise the activities of the police and too many, academics, media people and politicians, have encouraged the continuation, even development, of that view.

In reality the actions of the police, throughout, was to try and maintain normality in areas where there were people, led by highly politically motivated individuals, hell bent upon destroying the peaceful existence of others and in some cases determined to overthrow the democratically elected government. The history of only a decade earlier told them that bringing down the government was feasible. Anyone who was, or is, critical that the police did not seek to apply the law for the benefit of all has not examined all the facts and certainly had, or have, a very short memory as to what unrestricted trades union activities brought through much of the 1970s. We still have half a box of candles in our cupboard from those days and, I suspect, so does everyone who lived through that period. That the policing effort in this country has been heavily, almost totally politicised, causes me and many of my former colleagues great consternation but it is the action of politicians over the past twenty years, not in the 1980s, that have brought us to this position.

Before describing the start of the long and drawn out dispute it is important to explain what the Association of Chief Police Officers had developed into through the Twentieth Century. All Officers above the rank of Chief Superintendent were members of ACPO and the structure outside of the Annual Conference was of the lead being taken by ACPO Council, made up of the Chief Constables and the two Commissioners. Each year, at their Conference in September, the next President Elect was identified and would be a Chief Constable or Metropolitan equivalent. That individual would become the President a year later and then be Immediate Past President for a further year after that. Hence there were three Chief Constables, nominated by their peers from across the country, who supported one-another in the task of guiding the Service and liaising with other bodies, including Government, wherever this was required. There was a tripartite structured arrangement to bring ACPO into regular contact with, but not control by, the Home Office and the Association of Police Authorities. The small permanent office of ACPO was in NSY and administered by a full-time General Secretary, who in 1984 was a retired ACC.

ACPO President's Staff Officer on the first day in the NRC at New Scotland Yard March 1984

That the police service today is heavily politicised is a product of continued and intentional government activity, by all political parties, over the past fifteen to twenty years. I will return to this matter towards the end of this book but, in 1984 and for some ten years afterwards, the police could genuinely hold that they remained a-political. It is no exaggeration to state that the concept from the formation of the Metropolitan Police in 1829 had been an easily recognisable and routinely unarmed body. The Service was made up of professionals who were overseen by partly elected authorities, under several titles over the years, but were independent of direct central and local political control. The Service saw its role as being the day to day administration of justice and with the key objective being to ensure the maintenance of the Queen's Peace for the sake of everyone.

What has been described in the preceding paragraphs did not always suit the politicians, either at local or national level, but for decades they recognised the value of an independence from political direction within policing. The 'monitored autonomy' of Chief Officers served the people admirably and stood well beside the independence of authority possessed by all Constables within their Forces. In a period of over 150 years, with a wide acceptance of discretion in the administration of the law, the police were able to provide justice. In the past two decades, the more that politicians have sought to limit the independence of Constables of all ranks, the less the public has found that it can rely upon their police to be an ever-present and impartial supporting arm.

As I have said, all of this political destruction of a long-established and well respected service was yet to come in 1984. Indeed, at that time, for long before and for a while thereafter, the British Police Service was heralded across the World as the archetypal model to try and emulate. Many police services around the world were modelled upon what had become established in this country and visits by senior officers to Bramshill were still recognised by many countries as a very worthwhile investment.

On Monday, 12th March, 1984 activity by the NUM in an effort to force those who saw no purpose in the strike to 'toe the line' in Nottinghamshire indicated what was to follow. The Nottinghamshire miners had resented being called upon to strike without their views having been balloted. On the following day, what was feared in Nottinghamshire came to be and the Chief Constable had totally inadequate numbers of Officers to confront the miner-versus-miner confrontations provoked by the NUM leadership's actions. With the warnings from the previous twenty four hours having not been ignored by the police, the then President of ACPO travelled south to London from his 'home' Force and held brief discussions with the involved Ministries and the Commissioner of the Metropolitan Police. As a result he decided to ask the Commissioner to arrange for the 'mothballed' facilities of the National Reporting Centre (NRC) to be set up in NSY. The pair of meeting rooms on the thirteenth floor had their dividing partition folded back and the store room next door had the equipment brought out.

At that time the most efficient means of electronic communication throughout the Service was the messaging facility of the Police National Computer. A message was sent out to all Forces informing them that the NRC would 'go live' from the Tuesday morning but with a status of 'monitoring only'. Hence, all Forces were made aware of the current situation and could anticipate that there may be a change to the 'monitoring only' status. The President had been a Metropolitan Officer in his earlier days in Service, as a Sergeant he had been involved in the planning of the State Funeral of Sir Winston Churchill, and was now the Chief Constable of a northern provincial force. He was well aware that if the NRC was required to operate in a full mutual aid and coordination role, there could be some reluctance in the provincial forces if they perceived this as being 'run by the Met.'

He recognised the potential benefit of involving provincial officers in the running of the NRC and realised that to allocate this to his own Staff Officer, as had occasionally been done for the very few previous NRC activations, would deprive him of that very direct personal support. On the advice of the ACPO General Secretary, he sought the help of the body that had not been available on previous occasions, and which held officers well equipped to become involved with an activation where public disorder was a reason. The enquiry of the Chief Superintendent brought the three provincial officers in the Unit, the Superintendent from South Wales, Chief Inspector and myself into the NRC. The Superintendent and I were to remain. The Superintendent had not been in London very long, only weeks, and I was anticipating departing from NSY only a few weeks after this change of role. In the event my original nine month attachment at NSY was to be extended by another year, to a total of twenty months.

Having been preparing for another, expected to be my final, meeting of the ACPO Public Order Sub-Committee, I found myself on the afternoon of Tuesday, 13th March, 1984 familiarising myself with what the Metropolitan Officers, drawn from several parts of NSY, were setting up on the thirteenth floor. The Police National Computer (PNC) messages were constructed, approved by the ACPO President and sent out to all Forces in England and Wales. While this was happening, there was yet more unlawful 'picketing' by men mainly from the Yorkshire areas of those in the Nottinghamshire Coalfield area who had not accepted the NUM leadership's non-balloted edict to strike. The Nottinghamshire men were not to formally declare their rejection of that instruction until 5th April but in fact kept going to work at their collieries throughout. Later they were to be instrumental in the creation of the Union of Democratic Mineworkers.

The National Reporting Centre went 'live' at 'monitoring only' status, from 0700 hours on Wednesday, 14th March. That day, but rejected without much consideration by the NUM leadership, the National Coal Board (NCB) Chairman presented an offer of a 5.2% pay rise with the condition that the twenty "most uneconomic pits" be closed and that there be an overall reduction in the NCB workforce across the UK of 20,000, to be achieved through 'natural wastage'. While the NRC was being staffed by the Metropolitan Officers, the Superintendent from South Wales and I, together with his Chief Inspector Staff Officer from Humberside, accompanied the ACPO President to the Home Office so that he could brief them as to what it was he had decided upon and he offered them sight of a daily report which we, his Staff Officers, would prepare.

The preparation of these reports started the day after those meetings and continued throughout the activation of the NRC. In the very first few days, the ACPO President remained in London and even helped with the manual effort of preparing the morning report. Soon, of course, his Force command responsibilities demanded his return North and the Welsh Superintendent and West Country Inspector became his physical representatives in the Centre for the bulk of the remaining long activation. He and, from the September ACPO Conference his successor, coincidentally the Chief Constable of Nottinghamshire, visited as and when they thought the need was there but soon recognised that they had acquired two safe pairs of hands in their temporary Staff Officers. To add to the daily report and to meet the need for current information for the Prime Minister to use during Prime Minister's Question Time, then scheduled as Parliament convened on each Thursday, the requirement grew for us to produce a Statistical Return for the President and which he offered to copy to the Home Office each Wednesday evening.

To explain the process that developed a bit ahead of describing the events as they unfolded, the daily report was collected by a senior civil servant from the Home Office at about nine o'clock each weekday morning. That official then went to the Energy Ministry for a daily conference and, of course, was the most well briefed individual at that table. The compilation of the weekly statistical return was a collation of information relayed from all affected Forces. The daily situation report was a more spontaneous process with information gleaned over the telephone from affected areas and, importantly, the media by we two Staff Officers and the Metropolitan Information Officer (the only Met Officer to be continually at the NRC throughout the months of activation).

From anything between five and seven o'clock each day, we received calls on a regular basis from the researchers for the television and radio stations. When they enquired of us what was current, we always asked what they knew and that was often more than us! All across the colliery areas everywhere in the country, there were 'cub' reporters out and about looking for the 'scoop' of the day. These people knew and travelled their local areas looking for the current NUM activity each morning and frequently identified gatherings of 'pickets' before they were identified by the local police who had to have resources concentrated upon the collieries where men were trying to go in to work. These conversations with the television and radio researchers each morning became an invaluable source of 'intelligence' as to what was the most likely concentration of activity that day.

Back to the first full day for the NRC, with the Home Office briefed, the President of ACPO met with a few Senior Officers from NSY in the NRC. At about twelve noon a telephone call was received from the Force Control Room in Nottinghamshire and was answered by the Superintendent from South Wales. Hearing one side of that conversation, he asked for repetition having seized a pen and paper, saying, "I had better write that down." The request was beyond what anyone in the room would have imagined. At that time mobile Police Support Units (PSUs) had become standardised across the country for Mutual Aid purposes (refined by the activities for the street disturbances in 1981) and comprised two protected personnel carriers containing, together, twenty Constables, two Sergeants and one Inspector. Nottinghamshire were asking for 50 PSUs to be with them at their Sherwood Lodge Headquarters by 1600 hours – 1,150 Officers in just under four hours.

Pleased that we had primed Forces but conscious of the traveling time involved, we set the Metropolitan staff, mainly Constables and Sergeants from the Courts Administration Department in NSY, ringing around to find the manpower and send it on its way. The load had to be spread and needed to recognise the standard commitment under the Mutual Aid arrangements for

Forces. This standing commitment had been set for some time at a PSU for each 200 of a Force's establishment. Hence a Force that was 1,000 Officers strong, and that included many of the Provincial Forces, was expected to be able to produce a maximum of five PSUs. The exercise proved to be a greater success, much greater, that any of us imagined and certainly was in excess of what others, Home Office, media or across the Service, had considered possible. Of the 50 PSUs, one half was late making the 1600 hours deadline because its carrier suffered a puncture on the journey.

The request from Nottinghamshire had required the Superintendent to reach for pen and paper because it did not stop at the 50 PSUs by four o'clock. The further request, spread over the next 48 hours, was for 65 PSUs (1,495 Officers) on each of four deployments to Sherwood Lodge. All of the consequent requests to Forces had to bear in mind their capability to provide and their commitments either side of each deployment. The room at the NRC had deployment boards around the walls opposite the large windows to show what aid was available and where deployed aid was currently committed. The layout of the room was in two 'L' shaped arrangements of tables. On one side of the room the Metropolitan staff sat with the current senior officer, a Superintendent of Chief Superintendent, adjacent to the Welsh Superintendent with far less desks for the 'ACPO' Staff. The Met side became known as the 'Controller's Side' and that for ACPO as the 'Command Side'. The Controller's Side was manned by about six to eight officers of Constable, Sergeant and Inspector Ranks between 0700hrs and 1900hrs and the room held a Chief Inspector, Inspector and Sergeant between 1900hrs and 0700hrs to monitor any night time activity.

For the first few weekends the Superintendent from South Wales and I took turns to stay at the NRC just in case that proved necessary. It soon became apparent that we could get away with being absent and depend upon briefing from the weekend cover by the Met. Chief Inspector when we returned on Sunday evening. From then on the pattern developed of one of us departing for our home on Friday lunch time and the other later in that day, dependent upon what activity there was in the colliery areas. We almost invariably returned on Sunday in the early evening. With our replacements having been found within the Public Order Forward Planning Unit, the maisonette at Swiss Cottage could not house us all so we sought the assistance of the administrative staff who shared the twelfth floor with POFPU and the Metropolitan Receiver. They found us a flat in a block just north of Oxford Street, the rest of the building at that time still occupied by married officers. Fortunately it had a small parking area with a securable gate and we travelled, customarily at silly hours between 0400 a.m. and 0600 a.m. each morning in my Austin Princess car. The car became so well known by the night security staff at NSY that the basement car park barrier was usually raised before we needed to stop.

I am going to permit myself a small diversion at this point. Unusually, because I remained in London, I was to get to know my replacement on the Public Order Forward Planning Unit. He was an Inspector from the Royal Ulster Constabulary. On one weekend several weeks after the start of the NRC activation, I invited him down to Keynsham for the weekend. Gill and the girls thought he looked like Tom Selick, then famous for the TV series Magnum. He was quite insulted when Gill told him over Sunday lunch as he was keen to point out that the actor was significantly older! On the Saturday that he was with us we went in my car for a tour around Bristol. Not because we planned it, our youngest daughter, Emma then age eight, was in the back seat of the car. It may have been just as well as we travelled down Grosvenor Road so that I could show him the Black & White Café, start point of the 1980 riots. There was the customary large gathering outside but when they looked into the car they did not just see two men, had they done so there may well have been assumptions that we were on a police patrol. When we emerged from City Road to head up to the Downs and Clifton Suspension Bridge, the Irish Inspector, who had spent his police service thus far in Belfast, confided that he felt very uneasy and "would not want to work here!"

Once the NRC was in full activation the ACPO agreement was that all mutual aid requests must be dealt with through that Centre and the more normal, force to force arrangements should not occur. This was, of course, the only way that the NRC could be fully conversant with what the nationwide picture was in respect of manpower availability. Within that first week the Centre started receiving calls for supporting PSUs from a much wider sector of the coal mining areas than just Nottinghamshire and plans were soon necessary to minimise the considerable travelling time being incurred by Units from the more far-flung supplying Forces. The answer was to provide accommodation in the receiving Force areas and send Officers from their Home Force areas on a weekly basis.

Negotiations in most areas produced agreements with local military units for the police officers to be accommodated in Army and RAF bases. These personnel were then deployed each day by the local Force wherever they were currently needed. There was one exception to this arrangement and that brought about by local politicians setting their will against supporting the Chief Constable in his efforts to maintain some semblance of order in an extremely divided community. In South Yorkshire, the Police Authority was not prepared to enable the Chief Constable to accept what became known within the Service as 'Residential Aid'.

The need to try and keep secure those few individuals who openly resisted the NUM command to strike was added to by the even more complex need to adequately police the colliery communities. In these areas victimisation and intimidation of miners and their families by their neighbours and, so called, colleagues was rife. Some other arrangement to supply adequate numbers was required. The answer became the day-by-day re-deployment of PSUs from surrounding colliery Force areas across the boundaries into neighbouring Forces. Although it was an essential daily occurrence in respect of South Yorkshire, it became quite a common practice across other borders and proved to make far better use of whatever levels of Mutual Aid there was in the wider area over each week. Further display boards were set up in the NRC to enable the monitoring of the deployments of this manpower. This was no mean logistical feat and required continual monitoring and redeployment throughout many days of the activation. We at the NRC never directed what aid was to be taken but had to be in as best a position possible to anticipate those requests when they came in.

The week-by-week allocations to match the requests for the provision of Mutual Aid in the form of PSUs settled into a moving pattern but one to which the Centre could respond with a practiced relative ease. There were, of course, more spontaneous requests which had to be resourced directly unless the temporary transfer from another area was feasible. Some locations produced specially demanding public disorder situations, notably the Orgreave Coking Plant where the convoys of imported coal from the Humber became a regular target and at which there was to be one of the largest and most violent series of demonstrations through May and June, 1984. Here, and elsewhere on a slightly lesser scale, the Chief Constable called for Dog Handlers and their dogs and Mounted Officers and their horses. While dogs were available from every Force the number of forces with mounted sections were far fewer.

In the effort to dispel any media hype regarding the role of the NRC, both ACPO Presidents during their term in charge welcomed a restricted number of visits by the mass media. Several times television crews came in to the room with the only restriction being the deployment displays on some of the walls. We also received many visits from politicians of all persuasion and often were visited by senior police officers. One occasion that remains strong in my recollection was that of the Senior Command Course from Bramshill. One of those being developed for Chief Officer Rank commented to me regarding how fortunate I was to be in NSY and away from the confrontation experienced by many Officers out near the picket lines. I agreed. He then went on to ask what sort of hours I worked and somewhat changed his view regarding the comfort of my situation. The norm was a start around 0500hrs and travel back to the flat mid-evening. On Wednesdays, with the statistical return to be completed and handed to the Home Office on behalf of the President, it was seldom before 2200hrs.

The most unique aspect of my role within the NRC has to be the extreme level of responsibility which it would be difficult to imagine had, or has, ever been in the hands of an Inspector. The new President visited the NRC and our little office next door within a short time of his taking over from his predecessor. Although his Force had been the one which had so benefited from the efficiency with which we acted on that first day in March, he seemed still to wonder what we were doing. Within minutes of starting to enquire what we did he realised just how complex and demanding was the role which we two Staff Officers filled. The President in March was also the Chairman of the ACPO General Purposes Committee, of which POFPU was the executive arm of the Public Order Sub-Committee. He, therefore, and with the new President still experiencing heavy demands upon his time in Nottinghamshire, retained a close interest in what we were doing but grew to rely upon our judgement as the NUM Dispute rolled on month after month.

From the early stages, we had a 'Home Counties' Deputy Chief Constable present each morning in the Centre. The theory was that they gave a greater level of authority in support of our contacts with the forces around the country. In reality they usually brought a sheaf of papers to work through and left us to the task with which we had become so familiar. The 'rota' for these attendances by the DCCs was taken on by the then Deputy of the Cambridgeshire Force and he would fill any days upon which he was unable to obtain the cooperation of one of his counterparts nearer to London. We, therefore, got to know him very well.

An example of the type of decision making required of me as an Inspector came one Friday lunchtime. The 'duty' DCC had been required to return early to his Force and it had been my Superintendent fellow Staff Officer's turn to make a lunchtime departure. One of the Met. Sergeants called me to a telephone to confirm the request he had just received from the Durham Police. In the main, because of their distance north, we had facilitated very few mutual aid requests from other Forces in that part of the country with the local forces looking after each other but keeping us informed. On this occasion, such arrangements had already been made in advance of an anticipated demonstration but the Force now had information that they were also to see a large scale 'picketing' blockade at one of their collieries. Presumably the local NUM leaders had perceived the difficulty that two centres of activity would cause the Durham Police Force.

There being no-one with whom to consult and it, by then, being recognised as not the role of the Superintendent in charge on the Controller side of the NRC, it was a matter for me. I asked the Met team to contact all the Forces with residential aid that week to see what was still with them. Lunchtime on a Friday was 'going home time' for the residential aid PSUs and they seldom wasted any time getting on the road back to their respective bases once all was clear from any lunchtime colliery 'wind-downs'. Of all the dozens of PSUs that had been deployed across the north midlands and north of England that week only five remained. They were from a midlands Force and, because they had not too far to travel had remained for lunch before departing home. I instructed that they should be asked to travel north immediately. A minute later there was a call from their host force enquiring as to whether the request for the Units to travel to Durham was accurate and I confirmed that it was.

Later that afternoon, with everything as quiet as could be expected and with the five PSUs securely on their way north, I left the NRC and made my long way home. With the preciously small amount of time with the family, I gave no further thought to Durham until I arrived back at NSY on the Sunday evening. The duty Chief Inspector told me that the report back was that the PSUs had arrived just in time to support the local and other mutual aid units. They had then been accommodated in local hostelries overnight and had returned to their home Force on the Saturday morning. I went about my usually busy evening and was back in, with the Welsh Superintendent, the following morning to launch into another week of long days. Later in the morning a man whom I vaguely recognised came in to the NRC and demanded to have identified to him Inspector Leach. I stood and he immediately started to tell me what he thought of my action on the previous Friday.

Realising, now, who he was, I invited him to accompany me to the side office, leaving the rest of the staff in the NRC quite frustrated that they were not going to witness what looked like a blossoming 'roasting'. To deny them such an experience was, of course, one of my reasons for asking the Chief Constable to move to the side office. There was a more important reason. Earlier that morning the ACPO President had arrived and was catching up a few telephone calls in the side office. As my berator was giving forth while entering the room, the President looked up and asked him what was wrong. He told the President what I had done on the Friday and how it had interfered with his Force's plans for providing aid in this current week. The President simply looked at me and asked, "Was that necessary, David?" I told him that there had been no suitable alternative. He looked at his fellow Chief Constable and said, "There you have it, David says it was necessary!" I did not at all mind, in fact quite liked, making such decisions when my ability was that well acknowledged and we felt that we would be supported. The decision on the Friday had caused some disruption to pre-set plans and had certainly cost a lot of money in travel and accommodation costs. What, at that time, was most important was that it had achieved the objective and Durham had not failed their community.

I will not go into extended or greater detail about how the NUM Dispute continued, there is probably another book here, but it was marked by a slow recognition in most areas that strike action to sustain a subsidised industry was not going to work. More men started to reveal what many had probably felt from the earliest days, their desire to resume working and remove their families from their reliance upon benefits and 'food banks'. Alongside the policing of the unlawful activities from the NUM Dispute there were a number of other matters of policing importance through that NRC activation. Some required the arranging of mutual aid while some did not. They included the tragic murder of Woman Constable Yvonne Fletcher, on 17th May, 1984. The granting of an eviction order against the long-standing encampments at Greenham Common, on 12th September. The IRA bombing of the Grand Hotel at Brighton, being used by senior members of the Government for their Annual Party Conference, from which four people died, on 12th October. Newly focused CND demonstrations outside Molesworth Air Station in Cambridgeshire on 5th February, 1985.

After the extremes of violence, requiring considerable and sometimes very physical policing action, most heavily covered by the mass media at Orgreave in the June, the dispute had gone on far too long. The real anguish for the rank and file of the NUM membership was not what appeared at the time on the television, it was what their families experienced daily in most of the colliery communities. With a long history of being supported by the Union, it should not be surprising that so many men saw it as their duty to support the NUM in return. Many from the start, recognised that the industry was in the middle of a long period of decline and wanted to keep working for as long as the economics of the situation would allow. Only in Nottinghamshire and with a few elsewhere was there a preparedness to resist the Union leadership. As time went on, so more men and in more areas started to seek to go back to work.

Largely for historic reasons the South Wales coalfield area had been, at least overtly, 'solid' in support of the strike action. In the autumn a few demonstrating their desire to return to work changed that situation. Across England and Wales there were increasing numbers of miners, reaching their thousands, returning to work in defiance of the continued Union call. Most tragically, and resulting in two striking miners being charged with murder, a taxi driver taking a miner back to work was killed when a block was dropped on his car from an over bridge. The Chief Constable of South Wales Police was most conscious of the long historic memories of English Police Officers being deployed in the Welsh valleys decades earlier and told us in the NRC that he would, if it became necessary, only take mutual aid from other Welsh Forces. With his neighbours being two of the numerically smaller forces this could have presented a real problem. We, of course, sought to be prepared to comply with his request but always saw the Avon and Somerset Constabulary, a short drive across the Severn Bridge, as a potential support if things got overwhelming. Fortunately they did not.

As the New Year dawned and the move back to work was causing increased problems in South Wales, the Chief Constable asked that his Superintendent, most experienced in commanding public disorder situations, must be returned from London. Our close working relationship and lasting consequent friendship meant that his being told of his imminent return to South Wales was not hidden from me. The real question, for me, was what would his departure bring? Through the autumn of 1984, with the dependence the President was placing upon the two of us recognised, we received on four successive weeks a Superintendent from a Home Counties force to be familiarised with what the NRC Staff Officer role demanded. They, of course, varied in their personal abilities and team qualities but in a week, even of our long days, they acquired only a partial appreciation of what was required.

The Deputy from Cambridgeshire was given the task of speaking with me as he was first of the ACPO members to come to the NRC after the news of the Superintendents return. With the look of someone who knew what the answer would be, he enquired as to whether I was prepared to carry on as we had for the past ten months but with one of the Home Counties Superintendents substituted for the man from South Wales. I told him that the situation over the past ten months had been a 'double act', with us sharing everything, good and not so good. I was not prepared at this juncture, with the large numbers of miners returning to work and the end not in sight but evidently not too far away, to do all the work necessary to keep everything going as well as ever and for someone else to come in and be recognised as being 'in charge'. He had anticipated that reaction and offered another possible solution. Would I run the operation on the Command Side of the NRC single handedly? This, I agreed, was the best solution.

The ACPO Officers involved were not easy about the Command Side being seen to be in the hands of an Inspector and sought the support of my Chief Constable that he promote me to Chief Inspector. When I returned home that Friday evening, Gill told me that the Superintendent Personnel from Force Headquarters had asked that I see the Chief Constable at nine o'clock on Monday morning. With the Superintendent about to start his last week at the NRC before departing back to South Wales, I telephoned him at home and told him that I would not be back in London until the Monday afternoon. On Monday morning I paraded before the Chief Constable to be given quite a rigorous enquiry as to what it was I was doing in London. It has to be said that, except for occasional telephone conversations with the ACC who had sent me to the POFPU in 1983, there had been no enquiry regarding how I was getting on in all that long time away. After about twenty minutes of challenging interview, he ended by congratulating me on my temporary promotion to Chief Inspector. I went to the stores to pick up a handful of 'pips', rang Gill with the good news and drove back to London.

Within weeks, with the date for the end of the strike declared by the NUM Executive as being 3rd March, 1985, the close of the NRC took several days to accomplish. Coincidentally, Gill was significantly unwell and I found myself doing the trip between London and my home several times as the closure of the NRC was being accomplished. As we were 'decommissioning' the Centre, the former President and General Purposes Committee Chairman of ACPO came to London and asked if I would take on the task of coordinating the extensive de-briefing that ACPO felt was required. The side office had not been handed back to the Metropolitan administrators and I could use it. I explained to him that my original nine month attachment had already reached twenty months and I would be pleased to take on the task but from Bristol. He accepted my reasons and told me he would make the further request of my Chief Constable for my involvement and for office accommodation for me in Bristol.

When I returned to Old Bridewell the following Monday, I found that there had been no effort on anyone's part to find me office accommodation and my search around the buildings produced only the tea room on the top floor used by the Task Force Officers. They were kind enough to sacrifice this facility for my benefit and I managed to find a desk and chair and was issued by the stores department with a metal four-drawer filing cabinet. The cabinet was to follow me around for the rest of my time! There was still a considerable shortfall in understanding and appreciation within the Force as to what it was I was doing. It continued to be only the ACC who sent me to London who had any real recognition of what I had done and was still doing within ACPO.

The ACPO debrief of the extensive policing operations to meet the demands created by the NUM Dispute was split between eleven Working Parties. I became the 'secretary' for two of them, the one relating to the NRC and that for Mutual Aid. I also had the overall responsibility for the coordination of the reports from those and the other nine groups. Attending meetings and conferring with the Chief Constable Chairman of the ACPO General Purposes Committee meant a significant amount of travel. The office in NSY remained at my disposal and proved useful at times but, it has to be confessed, remained empty for much of the time.

My first rail journey to Hull resulted in my being picked up at the railway station by the Chief's driver and he took me for a trip across the Humber Bridge before depositing me at the nearby large hotel. The following morning the Chief Constable picked me up on his way in to the headquarters and we spent much of the day with me bringing him up to date with the current situation with the debrief groups. On return I was admonished by the Superintendent Administration regarding the extortionate hotel bill and was thankful that it had not been me that had made the reservation. On further such visits I arranged my own accommodation in a commercial hotel near the city centre and that proved much more satisfactory from the points of view of both cost and convenience.

Another occasional trip was to the Cambridgeshire Police Headquarters at Huntingdon but a quick examination of the options brought me to the conclusion that the car was best. I had piled on mileage on the Austin Princess while in London and changed it for an Ambassador when I returned to Bristol in the spring of 1985. Now I was doing the same to the odometer on this car! The mileage rates payable at that time, commonly known within the Service as 'public transport rate', were not overly generous but did make a small contribution towards the car's running costs, until the part-exchange for the next car was included in the equation.

The target date for all the debrief groups was set about a month before the September, 1985 ACPO Conference, scheduled to take place at Preston. With much of the material assembled, I spent four weeks living in 'single men's accommodation' and working at Hessle Police Station with the Humber Bridge visible from the office window. The Chief Constable's former Staff Officer had been promoted to Superintendent since the end of the NUM Dispute and we worked together on the overall ACPO Debrief Report. After the August Bank Holiday Monday, I travelled to start my four weeks and returned home each weekend.

The ACPO Conference presentation took place at Preston on 12th September, 1985 and I remained involved with the ACPO debrief at Hull and in London over the following nearly three weeks. This allowed for the full preparation of the Debrief Report for the Association and for the proper closure and handing back of the little office in NSY. I had, through the time I had been working for ACPO back in Bristol, also assisted my interested ACC with his research into changes to the Force structure. He it was who saw the obvious best place for me as my return to the Force proper grew nearer. With the ACPO commitment completed and my final return journey from Hull accomplished the previous Friday, I started in the new post on 30th September, 1985 – coincidentally our eighteenth wedding anniversary!

17 Force Logistics Office

I took up the new role as my predecessor moved out to take charge of a Chief Inspector Sub-Division, so we both did well out of the change. The role of Force Logistics Officer was one for a Chief Inspector and I anticipated my temporary promotion of eight months earlier would be confirmed within a short time. Despite a few enquiries of the Personnel Department this was not to be the case. That confirmation did not occur until the week of the anniversary of my temporary elevation. There was really only one conclusion to be reached, that the Chief Constable wanted to press home to me that he and not the President of ACPO was the promoting authority in the Force. His reluctance had been obvious at that earlier time but he later introduced me to the Lord Lieutenant of the County of Avon as his only 'field promotion'. It has always been a cause for wonderment on my part that a Force should have one of its number in what was a vital key position in the largest policing operation the world has ever seen yet only one ACC recognised its worth at the time and one other later.

Regardless of the 'acting' prefix to the rank for that further four months, I got on with the new task. The Logistics Office came within the Support Services Headquarters Division and, for some unknown earlier convenience, was shown as being under the Superintendent War Duties. This was, in fact, a Regional Appointment stemming from the continued concerns for Civil Defence throughout the 'Cold War' period. The War Duties Office consisted of the Superintendent and a clerk/typist, who was a real anchor for the role as the Superintendent was frequently away performing his liaison role with the Forces of the South West, various London based Government Offices and the military. He greeted me on the first morning and did so every day he was not elsewhere. Our team were an Inspector, who was really my working partner, and another Inspector with the specific post of Special Events. His main focus was planning for events, such as Royal Visits and large annual gatherings and readers will remember my earlier involvement with the role from Chapter Fourteen. In fact we worked as a team and our occasional visits from our Superintendent usually brought the greeting that we were his 'three degrees', all of us possessing degree qualifications.

The first few months in the post were a bit of an anti-climax after the engrossed involvement with ACPO, the Forward Planning Unit and the NRC of the preceding more than two years. We made a start, in what was to be a bit of a lull before a storm, in updating what were known as Permanent Operational Orders - contingency plans for known potential causes for concern. These included the actions necessary to confront a resurgence of disorder in, what was known nationally in all such areas, as the 'inner city' and various potentially hazardous locations such as the two nuclear power stations, one on the Somerset coast and the other beside the Severn Estuary in South Gloucestershire, and a number of specific sites around Avonmouth and in other parts of the Force area. Not being particularly keen on filing, this period did serve to 'bring me down to earth' and probably was good for me in the longer run.

As with some of the previous chapters, it is impossible to totally separate the description of what took place through my two years in the Force Logistics role either by topic or chronologically. I trust that the descriptions that follow will not become confused by this difficulty. At one point, after the activities in the office had become rather more demanding, and interesting, we were informed of a visit from Her Majesty's Inspector of Constabulary. Before his arrival, we received a visit from our Chief Superintendent, Support Services who was, of course, keen to ensure that the HMI's visit reflected well upon the Force, and him. With so many 'balls in the air' at any one time, (and my natural aversion to filing) we had developed a system whereby the currently active files rested on a table next to the desks used by me and the logistics Inspector. The Chief Superintendent was not at all content that these files were on display.

On the day of the HMI's visit, the files remained on the table and I could sense the unease of the Chief Superintendent and the Chief Constable when the HMI eyed the dozen or so files as soon as he entered our office. He enquired as to what they were and I told him that they were all relating to matters with which we were currently dealing and were left accessible as they were regularly being updated. He opened one and asked me to what it related. I was, of course, able to tell him in detail what the file contained, the current point we had reached in progressing it and what it was we hoped to achieve before it was completed and filed away. He reached for another file and we repeated the information for that and a couple more. He thanked us for our time and congratulated us on our attention to detail. The Chief Superintendent turned and winked as he left behind the more senior officers.

The more interesting aspect was that the ACC (Ops), he who had sent me to London two and a half years earlier, looked upon the three of us as his 'staff officers' and one of us attended his office, across the road in Old Bridewell, each morning to share in the briefing of the days either side of those sessions. In addition, there were a number of projects current at that time and my recent experiences, although still not widely understood, and the logistics role I now occupied seemed to make me recognised as a useful member of such groups. They included the ACC's on-going review of the policing arrangements within the Force (a topic to be revisited more than once in my remaining service and later), an air support working party and the identification of equipment and procedures for the tape recording of interviews (a new legal requirement for all police station interviews of potential culprits).

There were a number of visits back to New Scotland Yard regarding the finalising of files and storage of National Reporting Centre items. The ACPO Review Document, following the extensive debrief and ACPO Conference debate, were filed in the ACPO Office at NSY. That review had come to the conclusion that the name National Reporting Centre did not adequately describe what the Centre was all about. In truth the extent of the activities there through the NUM Dispute activation probably defied a brief but fully explanatory title. The conclusion was that it should, in future, be called the Mutual Aid Coordination Centre (MACC), a somewhat unfortunate choice as those initials already meant in police/military liaison terms Military Aid to the Civil Community, something to be seen on a surprisingly large scale during the 2001 Foot & Mouth disease epidemic. I say 'surprisingly' because I could not imagine the military being required by Government to take such a lead from the police even only ten years earlier.

There ran through that winter and into the next spring, the planning and liaison required for an anti-terrorist exercise. This involved contact with the many agencies who become involved with such occurrences and was to run through an overnight period at RAF Locking, near Weston-super-Mare. The process of planning the exercise rested largely upon the Inspector in the office as it was decided, at an early stage, that I was to act as Staff Officer to the night shift commander, being 'played' by the DCC from Gloucestershire. I purposely kept a distance from the Inspector's planning of the scenario so that our performance on the night in the middle of the exercise would be as realistic as possible. I also knew that, just as I would have done, he would have more than one possible scenario so that too great an anticipation of what was likely to happen next could be unwise.

It must be remembered that the planning and conduct of this exercise came only six years after the Iranian Embassy Siege, so its meaning was quite relevant to both the police and military who were involved at RAF Locking over those couple of days. Being on the night shift the DCC from Gloucestershire and I did not see the climax but were there for what looked as though it was the move away from the relatively static hostage situation overnight. It was not bad practice for the three of us from the Logistics Office as there was to be a real hostage situation during our time together. A prisoner at Pucklechurch Prison, a young offenders' institution since privatised and given a new name, took a fellow inmate hostage. The hostage negotiators, whose training had been established by my old boss in POFPU, now moved on to the West Midlands Police, were called upon. The usual tactic, if it can be permitted, is to play such events for as long as they do not escalate violently and, on this occasion, that succeeded after several hours.

Alongside of all his planning, for exercise and the real world, in April 1986 there came a significant problem at HMP Horfield in Bristol. This was alongside the concerns mounting nationally regarding impending 'industrial action' by members of the Prison Service. We held talks with the regional management, then based at Flowers Hill, Brislington in Bristol and visited prisons to see what may be required. The action at Bristol took its own course, with one wing of the prison being in nothing short of a 'prison riot' situation. The Inspector from the Office accompanied the ACC to 'C' Division to liaise with the Divisional Commander and then to the prison for discussions with the Governor. I went to the office adjacent to the Force Control Room for maximum access to communications of all types.

Mid-evening, the Inspector telephoned me and relayed a message from the ACC. The query was in regard to what was the 'authority' of the police within the walls of a prison? With totally inadequate manpower within the Prison

Officer establishment at Horfield and the later mobilisation plans within HM Prison Service not yet fully developed, it seemed that only a police intervention would solve the current situation but neither the Prison Governor nor the ACC were totally sure of the ground they stood on. With my little orange book still in my brief case from the recent long spell in NSY, I set about trying to find someone who would know. There was a number for the Prison Service Control within the Home Office but no response from that number. No Police Service out of hours liaison at the Home Office had been perceived to be necessary before all the civil servants had gone home earlier that evening. I, eventually, obtained a reply from one of the numbers in my little book and spoke with a man with whom I had some contact during the NUM Dispute.

Pleased to help, he promised to return the call after trying to find someone in the Prison Service corridors of the Home Office. When he came back to me I think that neither of us were really surprised by what he had been told. His relatively senior position in the Police Department had meant that he managed to gain access to the Prison Service monitoring centre. When he asked my question he was met by much shrugging of shoulders and the conclusion that it must have been so long since any police intervention on a significant scale was required within a prison that no one knew the answer.

I went back to the ACC with nothing more than an opinion - mine! If there is no precedent, the police must do what they have always had to do in such situations, exercise their discretion within their best judgement. With the required manpower already assembled outside the prison as a precaution against a 'break-out' the ACC had the necessary capability at his fingertips. More crucially, the blocks of 'low-rise' flats in the inner city area of Bristol had prompted quite a concentration of shield training for gaining access up the stairwells of such buildings. The only difference within the prison was that the stairwells were on the inside rather than the outside of the building. The plan was established and approved by the ACC and totally acceptance by the Prison Governor. The Officers made their entry to the affected block. Fortunately, and not really surprisingly, the obvious show of intent by the police officers brought an immediate capitulation by all the inmates, who returned with some haste to their respective cells.

The national concern regarding the Prison Officers' dispute brought a new activation of the old NRC, now MACC, and I was asked to go to London to assist the new team in getting things started. The request was only for a couple of days and I was, after my previous and significantly extended time away from home, determined that I would not get any more involved than was necessary. As it was, three days and couple of nights in London and I was back home, with a team in London who actually found that this activation was no great challenge. Its focus on this occasion was to monitor and liaise with Forces over the custody of prisoners sent from courts and not accepted by the prisons. Across the country, not least in Bristol, huge numbers of remanded and sentenced prisoners came from the courts each day and had to be housed in police cells where no prison was prepared to accept them.

An on-going problem over several years through the 1980s had been the crush and often accompanying violence around the traditionally peaceful celebration of the Summer Solstice at Stonehenge. In the run-up for several years, large gatherings of mainly young people, variously known as 'hippies' or 'travellers' had been in Wiltshire and the surrounding counties for some weeks before the end of June event. In 1986 I spent the weekend with a new ACC, who had started his police career in Devon & Cornwall, and we actually walked through the crowds on the Pilton (Glastonbury) Festival site for the first time in years. In 1987, I spent the Solstice eve and dawn in a liaison role at the Wiltshire Control in Devizes.

In 1985 there had been a significant confrontation between travellers and police officers in what became known as 'the bean field' and similar convoys of travellers in 1986 brought fears that there would be a re-run. This time the focus, in early June, was in Hampshire. Although not in the South West ACPO Region, the experience of the Forces surrounding Wiltshire and our own regarding the travellers roving around Somerset around the time of the 'Glastonbury Festival' at Pilton, meant Hampshire looked across the regional boundary for support. After several hours of preparation during the day, I was picked up at Old Bridewell Headquarters by a Traffic Constable, who was to be my driver as I took charge of our mutual aid of three PSUs (six personnel carriers) with which we rendezvoused at Junction 18 of the M4 at 2100 hours on Sunday, 8th June, 1986.

We travelled up the M4 then South to meet our Hampshire motorcycle escort into that Force's Netley Training Establishment. There we were all provided with a 'hot dog' and I attended the senior officers' briefing while the PSUs were shown a film of the activities a year earlier in 'the bean field'. It had, apparently, been the intention of the Hampshire ACPO group that this video should signify some of the confrontational issues to be avoided for the current day's policing operation. Soon, we set off in a huge and long convoy, equipped with aerial photographs which identified each contingent's area of the encampment for which we would take responsibility. Our objective was to clear the site, spread along and just a short way into the brush from a minor road. Our instructions were to move everyone on foot and for any vehicles to be seized under the conditions both of Common Law and the Eviction Order obtained by the New Forest Authority.

There was a minor problem in that the convoy had been carefully estimated so that our sector of tents and vehicles would be adjacent to where we ended up when the line of police vehicles stopped. Unfortunately, there had been the intention to include dog handlers and their animals but this had been reversed at a late stage. The absence of the dog vans in the convoy had a small impact upon where we stopped but we soon identified that we had to back-track a short distance to get to our 'sector'. The eviction was not much of a problem, provided we did not stand down-wind of a 'bender' (home-made tent of bent branches and canvas) as it was opened to reveal the unkempt group inside. All were gathered on the road and a contingent of Traffic Officers took the vehicles they could get started to a large parking area. Our main difficulty as a Force group was that we had to allocate one of our PSUs to accompany the walking travellers out of the Forest and towards Dorset. This, of course, split us up but the Inspector of that PSU was more than capable of commanding his Unit.

The remaining two PSUs, me and the Traffic driver were directed to a Dorset feeding van, also on aid to Hampshire, for refreshment, it now being after 1000 hours on Monday, 9th June. The van served up a cup of tea and a 'hot dog'. We then made up our own little convoy for the journey back to Netley. I attended a Senior Officers' debriefing which was somewhat premature as most contingents had at least one PSU still escorting the foot travellers. I took the opportunity of access to a telephone to report back to the Support Services Chief Superintendent at New Bridewell. I then joined the long queue for the food table but must admit to being somewhat disappointed that, after sixteen hours since we left our own headquarters and only two 'hot dogs', we were served sausage and mashed potato!

With the four protected personnel carriers making their separate ways back to their home stations and the PSU still committed expecting to do likewise before too long, the Traffic man took me at some pace back to New Bridewell. There, I updated the Force Control Inspector and, at 1600 hours (twenty two and a half hours after leaving there) was called upon to provide breakdowns of the events to both the Support Services command and, across the road in Old Bridewell, to the ACC (Operations). Another three quarters of an hour and I was able to 'sign off' and go home to bed. With Monday having run directly out of Sunday, on Tuesday I returned to the office a bit later than my usual time, at 7.45a.m., to set off for Hereford to engage with the Royal Army Ordnance Corps in a planning meeting for a series of 'Cider Nightmare' bomb disposal exercises.

I have not had a sequel for quite a few pages, and this is really more of an 'aside'. Before we moved our home from our first own house to the other side of Keynsham, I had sold the little Honda 90 before we moved and bought a 1961 BSA 650cc motorcycle after we had settled in at the new address. I almost invariably used the bike for the journey between home and New Bridewell when I was on shifts on 'A' Division but it was not often convenient in the Logistics role as I often had to use my car while on duty. We had a large group of travellers, before they reached the New Forest, encamped at Beach, between Bristol and Bath beneath Lansdown hill. Wanting to know what their intentions were, one evening I got the old bike out and in jeans and tee shirt rode up the lane between their encampments. The bike meant that I was immediately accepted by the travellers, many of whom had similarly old machines. I was told that they would be leaving in a couple more days and that turned out to be exactly what they did.

At one stage during the gatherings in 1986 around the Frome area, between Pilton and Stonehenge, we were told by a local farmer that he had seen that some of the travellers were carrying crossbows. Our immediate question to be answered was whether the police riot shield then produced for police use would be protection against such a weapon. Reaching, once more, for my little orange book of telephone numbers, I contacted one of the doctor scientists at the Home Office Scientific Branch at Sandridge, St Albans. Having explained the dilemma, he promised to get back to me as soon as possible with the result of their findings. They purchased what was said to be the most powerful crossbow on the market at the time and fired it at a standard police riot shield. They discovered that the crossbow bolt penetrated the shield but became lodged before it had passed half of its length through the polycarbonate. Apparently, polycarbonate when penetrated seeks to bond back together immediately. What was discovered was that the 'healing' process was so rapid that the polycarbonate was squeezing the bolt immediately that it had penetrated the shield and the friction caused by this process slowed the bolt to a stop well before it had reached a point where it could pass right through the shield. Some comfort and a piece of information we immediately shared with all other Forces.

The largest operation for which an Operational Order was required during my two years in the Logistics Office came from a meeting in the ACC (Operations) office at teatime on Thursday, 4th September, 1986. A new Superintendent had recently been posted to command the sub-division at Trinity Road and it had been identified to him that the premises subject of the drug and unlicensed alcohol sales raid in 1980 was re-emerging. The 'softly-softly' approach encouraged by the most senior officers, to seek to avoid another riot, had brought the unintended resultant feeling among the drug dealers that they could operate with impunity. The Superintendent had brought the issue to the ACC as he was not prepared to allow this trade to continue but needed support in order to combat it. The Deputy Chief Constable was asked to the meeting, as were senior officers from the Community Relations Department and Traffic Department. It was decided, in a short meeting, that action was required but it would need to be well planned and there would need to be a significant element of surprise if it was to be successful. The following morning, the outline of the prospective operation was presented to and agreed by the Chief Constable.

The team, with me acting in the coordinating role, went about furthering their respective parts in the plan. The local station at Trinity Road found and manned an observation point with a view of the section of Grosvenor Road in front of the Black & White Café. The Traffic Department set about hiring coaches and, crucially, three soft sided lorries and established timings for the journeys to Grosvenor Road from variously distant holding areas, one some miles away out near J1 of the M32. In addition to drawing together the overall operational order, with which I received the assistance over the weekend of the War Duties clerk typist, I had to plan how we were to draw together the largest single deployment of our force manpower on the targeted day, Thursday, 11th September.

Our presence in the Logistics Office over the intervening weekend could not go unnoticed as there was a routine for the Control Room staff to carry out security checks of all the floors in New Bridewell. The visit from a Constable was soon followed by one from the duty Inspector, hoping that I would tell him more, but there was a real need for the number of people knowing what we were doing to be extremely limited. It was a tradition at the time for all planned operations to carry an invented title which had the same initial letter as that of the Division on which it was to take place. In recent months the repercussion of the newspaper dispute in London, as production moved away from Fleet Street, had been demonstrations at a distribution depot near J18 of the M4 at Old Sodbury. We, therefore, called it 'Operation Delivery' and all bar those on 'D' Division seemed to have accepted, as more had to become involved, that the newspaper transfer point was the venue. Those on 'D' Division were sceptical that they would gain such support!

With a draft order and the other departments having been busy, the next phase of this unusual operation was agreed by the ACC. Over preceding months he had held, with some significant input from our office, a series of seminars to familiarise senior officers and key players from all parts of the Force, especially headquarters departments, with what was required to confront large scale operations. This training now brought its full benefit as he called the many sector commanders and their deputies to Kingsweston House on the Wednesday. I had, the day before, contacted all Divisional Commanders with the 'shock' request for many more PSUs than they would normally be able to supply. Their relief was audible when I explained that the overtime bill was to be handled from headquarters. This contact also required the senior officers they nominated to be at the pre-briefing on the Wednesday. Knowing that our internal demands for manpower would exhaust our capabilities, I contacted the ACC Operations in each of our neighbouring Forces to pre-warn them, confidentially, that we may be seeking urgent support from them on the Thursday night.

The sector command teams were provided with copies of the overall plan which the War Duties clerk/typist had produced from my dictation and were required by the ACC to go to separate training rooms in Kingsweston House to create their own micro-plan for their own part of the operation. They then returned to the conference room and presented their 'bit' to the rest of us. With some minor fine-tuning, their sector plans were incorporated into the overall Operational Order. This necessitated another late night, there had been no other kind since the previous Thursday, and the production of a composite order for the final briefing on Thursday lunchtime. The benefit of the process adopted by the ACC was that every sector commander had a really intimate knowledge of his own planning within his area of responsibility and had heard more than he would have read from the Order through the presentations in the conference room.

The timings by the Traffic Department proved to be invaluable and, when the time to move was established, each holding area sent its units away at appropriately slightly different times to reach their locations in the St Pauls area on time. The three soft sided lorries had to take the journey from the M32 J1 slowly as each contained three PSUs, a total of 69 Officers. The intention and briefing was for them to stop in Grosvenor Road, one directly in front of Brighton Street and the others front and rear of that vehicle. They arrived in the road with the first lorry outside the Black and White Café and the others close behind. Although the slight variation from the intended point at which the Officers jumped from the lorries was not overly problematic it did point up for the debrief the importance of adequately briefing such key personnel as the three Constables driving the lorries. A mixture of hired coaches and our own crew busses brought officers to other strategic points from different start-off points and coaches were used again to convey the relatively few arrested back to Trinity Road Police Station.

The timings by the Traffic Department were 'spot-on' with all of the near 600 Officers deployed to their planned locations within less than a minute of each other. The surprise element was achieved by the use of the lorries, which had been very easy to obtain by Constables with HGV licences simply hiring them for the day. More difficult, certainly in 1986, was the obtaining of coaches. All coach operators hired out their coaches complete with their own employee as driver. The Traffic Department managed this aspect by going to coach operators well outside the Bristol area and offering the owner an operational necessity argument for our own qualified drivers to have the vehicles for the day.

We had looked at avoiding the mid-afternoon, mindful of that timing problem in 1980, but had to 'go' when the observation point told us that dealing on the street was visible. Despite the timing difficulty, the operation itself was a resounding success and the disturbances that followed it, which lasted a couple of evenings were contained. A point of self-criticism had to be that we stuck too long to the sectors and deployments for the operation which made redeployment to confront the moving street disorder situation less fluid than was ideal. On the plus side, of course, there was no shortage of immediately available, equipped and trained, Officers and, thanks to the seminars at Kingsweston, those capable of commanding the units. As the situation went on beyond what was really the end of the planned operation, I made the calls necessary to bring in the mutual aid from the Forces I had contacted a couple of days before and all arrived to look after the night shift and, importantly, relieve much of our own manpower after a long, and in places strenuous, day.

One of the lessons learned from 1980 was the importance of fully debriefing the operation and its, fortunately not too serious, aftermath. This we most certainly did and involved most of the key players in the exercise. The most significant effect of the operation was that it restored police authority in an area where it had definitely slipped and made the task of the local Officers somewhat easier. The operation had demonstrated to the law breakers and, more importantly, to the law abiding in the area that policing the street had returned to what was, then, the expected norm. In the early aftermath, we set up foot patrols around the immediate affected area with Officers in pairs but each pair monitored from a visible distance by a Task Force Unit of a Sergeant and five or six Constables. A few days working in that way to safeguard the patrolling Officers soon enabled us to reduce the back-up.

An aside – a comment on the evening of Operation Delivery demonstrated to me that it is never safe to speak too soon. With the small control room at Trinity Road monitoring a successful operation as we reached teatime on that Thursday, I went into the side office in which the Logistics Office Inspectors were ready for what may come next. At the time there was a popular programme on television called The 'A' Team and I quoted one of the common sayings from it, "I do like to see a good plan coming together!" Almost immediately from behind me the noise level in the little control room grew louder as the follow-up disturbances started.

The longer term consequence for me of this operation, coming less than a year after my closing down my involvement with ACPO after the NUM Dispute, was the demand from elsewhere for me to share the Avon and Somerset experience with others. Most immediate were talks to the Public Order Command Band courses, emanating from the Hendon trainers' training in 1984 and delayed in rolling out by the demands of policing the disorders from the NUM Dispute and inner city disturbances in 1985. To remind the reader, these courses were for those of Chief Inspector up to Chief Superintendent ranks to enable them to take command roles in large scale public disorder, with the additional knock-on benefit for command in all types of major incident.

My input, describing the best structure and logistical issues, occupied an afternoon session on each course at Devizes for the South West Region and a full morning at Bridgend for the Wales Region. At that time a former Sergeant, who had been a Constable on my Group at Central Police Station a few years earlier, had resigned and taken up a post as a lecturer at the University of South Wales in Pontypridd and was running the course for Officers from several Forces, including our own, to obtain a degree. I attended on numerous courses to speak about the logistics and command of policing large scale events. Less auspiciously, the Superintendent from South Wales had, since 1985, given a presentation to the large Inspectors' Course at the Police College at Bramshill. On one occasion he was unable to match the date and telephoned me requesting that I fill the slot. He sent the papers which he used across to me by the kind cooperation of a South Wales traffic motorcyclist, who I expect enjoyed his trip 'abroad'. I did some homework and went off to Bramshill with his package under my arm. The visual aids technician took the slides from the pack and, after a full lunch, I stood in front of an Assembly Hall containing about 130 Inspectors from all over the UK.

I could see, about half an hour in, that the lunch and the fact that it was a Monday and many would have driven many miles since that morning were having a soporific affect. It was plain to see that one or two were struggling to keep their eyes open and others were apparently straining to see what was on the huge screen behind me. When I checked, I found that I could only just make out the wording on the slides of the display boards from the NRC. I asked for those in the audience to tell me whether they could see what was on the slides and a few responded, all negatively. I called a halt at that point and invited the audience to take the ten minute break between the double period session early. When we all returned, I abandoned the notes and the projector and spent the next hour and a quarter wandering around the platform talking about the NRC activation purely from that recent memory. That was better!

Other than the on-going Review of Policing Structure with the ACC and my interesting involvement with the Air Support Working Party the only other really significant event was a gas explosion at Wickwar. A serving Constable returned home from a night shift early on Thursday, 8th January, 1987 and smelt gas as he entered his home in an old house close to the centre of the village. He immediately got his wife out of the house and awakened his neighbours for them to also evacuate. Shortly afterwards, it was concluded that it was probably when his central heating systems started up, there was an explosion causing extensive damage. Thanks to the quick thinking of the Constable, no-one was hurt and he was, later, awarded a BEM for his prompt action.

When I arrived at Wickwar to assist with the 'major incident' arrangements, the ACC, who had arrived separately, wanted to know why the senior officers from the Fire Brigade and Ambulance Service had mobile telephones while he did not. I knew that there was, at that time, one mobile telephone held in the emergency cupboard in Force Control and arranged for it to be ferried out to us by patrol car. It has to be said that in those times the coverage from the cellular telephone system was quite poor and the telephones were a handset atop a battery nearly the size of a breezeblock. They were so heavy that they came in a satchel with a robust shoulder strap to enable their transportation while on foot. After the event, the ACC insisted that I obtain another such telephone to be taken out for use on any future operations and held in the Logistics Office. I arranged for the Chief Inspector in Communications Planning to purchase a telephone and, at his insistence, funded it from my emergency equipment budget. I have surprised many over the intervening years by identifying that this piece of equipment cost, in 1987, a handsome £1,999.

Throughout my time in the Force Logistics Office I was periodically contacted by ACPO, New Scotland Yard or individual Forces from around the country to check the records that I had retained in the four-drawer filing cabinet issued to me for the Debrief Review of the Policing of the NUM Dispute. These enquiries were usually to settle confusion as to what mutual aid had been provided on any given week by one force to another. Such enquiries actually continued for close on three years after the end of the NUM Dispute, into 1988.

My more Senior Officers, particularly the ACC who sent me to London in 1983 and the DCC who had seen my involvement in Operation Delivery, responded to the perceived need on the part of the Chief Constable for me to gain operational command experience. An exchange was arranged between my headquarters position and the Chief Inspector's Sub-Division at Chipping Sodbury. I will relate in the next chapter how that experience was to last a further three years, largely, I think, because these two 'sponsors' moved on. The ACC retired and the DCC moved up to Merseyside, where he became their Chief Constable. No regrets as running a sub-division proved to be an enjoyable phase in my career and the experience just related of having been involved in every major job in the Force at that busy time brought its own rewards in many ways.

18 Chipping Sodbury

Before my transfer to Chipping Sodbury, I paid a visit to tie up with my predecessor and for us to exchange at least some of the information each of us would need to take up our new roles. There were, of course, a few telephone calls between us as we settled in to our respective offices but we, of course, each approached the other's former role by applying our own 'stamp'. My predecessor had favoured a very formal application of his command over the sub-division, accurately informing me that I would find that everything was fully recorded in the files within the office. I favoured an approach which relied far more on delegated authority, with Officers, particularly the Sergeants assuming more responsibility for day-to-day decision making. Whereas my predecessor gave most of his instructions by way of written reports requiring action by the Sergeants or individual Officers, I tended to rely upon them to respond to a verbal instruction or, even, take action without always seeking my view.

At that time and for most of my police service, I smoked a pipe and, in those days, smoking in the police stations had not yet been seen as a problem, although it may have been by some non-smokers throughout time. I found that tea breaks and a smoke with the other Officers enjoying the breaks was an excellent time to get to know people and, just as important, for them to get to know me and my general attitudes and expectations. I adopted a practice that my office door was wedged open, using a piece of cardboard previously indicating on the door whether it was alright to enter. On the first morning, my deputy, a female Inspector who was to go on to become the Deputy Chief Constable of the West Midlands Police, upon seeing my office door held open apologised for her absence for a minute while she did the same to her outer door. Her next enquiry related to the full-wall sized photograph in her office of the current Bristol City football team. Did I have any preference as to which weekend I wanted to provide the senior officer cover on the sub-division? With no preference, she chose those weekends when Bristol City were away as traveling on the supporters coach was usually an all-day event. The home games she could attend between morning and evening attendance at the station on the, then familiar to officers in our position, 'split shifts'.

I had two important matters to which to attend on my first duty weekend and a third came without much thought. On Monday, 7th September, 1987, I arrived at my customarily early time, a habit that 'beating' the traffic had brought while working in central Bristol, and gave the early turn Sergeant a bit of a surprise. Each shift Sergeant soon got used to being ready to brief me as to the current situation and what had happened overnight as I made my way to my office each morning. The important items I had in mind were to demonstrate that I was still a practical copper and, because of the current climate of antagonism between hunt supporters and those opposed, to have a meeting with the Master of the Beaufort Hunt, the Duke. The matter that simply came of its own accord was my regular foot patrols in uniform of Chipping Sodbury's main street.

Chipping Sodbury Police Station (taken in 2015 but externally largely as it was in 1990)

My appearance on my first Friday evening, a choice of my own because I had in fact already been on duty throughout that day, was not quite such a surprise for the duty Sergeant and the Constables as I had made a point of returning to see them on my first day. The shopping precinct at Yate then had a night club, the only one on the sub-division, called Spirals, after the staircases inside the club. It was, inevitably, the focus for activity after midnight, with the club emptying out at 0200 hours on Saturday and Sunday mornings. On that very first night with the duty Sergeant we encountered an assault directly outside the club leading to an arrest and much advice to a large group to disperse or risk also being arrested. The best bit as far as my credibility with the Officers on the sub-division came directly after this fracas.

One of the Constables who worked his own beat skirting Yate, had, as was expected practice, made sure that he was in the large car park to support his shift colleagues. These Officers commonly worked shifts of eight hours between 0800 hours and 0200 hours, to provide a mix of cover to their areas. As the Sergeant and I were returning across the car park to our car, still marked with the 'panda' colour scheme all those years after the Unit Beat Policing system had melted away, I suddenly realised that the Sergeant had detoured and was some distance behind me talking to the beat Constable beside his Ford Escort van. I retraced my steps and the pair moved away from the van. I asked what was happening and the Sergeant replied, "You don't want to know, Sir." Wrong reply! My next was, "I want to know everything." This latter can be a dangerous principle to adopt as it means taking responsibility but it was my natural way. They reluctantly informed me that the radio handset had been taken from the van.

In response to my unspoken question, the Constable said, "I could see you and the Sarg. had your hands full, Sir, and wanted to come to your help quickly. I must have forgotten to lock the door." I looked at him in a way that indicated my scepticism that his error was born of his concern for me and the Sergeant and took a look inside the van. The handset plug was still in its socket but the lead and handset, not much use other than as a 'trophy', had been torn out. Knowing that the Constable was already a little late for the end of his shift and suspecting that he would not be scheduled to work later that Sunday morning, I simply told him to see me in my office on Monday morning. First thing on Monday, I telephoned my good friend the Chief Inspector in Communications Planning and, after not much explanation, obtained from his stock a new VHF radio handset.

The Constable soon arrived after his 1000 hours shift start and stood to attention in the open doorway of my office. I invited him in and for him to close the door as he entered. He did so and again stood firmly to attention directly in front of my desk. I asked if he had any specific commitment for the rest of the morning and he told me he had not. I then told him to take his van to Headquarters, in New Bridewell and to report to the Communications Planning Office to collect the replacement handset. The relief on his face was immediately apparent and he simply said, "Thank you, Sir." There had never been much, if any, prospect of us finding the damaged handset, which would have been as costly to repair as was the price of the new one. The worth to my credibility on the sub-division as a 'coppers' copper' was, however, immeasurable.

The matter of the hunt, with problems going back some distance in time, had to wait a couple of weeks until the Duke was available for us to meet on a Saturday evening almost four weeks after my arrival on the sub-division. The local detached beat Constable from Acton Turville had arranged the meeting and accompanied me that evening. We were greeted by the young butler, who had not long previously 'inherited' the role from his father, and were escorted to meet the Duke in his study. David Somerset had inherited the title only a bit less recently, in 1984. We were offered a drink and a cigarette from a box on the small table beside the Duke's chair. Both the Constable and I declined the cigarette but asked if we could smoke our pipes. The study was lined with oil paintings of many sizes, so much that many stood on the floor through lack of wall space. The Duke had been an international art dealer for many years before inheriting the title. I did have some concern as to what the build-up of nicotine in the room was doing to these paintings as the Duke often lit his next cigarette from the 'stub' before placing it in the ever-filling ashtray.

We discussed his art business and his private twin-engined aircraft for which a grass airstrip was maintained and used by local flying enthusiasts. After a most convivial half an hour or so the Duke enquired as to what had been my real reason for asking to meet with him. He was not the least surprised when I told him that my main concern related to the Beaufort Hunt. He asked me what my stance was and I told him that we would, as in all things, seek to be even-handed and deal with problems from whichever direction they originated. I explained that where we detected hunt saboteur activity that breached the law those people responsible would be dealt with accordingly. I also emphasised that should there be any member of the Hunt found to be in breach of the law or provoking a breach of the peace they, too, would be taken before the courts.

The Duke, as should be expected, accepted what I had said without challenge and, after a few more casual bits of conversation, we left. The Constable came to my office a few days later and reported that those involved with the Hunt had been addressed by the Duke. He had identified my emphasis upon even-handedness and indicated that he wanted his staff and those who rode to the Hunt to respect that position. There were those among the fraternity who showed some resentment that I had not been 'on their side' but the policing of the hunting days proved reasonably successful. To support the conversation with the Master of Fox Hounds, I arranged for the first several weeks after the September 'Cubbing' to have more than adequate police resources available. A few telephone calls to the Headquarters Departments with which I had so recently been involved, brought Task Force support and Mounted Section Officers. The police horses could not keep up with the hunters but were able to provide a much better picture when they went off across the fields.

On one Saturday morning, I had been informed by Force Control that HRH The Prince of Wales would be riding with the Hunt and accordingly briefed the Task Force units that came to Chipping Sodbury. There were no untoward incidents reported, although as may have been expected, the press were more a hindrance to the hunt than any 'saboteurs' that day. Back in the office on Sunday morning, I received another call from Force Control, this time telling me that there was an angry Chief Constable on the line wishing to speak with me. I picked up the transferred call with a cheerful, "Good morning, Sir!" I, of course knew the Chief Constable as he had served not long before in our Force. His response was not at all cheerful but he enquired, seemingly expecting I would answer in the affirmative, whether I had seen the front pages of several Sunday newspapers.

I explained that I had not had the opportunity of reading a newspaper as I had been out with the personnel the night before and back in to the office ready for the usual session of cautioning juvenile offenders. Sweeping that aside, he explained that these pictures were of Prince Charles changing his riding breeches beside a Range Rover and with a police personnel carrier, that of one of our Task Force units, easily visible with its Avon and Somerset badge on the door. He demanded to know whether it was under my instructions that our Officers were well inside his Force boundary. He was not wholly content when I told him that my brief to the units had been to 'keep an eye' on His Royal Highness. He was less content when I suggested that they probably thought that they had better keep close if there were no other Officers in evidence.

Not long after my arrival at Chipping Sodbury, I was returning from the amenity area after my morning coffee up the wrought iron spiral staircase which someone had thought would become an architectural feature but was in fact a bit of a liability with bright tape signifying where people had knocked their heads on it. This took me through the small Administration Office in which worked a Sergeant and Constable. I enquired as to what was the norm in regard to the allocation of duties over the Christmas period and was told that nothing special had been arranged in previous years, with Officers simply doing whatever shift the normal roster brought. I told the two that I wanted to see a minimum cover on both bank holiday days, with Officers with young children off on Christmas Day and those without on Boxing Day. The Constable recognised, correctly, that this would take a little effort to arrange but could see the reason. The Sergeant took the opportunity to enquire as to what would be my requirements for New Year.

He also enquired as to whether I would be in the Divisional Control Room at Staple Hill on New Year's Eve. When I enquired as to why I would want to be at Staple Hill, he told me what had happened at Chipping Sodbury on New Year's Eve at the turn of that year. A large crowd of youths had 'laid siege' to the police station forcing two detective constables inside the building to resort to the use of the cues from the pool table to defend the back entrances. He went on to explain that the wide main street along which the police station stood about mid-way on the southern side, behind the huge town clock atop the public conveniences, was always thronged on New Year's Eve. On the last occasion the situation had become really nasty with young men with too much drink focusing their efforts upon the Station.

I had, having been in the Headquarters Operations role (although not called that in our Force), heard nothing of this incident and it was apparent that the information had not been fed back to headquarters. Almost immediately I had moved to the sub-division we had needed to appoint a new Special Constabulary Sub-Divisional Officer (SDO) and my female deputy and I had interviewed all the Section Officers and made the appointment from among them. I told the Sergeant to get the SDO to call in to see me and to ensure maximum cover of the regular Constables through till 0200 hours on 1st January. The next day, the SDO called in on his way home from work and I told him to muster as many Special Constables as he could.

On New Year's Eve at the close of 1987, the wide street outside the police station was thronged with hundreds of people cheering as the Church clock, just behind the buildings on the north side of the street, struck twelve. Among the hordes, wherever you looked, police helmets were prominent. Everyone, including the police officers - Regulars and Specials, enjoyed a great celebration and, after not too long, made their way home. I had, as I had learned many times over throughout my involvement with public disorder policing on much larger scales, applied the principle that a strong police presence deters criminal or disorderly activity. Not a bad principle to revisit today but somewhat frustrated by cut-backs and excessive bureaucratisation.

Another lesson from the past that looks in danger of being ignored has brought the 'centralisation' of custody units to Avon and Somerset. Time will tell as to their efficiency but in 1987 I had real concerns over the travel and Officer time committed to conveying prisoners the dozen miles or so to Staple Hill. With not too much resistance from either the Divisional Commander or Headquarters, I kept chipping away at the edifice of the Force establishment for a couple more Sergeants on the sub-division. Eventually this was granted and we had two for each shift when at full capacity. With some adjustment it was possible to maintain street supervision and retain a Sergeant on the station for all but the latter part of the night.

Following the inner-city disturbances in 1985, which had little impact in Bristol, a conclusion of the reviews that took place was that all sub-divisions should have a Police Liaison Committee. With the regular attendances that I achieved, in common I am sure with all other sub-divisional commanders, at local council meetings and other organisations, the need for such a liaison committee at Chipping Sodbury was actually nil. But, thanks to the broad brush often injudiciously applied at central government level, we had one. The very mixed Committee was largely supportive and they were chaired by a lady who kept proceedings in order. Quite rightly, I felt that I could be challenged but would be listened to and, largely, understood.

The same could not be said for all the councillors I encountered at their meetings. Too many saw their participation as their first step to becoming Prime Minister and were determined to try and catch me out. At my first meeting of Yate Town Council, I had been told what a good relationship they had held with my predecessor and then was asked what changes I intended to make to policing in the town. My reply was that if their relationship with the previous incumbent had been so good I was sure that they would want me to change as little as possible. The councillor who had tried to trip me with the question spoke with the local beat Constable after the meeting and offered an indirect insult, although he may have intended it as a compliment. He had the nerve to say that I would make a good politician – diplomat may have been more acceptable!

My regular Saturday morning patrols in uniform along the wide main street of Chipping Sodbury, referred to early in this chapter, seemed to go down quite well. I met people, some well known in the town, and stopped for a chat. On most of these alternate Saturdays, I ended up at the top, Yate, end of the street. The Constable with whom I had joined who came from the Forest of Deane, had resigned from the police in the rank of Sergeant when we each had about eleven years' service. Keeping in touch by Christmas cards, I had met him quite a few times when an Inspector on 'A' Division as he was then senior security officer for one of the large central Bristol department stores. By 1987 he had set himself up in business with a small antique shop where he also undertook furniture restorations and had been elected to Chipping Sodbury Town Council. Over a cup of their coffee, we would often exchange conversations about what was current within the council and the police and how one could be helped to support the other.

Some many months after the Wickwar gas explosion, referred to in the previous chapter, the Constable who had raised the alarm before his house was demolished received his BEM from the Lord Lieutenant of Avon. The arrangement was for the community hall to be the venue so that as many local people as possible could be present. The Dowager Duchess of Westminster lived close to the village and invited everyone for tea. The Chief Constable introduced me to the Lord Lieutenant as his "only ever field promotion!" The dowager Duchess was a very popular local character who sometimes called at the village police station for a chat with the resident Constable's wife. As a certain former colleague of mine would say, "When things was proper!"

I had been at Chipping Sodbury for some months when one of the Constables who spent much of his time around the Yate shopping centre came to me with a concern regarding drug dealing in the night club. We visited the club out of operating hours and discussed the situation with the manager, leaving him in no doubt as to his potential liability. We agreed that he would do what he could inside and I would do what we could outside. The information we collected indicated that the police activities in central Bristol, largely made possible following Operation Delivery, as related in the previous chapter, was forcing the suppliers of drugs to seek new markets. With the support of the Task Force and Traffic Department, we set up static checks on the roads between Bristol and Yate, at a time when there was not the unbelievable requirement for such checks to receive a Superintendent's authority. Only a few stops and arrests for possession with intent to supply halted the trade. At one of the Command Band public order sessions at Bridgend I was later spoken to by a Superintendent from Newport who told me that after our successes they had become the next market area.

One lunchtime we received a call from Leyhill prison, reporting an escapee. The open prison concept seemed to work for most of the time but when a prisoner felt the need to escape it could not really have been easier. This man, as was too often the case and I think has become even more prevalent, was not the well-mannered fraudster type of prisoner but did have a record of occasional violence. My main concern was for the small junior school not very far from the prison so we ensured that they received a warning and a visible police presence. We then set about trying to search the immediate area. This was easy over the open fields but not as exact a science through the large acreage of woodlands. After the expending of much police time he turned up wondering why we were concerned.

The early summer of 1988 brought a repetition of a large gathering of travellers, waiting for the Solstice and Pilton Festival, to Inglestone Common north of the town and under the escarpment of the true start of the Cotswold Hills. More were arriving each day and a large convoy was reported by the Gloucestershire Constabulary to be making their way south through Dursley. There had started another move from Inglestone towards Wick and we set up a temporary communications facility at the Tracy Park Golf Club. Not at all sure where were all the vehicles being used by the travellers and knowing that Wiltshire Constabulary had a helicopter ready for the Solstice gatherings, we requested that we receive their help in getting an aerial view.

I gave the coordinates of the football field near Wick Junior School, having got someone to check that it was not in use that Saturday morning. I then drove a marked car to the field and placed it with its back to the slight wind and near one of the goalmouths, leaving the entire pitch as a landing site. The helicopter appeared and the pilot seemed to take ages to weigh up his approach but eventually came in to land. I boarded the aircraft and off we went. We landed briefly near Dursley for me to speak with the Gloucestershire Inspector leading the Officers escorting the travellers south and then, after a quick flight over the rest of the area and especially Wick quarry, we returned to the football field. Now, I could see why the pilot had been so hesitant on his first approach. Much of the area around the edge of the field was covered with trees and that full-size football pitch looked no bigger than a postage stamp until we were close on top of it. As they had in previous years, the travellers moved on before the Solstice, leaving the Common Commissioners and Town Council with another rubbish clearing operation.

There were two 'standing' annual invitations for the Sub-Divisional Commander at Chipping Sodbury. One was to the Islamic School right on the southern edge of the sub-division's 98 square miles of territory, near Colern airfield. The airfield was on the opposite side of the steep road from Bath and in Wiltshire. The invitation was for Gill and I to attend their Open Day, combined with what at my old school had been called Commemoration Day. The young people put on a range of demonstrations of their work and art, including very accomplished dancing. The afternoon included a sumptuous buffet with some foods neither of us had tasted anywhere else.

The other event was to attend the British Legion annual dinner and I attended two of these while at Chipping Sodbury. On the first occasion, the Secretary telephoned after he had received the letter of acceptance to inform me that I would be expected to announce the toast to their Branch. With National Service ending in 1960, I missed it by three years and the nearest I got to military service was in the Combined Cadet Corps at school. At about fifteen years of age, that would also have been in 1960, I went on a Royal Signals course in my summer holiday to Catterick Garrison in Yorkshire. I used that recollection in my short speech before proposing the toast. The aged ex-Brigadier who was President of the Branch spoke to thank me and announced that he had been a Lieutenant Colonel and officer in charge at the Signals School at Catterick at about the time I had been on my course.

At the same dinner the following year, Gill was not feeling too well so our middle daughter, Cathryn, then sixteen years old, accompanied me. She was then looking towards starting her course to train as a nanny and got into deep conversation with another guest, the wife of the local vicar, who had gone through that training some years previously. When it came to the time for me to speak the Chairman introduced me and explained that my wife was not well so I was accompanied by, "my daughter for the evening!" When I stood, I hastily explained that this young lady was not just my daughter for that evening. With Catterick the first year and the slip about Cathryn the second, I had managed to successfully hide my poor performance as a public speaker.

By far the biggest annual event for the Chipping Sodbury Sub Division was, still is, the Badminton Horse Trials. Although the date has shifted slightly over the years, it was always held in May and, in the three years while I was there, after having been cancelled because of the rain in 1987, was bathed in sunshine. In the first year, 1988, Lt. Col. Frank Weldon was the Director and had been since 1965, but the following year he was succeeded by the man who still leads the team that runs the event. Instead of simply asking for support for the event, I took pains to ensure that the sub-division was covered by our colleagues from Filton and Staple Hill so that all the Chipping Sodbury personnel could be at Badminton Park for the three day event and the day either side when policing attention was also necessary.

For some years Her Majesty the Queen had been a regular attender at Badminton but she must have thought it particularly safe hands for the three years of my time there as she did not make an appearance. Other members of the Royal Family did attend but they visited the estate quite frequently on other occasions so that was not unusual. The policing arrangements were quite comprehensive as the Force could not be seen to be lacking should anything untoward happen with the mass of publicity the event attracted. We had a large compound beside the 'tented village' in which all the sales marquees were sited and between the show ring and the house and stable blocks. It was good to be able to get Gill and the girls up on the Saturday to see the cross country event, especially as Cathryn had and still has a love of horses.

On my final occasion as sub-divisional commander at a Badminton Horse Trials, the Traffic motorcyclists brought two Armstrong trail bikes to the compound to permit access across the park if required. I ensured that my police motorcycle authorisation was renewed by one of the Sergeants and we spent a most enjoyable hour patrolling the route of the cross country on the Sunday morning. When we returned up Kennel Drive to the compound to stand the bikes on the 'duckboards' the young Constable on the main gate had a shock when he saw who was riding the first of the two machines. When we reached the compound I saw that the Divisional Commander was waiting for me together with one of our Assistant Chief Constables. They both looked somewhat surprised as I took off my helmet and I felt obliged to offer some explanation. When I told them how important it had been for me to check the perimeter of the park neither looked really convinced.

Just a few miles from Badminton, near junction 18 of the M4 motorway, lies Doddington House. During my time at Chipping Sodbury, it was owned by a well-known builder. Also with a daughter enthusiastic about horses and with the kind of bank balance required, he set up their own one day horse trials. The family and I were on the invitation list and a number of well-known show jumping personalities were demonstrating their prowess or notable among the spectators around the course. Our invitation included a ticket for the excellent buffet luncheon laid out in the hall of the house and our youngest daughter, Emma, then twelve years old, followed me around the food on display trying to decide what to eat. The young lady standing behind a huge salmon watched as I asked Emma if she would like some salmon. Loud enough for me not to be the only one who heard her she said, "Don't they have any tuna?" The waitress looked so understanding!

During the afternoon of Wednesday, 28th December, 1988 there was a fire in a Dutch barn on a farm to the north of Pucklechurch with which the Fire Brigade experienced some difficulty. Although we had become involved because arson by local youths was suspected, I only attended as it was on my route home. At the entrance to the farm I was met by one of the Constables and the Detective Sergeant but they were keen to get my involvement because the senior fire officer had called for the attendance of a representative from the council's environmental health department. The debate was whether the smoke from the fire was a danger to the traffic on the M4 motorway, about a mile away, or to Yate a couple more miles further north. I asked the environmental health man what he thought were our options and he agreed that there were only two. Either we did nothing or we went for a closure of the M4 and a full evacuation of the thousands of homes in Yate. Neither of these courses of action were in any way attractive but he and the fire officer now were able to comfort themselves that it was I that had seen them as impracticable.

When I arrived home I was contacted by telephone and told by the Divisional

Control room Sergeant that the incident had been escalated by the discovery that the roof of the barn was made of asbestos. The discovery that asbestos dust was potentially seriously injurious to health was relatively new at that time and there was some level of panic over this discovery. I returned to the scene only to reiterate my earlier decision. The plume of smoke was not thick and the most likely potential danger was to people leaving their homes at a time when most of them would be settling down for the evening before going to bed. I returned to Chipping Sodbury to tie up with the Detectives regarding their suspects for the arson and liaised with the Fire Service headquarters to confirm my view regarding the fire. The best outcome came late that night, after I had returned home again and gone to bed, it rained and no fire or danger of breathing in asbestos existed by the time those people not on holiday set off for work. The important point was that, as the sub-divisional commander at that time, I saw no need to refer to any higher authority for the decision and was confident that my initiative would receive the support of my more senior officers.

Early in 1988, the Superintendent Deputy Divisional Commander moved back to his beloved Traffic Department and was, somewhat contentiously, replaced by a newly promoted Officer who transferred from the Metropolitan Police. This appointment was contentious as the norm was for Divisional Deputies to be selected from those who had been Sub-Divisional Superintendents, while this man was promoted directly into the post. I happened to be visiting Staple Hill on the day the new Superintendent arrived and we were introduced by our Divisional Commander. A couple of days later we were together again, with the other two sub-divisional commanders and the Divisional Administration Officer, for the Wednesday morning weekly senior officers' conference. During the meeting the new man spoke several times regarding how matters we were discussing would have been handled at his last station. After the meeting, I took the opportunity to privately ask him, for the sake of his acceptance in the Force, not to relate how things were done in the Met. When I explained my significant experience of working alongside Metropolitan Officers, some very good and others with lessons they too could learn, he took the well-intentioned advice.

I was called down to Staple Hill for a few weeks to gain the valuable entry for the annual staff appraisal return as acting Superintendent on that Sub Division. The full time incumbent was on a course at Bramshill at the time. At the end of the period, which had been quite uneventful, I was interviewed by the Chief Superintendent, who asked me how I thought I had got on. I told him that I thought I had done alright but pointed out that the role of my usual post and that at Staple Hill were scarcely different. He asked in what small way they were different. My reply was that at Chipping Sodbury it was like being a Lieutenant Commander on a Frigate while at Staple Hill it was like being a full Commander on a Destroyer - but the destroyer had the Admiral (himself) on board. There was no doubt that, although numerically smaller in establishment, my role at Chipping Sodbury, like any on a detached sub-division, meant that the responsibility for what went on rested with me.

While in the last year at Chipping Sodbury an old colleague from the Special Course in 1973/74 arrived as one of our new ACCs. I had met him a few times in London when he was one of the Commissioner's Staff Officers at the time that I was fulfilling that role for the President of ACPO. Recognising that I had been sent to Chipping Sodbury to gain operational command experience and that this had been accomplished, he nominated me for the first ever Home Office Scrutiny to be conducted by the Force, in our case into the force Communications Structure. To do the job properly I was provided with a team and temporarily replaced by another Chief Inspector who only needed that type of experience to become eligible for advancement. I am devoting the next chapter to the Scrutiny and will round-off my return to Chipping Sodbury before dropping back the few months to relate how the scrutiny was conducted. I was absent from the sub-division for four months, although I did have some contact in respect of staff appraisals and assisting my most capable stand-in on a few occasions.

I returned, full-time, to Chipping Sodbury from Monday, 12th February, 1990 but, as is usually the case with such matters, the Scrutiny remained part of what I was doing on occasions. Even through the Scrutiny I had continued my inputs to the Public Order Command Band training at Devizes and Bridgend and the even more occasional visits to the College at Pontypridd. Not too long after returning to my normal task, I was in my office when the Divisional Control room staff told me that Yate Magistrates Court had a problem. As was the case in most Magistrates Courts there would be a sitting on a Saturday morning to deal with any people arrested overnight. The police escort had taken three young men arrested during the night and one who had responded to a warrant issued by the North Avon Magistrates. The warrant was within their domain but the three arrested overnight needed the attendance of a solicitor from the Crown Prosecution Service (CPS). No one from that Service had attended.

I related in Chapter 14 my early involvement at Bristol Magistrates Courts as the move towards the establishing of the CPS was starting but by 1990 this body was firmly established as the public prosecuting authority throughout the country. I went to the Court building and spoke with our escort team who had brought the prisoners from Staple Hill. I then spoke with the Magistrates' Clerk regarding the dilemma. With it having been some years since Police Officers stood before Magistrates to prosecute the accused, the Clerk was in some difficulty. He had tried to contact the CPS local office but received no reply and was not at all sure where we would stand if I undertook to proffer the prosecution case against the three, one of whom was charged with violent offences and we wanted him to be remanded in custody.

Eventually we came to the conclusion that the prisoners had to be brought before the Magistrates but there was still the doubt as to my status before the Court. The way forward we decided was for me to offer to present the prosecution case and for the Magistrates to determine whether they were prepared to hear me. With precious little alternative and that I am sure having been explained by their Learned Clerk, they accepted that I should present the cases for their consideration. This I did and two of the overnight arrested men were granted bail while the third, and the man who had surrendered to the warrant, were escorted on remand to Horfield Prison in Bristol. I went back to my routine.

On Monday morning I received a call from the Chief Superintendent at Staple Hill and then spoke with one of the ACCs at Headquarters. I was astonished to discover that the Chief Prosecutor for the CPS in the County of Avon had actually complained to the ACC about my improper assumption of the prosecuting role at Yate the previous Saturday morning. I explained the position I had discovered at the court on the Saturday and told him that, far from feeling there was any grounds for the complaint against me, I would look forward to an apology and their thanks from the CPS. Neither, of course, came but I heard nothing more about the matter.

In late June, 1990, the Chief Inspector in charge at Filton, Superintendent from Staple Hill and I were given our first information from the Force Reorganisation team who had continued their work after our Scrutiny had been completed. It had been decided that our Division, the South Gloucestershire part of Avon, would be used for a 'pilot' for the proposed organisational and structural changes. Effectively, the Division would become the first new District and the Sub-Divisions would become Sections with an Inspector reporting to the District Command Superintendent. Hence, my post was to disappear.

There was only one other notable event, and that only really locally important, before my tenure as Sub-Divisional Commander was to cease. The flying club that used the air strip on the Badminton estate, maintained principally for the Duke of Beaufort's benefit, decided to run one of their occasional Air Days on Sunday, 22nd July, 1990. Our involvement was not great but there was a need to ensure that the roads leading to the airstrip were safe. There were also a number of dignitaries, including members of the Royal Family, who had accepted invitations to attend. So too had a number of performers well known in aeronautical circles for their aerobatic skills. The day turned out to be fine and the displays most impressive. The down-side was a local inhabitant decided that the noise was inappropriate, apparently a resurgence of a long-standing objection which he had held against the air club since buying his country home. We had not seen the need for any noise monitoring on the day and he had no 'evidence' either so the matter had to rest.

I must say that, while the promise of early further promotion did not materialise after my move to Chipping Sodbury in 1987, the nearly three years of being in charge of 'my own' sub-division proved as enjoyable as any period in my Service. With nearly twenty two years of very mixed police service behind me I felt totally confident that I would not encounter anything I was unable to handle and found the relationships that were built up in a team totalling fifty Officers and just a very few civilian support staff were excellent. Nothing is good all of the time and it is inevitable that there will show up differences of opinion from time to time but these were rare over those three years.

The files which had accompanied me from London, through the preparation of the debrief from the NUM Dispute and were still referred to quite often in the first year or so at Chipping Sodbury were now, largely, redundant. Rather than take them on to my next engagement, we set about firstly shredding and then burning most of the papers. Fortunately, there was a long and rather overgrown 'garden' behind the Police Station and our handyman helped me to destroy the papers. With a fairly 'clean sheet' I left the Sub-Division, as it ceased to exist as such, and started in my new role back at Headquarters on the penultimate day of July, 1990.

19 Communications Scrutiny

The Home Office Scrutiny system was quite strictly set out and we were visited by a civil servant to be briefed. The 'pure' model for a scrutiny stated that the Officer appointed should be allowed to select his team but I had them nominated. In the event, the Sergeant and two Constables performed well, in two cases exceptionally well, and, importantly, we got on well and bought in a variety of typist support through a temping agency. Our brief was to analyse all aspects of the communications infrastructure of the Force, report our findings and make recommendations for change. Our reporting up line was direct to the Deputy Chief Constable and the structure from the Home Office gave us 90 working days, about four months, to complete the task. We moved into offices that used to be the bedrooms of a police house at the rear of Filton Police Station and spent the first few weeks sorting out our plan as to how we would best meet our required target.

We used my car for much of the more local travel and, in the first weeks, visited many other Forces and Agencies throughout the southern part of the country to discover what others did differently to ourselves. The first few days spent making contact by telephone meant that not too many of our journeys were wasted and it was quite an eye-opener to discover how many variations on a theme there could be within Services with such similar communications requirements. Because I was not and still am not in any way qualified to do so, I will not seek to explain the technologies involved. We were fortunate to have, in Force and through the Home Office Radio Workshops at Shapwick, near Street in Somerset, those with the requisite skills and knowledge. Our brief was to present our findings with a 'user' emphasis. The principal difference we discovered was that Lancashire and Scotland had taken a different path in terms of radio modulation, the Home Office Forces (including most Fire Brigades) had pursued Amplitude Modulation (AM) while north of the border and, for historic reasons, Lancashire employed Frequency Modulation (FM) systems.

Although we had to delay Lancashire until the week afterwards, by the sixth week we had plotted out the benefits of a closer look at the Scottish models. Using one of the Force Staff Cars, the four of us spent that whole week in Scotland. Two of us were qualified to drive the Ford Granada and shared the task. We started with Strathclyde, in Glasgow; moved on to Fife, at Kirkcaldy; and ended the week at Lothian and Borders in Edinburgh. As an aside, given how motor car technology has progressed since November 1989, we were amazed to discover that the Granada presented an average consumption with the four of us and our luggage of just over thirty miles to the gallon over that week. The next week was also spent traveling, with visits to British Transport Police in London; Lancashire Constabulary at Preston; South Yorkshire Police at Sheffield; Hampshire Police at Winchester and Thames Valley Police at Kidlington. The combining of findings in all of these areas greatly assisted our capability to draw out from our existing Force structure what was good and what could see improvement.

An important part of the Home Office Scrutiny process was that link with the Home Office which its title implied. I have already related that we received a visit in the first few weeks from a Civil Servant well versed in the process but our on-going link was through the office of the Technology limb of Her Majesty's Inspectorate of Constabulary. A Chief Superintendent, Staff Officer to the HMI (Technical) visited us on several occasions for updates. Consultation with the people at Shapwick and with our 'in house' experts ensured that we were not in danger of floating off into the realms of unattainable fantasy but our, particularly my, lack of previous close involvement in communications, other than as an end-user, was an important part of the process.

We were, of course, not only looking at radio technology but our remit took us into areas which were, in 1989/90 rapidly changing with the move into the digital and computer age. We examined and produced a plan for a revised force digital telephone and data network, at an opportune time as the plans for the construction of the new Headquarters at Portishead Down were well advanced and how that sat within a revised forcewide network was vital. We also, with the special importance of user access and staff economy, examined the structure of the communications centres within the Force and the new technologies in respect of 'command & control' computer systems.

Throughout this process at our offices at Filton and notwithstanding an excellent 'caretaker' job being performed by the Chief Inspector cast in my place at Chipping Sodbury, there were commitments beyond the Scrutiny that I could not avoid. These included matters back on the Sub-Division, especially in respect of the continuity of staff appraisals of officers and planning for the 1990 Badminton Horse Trials. Elsewhere, my logistical input commitment to the Regional Command Band training at Devizes and Bridgend did not go away, nor did I want them to as these were sessions in which I really enjoyed being involved.

The changes to radio technology were some years into the future when we were undertaking the scrutiny and within the VHF (mainly vehicle sets) and UHF (personal radio) structure the Force was quite robust. Under the guidance of an excellent Communications Planning team, headed by a most knowledgeable Chief Inspector, the Force had made an early swap from VHF to Microwave linking for the 'figure of eight' hilltop site system feeding the VHF transceivers. This had included a link to the Independent Television mast in South Wales to provide full coastal cover from Porlock up to Avonmouth. The Fire Brigade, although they had ceased to share a frequency with the Police remained on the microwave linked system and were jointly taken care of by the Home Office engineers from Shapwick. All would change in the late 1990s but more of that in chapter twenty one.

With the new Force Headquarters being a 'future' our plans for changes to the operating infrastructure were based upon three communications control centres. We took care not to claim that these centres controlled policing effort across the Force as this, quite squarely, rested with the command structure, which as I have said was being examined by another team, headed by the formerly Metropolitan Police Superintendent who had arrived in the Force at Staple Hill. It was important that we liaised with that team regularly and tried to complement each other as we worked towards our recommendations. Our communications rooms up until that time had developed from before the Forces amalgamated into a divisionally based structure. Each of the eight territorial divisions had its own control room and there was one for the Traffic Department, based at Almondsbury and an overviewing 'Information Room' known by 1989 as Force Control. Hence, ten communications centres.

From what we saw elsewhere and with an eye to slimming down the number of police officers in these rooms, with a view to bolstering their availability for patrol duties, we arrived at a three-centre configuration. Although in recent years, the Avon and Somerset Constabulary has further reconfigured by drawing all communications control into Headquarters, we were more cautious against the possibility of system failure. Our examination of this aspect brought us to three centres, in the view that the failure of one centre could be accommodated by a temporary increase in workload to the tune of 50% in each of the other centres. This, we believed, gave a sustainable level of resilience.

Without determining exactly where, that was to become another responsibility for me a little later, we concluded in our report that the centres should be at New Bridewell, still then alongside Force Headquarters; in the Taunton area and north of Bristol, with the longer term prospect that third centre being replaced by a new facility at Portishead Down. The broad recommendation, not universally popular at that stage, was for a greater emphasis upon support staff as operators but retaining a minimum level of Police Officers in each centre and with the supervision being by Sergeants and an Inspector (in the centre still carrying the Force Control responsibilities).

With the plans approved by the Deputy Chief Constable and accepted by the Staff Officers to both the local HMI, based at Bridge House, Clifton, Bristol, and HMI Technical in the Home Office, we set out to present them to the Force. The other team, examining the operational command structure of the Force, had followed an approximate scrutiny format but were not linked in to the Home Office. We, in the final stages held further meetings with them to ensure compatibility between what was being put forward as they were, largely pursuing a new national trend, looking towards a Basic Command Unit (BCU) single tier approach. We tried, fortunately with some success, to come up with a communications command and control structure which would be compatible with most territorial structures that may evolve.

Having submitted copies of our report, with all its various areas included, to the Chief Officer Group and, with their approval, to the HMI, our first presentation at Kingsweston House was to the Divisional Commanders. With the prospect of losing direct sway over their divisional control rooms they were, inevitably, a very sceptical audience. That they had already received enough feedback from the activities of the other review group to reveal that the days of Divisions were numbered probably mitigated some of the critical comment we would otherwise have received. Later that same week, the penultimate week of our time at the offices at Filton, we repeated the presentation, inevitably honed through the earlier experience, to the Chief Officers and Regional HMI. The HMI Technical was represented by the Chief Superintendent Staff Officer with whom we were, by 2nd February, 1990, well acquainted.

In the final week we set about drawing up the final report, having taken on board any significant comments drawn from the presentations. This report had, under the Home Office Scrutiny rules, to include broad budgetary assessments for each recommended course of action. This we had, of course, been aware of throughout the scrutiny timetable and had assessed as best we could as we developed each area for recommendation. The final day, because they were such an important group to 'carry' with the Scrutiny Report, was again with the Divisional Commanders.

On Monday, 12th February, 1990, the team split up and I returned to Chipping Sodbury, as related towards the end of Chapter Eighteen. There were further aspects to be considered, especially with regard to the costing exercise, which necessitated my having further meetings with the DCC and HMI's Staff at Bridge House. This aspect was followed up by a, thankfully not critical, response to our report from the Audit Commission the following July. By that time my days were numbered as the Staple Hill Division had been chosen for the 'pilot' move to a District, single tier, structure with the Chipping Sodbury Sub-Division becoming an Inspector's Section commanded from the former Divisional Headquarters.

20 Regional ACPO

On Monday, 30th July, 1990, I was back in Headquarters, not really further advanced than when I had left three years earlier but enriched by some very interesting and, mainly enjoyable, experiences. With the prospect of being 'redundant' not a pleasing one, another officer's advancement had created a vacancy. The ACC who had returned, after many years and had shared my time on the Special Course at Bramshill, had assumed the role of Secretary to the South West Region of the Association of Chief Police Officers (ACPO), an organisation with whom I was familiar as described in Chapters Fifteen and Sixteen. His regional role brought with it the entitlement to a Staff Officer and my new role was to take up that task. The current post holder had been successful in achieving promotion to Superintendent in the Hampshire Force but there was a theoretical overlap before he departed from our Force.

In fact we both had summer leave planned so spent very little time together. Thankfully that time did include an agenda planning meeting with the Gloucestershire Chief Constable, then Chairman of the Regional ACPO Group, in preparation for my first Regional ACPO Meeting at Middlemoor, Exeter on my return from holiday on Monday, 3rd September, 1990. My predecessor's move to Hampshire was the start of a rapid climb through the rest of the ranks and he was to return to Gloucestershire and become their Chief Constable just over a decade later.

The largely administrative aspects of my Regional Staff Officer role were not to my best liking but there was enough of greater interest surrounding the post to compensate. The full meetings of the Regional ACPO Officers were shared around the Forces in the Region, Avon and Somerset, Devon & Cornwall, Dorset, Gloucestershire and Wiltshire and took place about once a calendar quarter. In between the contact between the Forces at this, highest, level continued by correspondence and less formally over the telephone, this was of course before the advent of universal e'mailing. Preparing for the meetings involved quite a bit of paperwork generation as each member had become accustomed to finding a full file in front of them when they arrived for the meetings. An audio recording kit had also been obtained some time before I took over and that had to be set up in the appropriate room before a meeting commenced.

The ACC's Secretary had also found herself a promotion, within the Force, and was replaced by a young lady who had only been employed by the Force for a relatively short time. We proved to be a good team and became lasting friends. Not long after the move to Portishead she married and moved to Dorset, where she obtained a similar post in that Force's Headquarters. She accompanied me to the ACPO Regional Meetings and that, with the tape recordings, helped a lot in terms of our correctly constructing the Minutes of those meetings and preparing the resultant latters and other papers. The Regional ACPO Group had, in addition to sharing discussion of all policing issues between them, several specific responsibilities for Regional Functions. These included the Regional Crime Squad, referred to in some detail in Chapter Thirteen; the Regional Driving School, my attendance at which was related in Chapter Seven and the Regional Training School at Chantemarle in Dorset, mentioned in Chapter Two.

Although my role was the result of his regional responsibilities, I acted as the ACC's Staff Officer in all other respects but it was not the level of operational involvement I had experienced when working to the ACC (Operations) a few years earlier. One regular meeting in which I was involved was the monthly session between the ACC and the Detective Chief Superintendent who was the Regional Coordinator for the Crime Squad. Their offices had moved from New Bridewell since my attachment to them in 1977 (Chapter Thirteen) but were only a short distance from the Old Bridewell Offices then occupied by the Chief Officers. These meetings were most interesting as they kept the ACC, and me, fully up to date with the wide range of activities of the Squad and brought us both closer to 'real policing' than much of the administration with which I was involved.

To fully fulfil the Staff Officer role, I independently visited both the Regional Driving School and Chantmarle to liaise with their respective Senior Officers and report back to the ACC. On rare occasions I would also accompany the ACC on visits to neighbouring force headquarters, and further afield, when he had discussions with his counterparts in between the full Regional ACPO Meetings. All in all, these more than compensated for the administrative routine that I accomplished rather than wholly enjoyed. My first independent visit to Chantmarle was most enjoyable as it was my first visit there since I had left my initial training course in 1966, twenty four years earlier. After the updating session with the Chief Superintendent who was the current Commandant of the establishment, he invited me to take lunch before making my return journey to Bristol. As I joined him on the 'top table', literally slightly raised from the main floor of the dining room, and the young students were enjoying their lunches and conversations, the thoughts of my days at, then, scrubbed wooden tables flooded back.

The Communications Scrutiny had not gone away although it seemed that what it recommended had been held in suspension while the main focus of attention was on the Review of the Force Structure and the preparations at Portishead Down for the New Force Headquarters. The 'status' of the Communications Scrutiny findings were to be drawn back into focus towards the end of the year in order that their implementation could be coordinated with the other massive changes following on from the 'pilot' Staple Hill District. My appointment to the role of Superintendent Communications turned out to be quite a comical episode. Not even this, wholly in-Force controlled, promotion was to be straightforward, following the pattern set on the previous occasions.

On Friday, 9th November, 1990, I arrived at the secretary's office at the usually early time and we were chatting about what the day promised when the ACC breezed in, as was his usual fashion. He wished us both "Good morning!" then asked me if I had seen the DCC, who was another customarily early starter. I told him that I had seen him but only for long enough to wish him the time of day. He immediately told me to go down to the Deputy's office. When I entered the DCC's secretary's office she called through the open door to inform the Deputy that I had arrived. The Deputy said that he had not asked to see me but as the ACC had not told me he supposed that he had better do so. He explained that the Chief Constable would not be back in the Force area before late the following Monday other than to attend the Officers' Mess Dinner at the Bristol University Assembly Rooms that evening. He informed me that I would be expected to see the Chief on Monday afternoon for him to promote me to Superintendent in charge of the Communications Department. In the meanwhile I was to say nothing to anyone.

As I walked through her office, the DCC's secretary congratulated me, as did the ACC's secretary when I returned to her office. Both, of course, were 'in the know' but as would all good secretaries kept it to themselves, even the one with whom I spent quite a bit of my working time. The ACC was grinning all over his face when I thanked him for the support that had started when he had nominated me to perform the Communications Scrutiny over a year earlier. The real difficulty came when I attended the Officers' Mess Dinner that evening. Before departing from the Force area on the Thursday, the Chief Constable had presided over the latest of the bimonthly Divisional Commanders' Conferences. He had told all the Chief Superintendents and ACPO rank Officers of his intention to promote me on the following Monday. On Friday evening, sworn to secrecy, one Chief Superintendent after another quietly congratulated me!

On Monday afternoon, all was back on an even keel when the Chief Constable told me of the promotion. He added that his challenge for me was to implement all the agreed recommendations from the Scrutiny Report but not to expect him to have to spend any money in the process. We both shared a knowing grin regarding the latter comment, knowing full well that the cost of the changes was not going to be small. On this occasion, the promotion was not only to be unusual in the way it came about but was to be tinged with much personal sadness. When I returned home, having already telephoned Gill to give her the good news, I immediately telephoned my parents to inform them. As she usually did, my mother answered the call and was, of course, thrilled to hear the news. Having worked until she was 65 years of age, five years beyond her retirement age, and not being in the best of health since she was 70, within a couple of days of that telephone call she was in Musgrove Park Hospital in Taunton and two weeks later she died. The woman who had driven whatever ambition I held right from my childhood had, at least, known of my latest modest success before her departure.

21 Headquarters Communications

Having spent the couple of weeks since I had received the promotion news between running down to Taunton to visit my mother and introducing the new Regional Staff Officer to his role, I was unsure why it was mid-week but moved up to the rank of Superintendent on a Wednesday, 21st November, 1990. The ACC could not have been more helpful in terms of my being absent at Musgrove Hospital and checking in with my father, perhaps because I did try to ensure that all my duties were attended to by working longer hours when not absent. Just as there had been in the previous instances, I suppose always are unless moving out of a role is terminal, there was some 'overhang' with certain aspects of the old job still needing occasional attention.

I discovered, very quickly, that the job I actually inherited, in an office hidden away from the Force Control Room, was about as routine, even tedious, as any task I had ever undertaken in the Service. It was, unfortunately, to be some weeks before other aspects were in place and I would be able to launch into the closer planning and implementation stages of the Communications Scrutiny. Meanwhile my main focus was the unbelievable levels of casual sickness in the Department. Remember that the Communications Department was entirely headquarters based and still separate from the Divisional Control Rooms and Traffic Centre at Almondsbury.

There were many exceptions but a significant proportion of civilian support staff and a few of the Regular Officers in the Department had shocking records of repetitively taking the available three days uncertificated sickness. I am not sure whether I had ever noticed it before but, with my 'inherited' inspections of the sickness records of the four groups, I discovered a Bristolian trait. There were a few police officers in the department who had found their way to the Bristol area from elsewhere but most of them and virtually all of the civilian support staff were local to the city. Their reasons for taking the three days uncertificated sickness were, more often than not, shown as 'flu', scarcely ever 'cold' or 'head cold'. I could only assume that few of these individuals had ever experienced a real dose of flu! The other noticeable trend, other than the repeated appearance of certain members of staff, was how often these 'sick days' were taken immediately before or after the rostered rest days. I could never have envisaged that my promotion to Superintendent would bring me to a primary focus upon departmental sickness!

Thankfully, for me, the winter of 1990/91 ended with my becoming directly involved in the implementation of the Scrutiny report recommendations and my deputy, a Chief Inspector, received the distinct reward of standing in for my daily routine for long enough to benefit from that upgrade to his pay for the purpose of his pension base-line. There were five Inspectors, one each on the four groups that provided the shift cover and a 'spare' who filled in where necessary. That 'spare' Inspector also received the lesser increase as Acting Chief Inspector for long enough to benefit his pension calculation.

With the outline plan being to retain the 'northern' control at Staple Hill, to also cover Bath, pending the completion of the Operations Building at Portishead and a re-vamped facility in New Bridewell to cover the Bristol Districts, the focus for me at first was to identify suitable space at Taunton. The Taunton Centre would need to be of a size to accommodate the then current Divisional Controls at Taunton, Weston-super-Mare and Yeovil. While spending time in the buildings behind the old Somerset Headquarters at Taunton, one room that looked to have promise was then well packed with all sorts of historically interesting items. One thing that caught my eye was a pile of Annual Reports from the Bristol Constabulary for the year in which I had joined the Somerset Constabulary, 1965. With the figure still fresh in my mind of the Chipping Sodbury Sub-Division's recorded crime for 1990, I was amazed to discover that it was close to identical to that for Bristol twenty five years earlier. I cannot help be sceptical when I hear over recent times the constant reference to 'lack of resources'. At Chipping Sodbury in 1990, with a total Sub-Divisional strength of 50, we had maintained a creditable level of crime related service to the population which in Bristol in 1965 had been achieved but with an establishment more than twenty times greater!

Fortunately, before I had taken any real measures to clear space at Taunton I was called to the office, in Old Bridewell, of one of the ACCs, who would later go on to become Chief Constable of Merseyside Police. He had been to a recent seminar involving the relatively newly formed Nuclear Electric, formerly a limb of the Central Electricity Generating Board (CEGB). In discussions outside their meeting the project manager, based then in the CEGB offices on Bedminster Down in Bristol, related to our ACC that they had been directed by the Government to create Local Emergency Centres (LECs) for each nuclear power station across the country. Avon and Somerset had within its boundaries two nuclear power stations, one at the extreme north on the side of the Severn estuary at Oldbury and the other beside the Bristol Channel at Hinkley Point, south of the estuary of the river Parrett.

Nuclear Electric had reached the point at which they were eying up some land near Walford Cross, south of North Petherton, for a new-build LEC for Hinkley Point but the ACC suggested to them that they may like, instead, to invest in a joint effort in conjunction with our proposed new Communications Centre at Taunton. With the outline costs of the new-build looking quite massive, the Nuclear Electric manager immediately saw the potential benefits of the joint effort. These benefits were not just financial for Nuclear Electric. Even a brand new 'mothballed' centre would, in time, suffer from deterioration of the electrical and electronic equipment due to long periods of standing idle and some form of, costly, regular attention would be required. Within a fully active Police Communications Centre their equipment would only require occasional testing and exercising.

Hence, I ended up making another visit to Taunton with a somewhat different brief, and a promise of Nuclear Electric cash to help the process. Inside one of the wings of the early nineteenth century prison block and long since used as an undercover vehicle storage area, was a large space as all the floors had long-since been removed. We engaged the assistance of the County Architect from County Hall nearby and he created a rough plan of what could be included inside the space. I looked at the plans and created my own suggestion on a piece of A4 paper. My version had two floors with higher ceiling levels at one end and three floors with normal room heights at the other. The architect kindly revised his accurate plans to provide what I had outlined.

An early assessment brought the conclusion that the Grade A listed building, although the walls were several feet thick, was not strong enough to support the floors, equipment and activities within a new centre. The solution was to build a girder supported structure inside the old building with panels providing surrounds to the windows to secure as much natural light as was possible. The old outer walls' only 'load' was the roof. At the end with two floors, the upper was the new 'Area' Control Room space and below it a similar sized room which was intended to become the call handling centre. Our intention, from the Scrutiny, had been to separate call reception from radio dispatching with a view to trained staff with modern command and control computer systems 'fielding' as many calls as possible. A database was started for operators to be able to find the answers to as many telephone enquiries as possible without having to send a police officer.

The latter aspect, call handling, required an increase in civilian support staff and their appropriate training. To facilitate financing these posts, the moves into the three centres from the former eight local control rooms, Almondsbury and Headquarters Force Control, 'saved' a significant number of Constables and Sergeants. For good practical reasons not associated with the communications changes these Officer posts were redeployed so the money to pay for the large number of call-handlers was not realised for many years after the changes between 1993 and 1996. Because of this the full potential of this aspect of our review was not fully realised.

The best bit about the Nuclear Electric involvement was that the Force had a new centre capable of dealing with all the communications for the two Police Districts in (post 1974) Somerset and the Weston-super-Mare District within Avon. What is more both organisations had benefitted. Nuclear Electric had a secure LEC with the police on site for any exercises (no one ever wanted to see a live operation) at a small proportion of the cost of building and maintaining their own centre. The Avon and Somerset Constabulary had saved the cost of the Taunton build. What is more, the Nuclear Electric need for an LEC for Oldbury was incorporated into the plans for the new Force Headquarters (NFHQ) Communications facility at Portishead Down for a much more modest contribution from that company.

There were two aspects of the liaison with Nuclear Electric in the old CEGB offices on Bedminster Down which struck me as amusing. Nuclear Electric moved out of that complex not many years after our meetings to re-locate to Barnwood near Gloucester. Years earlier when the Bedminster Down building was constructed, the architects had included what was then a very modern form of air conditioning that required a large capacity of stored water. This they created in the form of a swimming pool for the use of the staff. More directly related to my liaison was that they always insisted that my visits were late morning and incorporated a lunch in their staff dining area. I would meet with only a handful of their staff but we would collect their colleagues as we went from the meeting room to the restaurant, so that all could be included in the 'hospitality'. So much reminiscent of my visit to Derbyshire, related in Chapter Fifteen.

Part of the plan was for the operators at the new consoles to have two screens before them, one containing the computer data and log for the current incident and the other a map of the affected area. In the early 1990s there were still some advances to be made before we reached the mapping technology we all now take for granted. The best at that time was contained on large discs and relied upon Ordnance Survey coordinates for locations, with quite cumbersome searching processes. One of the pioneer companies involved in this technology was based not far from our county boundary in Wiltshire and another further away in Surrey. Our visits demonstrated that our desired way forward was still in the developmental stages at that time. By the end of the 1990s, after I had 'moved on' the technology blossomed and I have never been able to understand the complaint I occasionally hear from people that a police operator "did not even know where I was!"

In early 1991, I started to get involved with the architects for the NFHQ phase two, the Operations Building, which would house the new Communications Centre, and stand beside the communications tower at Portishead Down. Their offices were off the bottom of Park Street in Bristol and, with the small project team we had assembled, of which more to follow, we visited them with the Chief Inspector NFHQ Project Manager. They were entirely looking to us for a steer regarding the tower and the plans for the Operations Building showed a large circular area in its centre. My enquiry revealed that this was to be 'the atrium' and would be "a pleasing architectural feature". When I further enquired as to how cabinets would be located on the curved surfaces on the other side of the atrium walls, the atrium was re-drawn and built as a rectangle. In later years, long after I had departed, this atrium was occupied by fabricated office accommodation, how would that have been if it had remained round?

One of the innovations within the new, large, communications room at Portishead was to do away with the constant complaint from the staff about the draughts created by ceiling or wall mounted air conditioning systems. At NFHQ a new system was installed of 'chill bars' which were thermostatically controlled and relied upon the natural convection of air being chilled at higher levels gently permeating the space and being replaced by the warmer air rising up to, in turn, be chilled. This proved to be a most successful advancement. The implementation project team comprised two technically well versed Officers, one a Chief Inspector whom I had worked with when he was a Sergeant on 'A' Division and the other an Inspector, who had been with me as the Sergeant on the Communications Scrutiny team.

We went, with the Information Systems Manager, to visit several communications towers and to discuss their respective good and bad points with local communications staff. The outcome was a recommendation that the architects took forward for the cylindrical tower in four long sections still visible for many miles from Portishead Down. There was a need for a specific height because we still had the microwave link to the VHF coverage provided to the Somerset coastal areas from the commercial television site in South Wales. One of the more comical aspects of the massive NFHQ project came from this tower's introduction to the site. At the time there was much talk in the mass media regarding a 'super gun' for Uganda. A few, seeing the sections of this tower being brought by road towards Portishead, 'warned' the media people of the super-gun being transported to the local docks!

Alongside the project and regular contact with my 'stand-in' looking after the day-to-day running of the existing communications, I still enjoyed paying visits to the Pontypridd Police Management Studies Course to give talks on the logistics for large-scale operations. With many Officers in the Chief Inspector to Chief Superintendent ranks having gone through the Public Order Command Band Training, the courses at Devizes and Bridgend became far fewer and, eventually, ceased as in-Force arrangements took their place.

In March 1991 I was asked by the ACC who had found our Nuclear Electric link to stand in for him at a seminar at the European Centre for the Study of Policing, part of the Open University at Milton Keynes. The ACC did not have much idea as to why he had been asked to attend but did not want to totally renege upon his agreement to do so. As far as I could tell there was only one other serving officer present, I believe from Bedfordshire, but a room full of academics and representatives from local authorities and government departments. The only item I found memorable was a presentation by a young woman, recent recipient of a PhD, presenting her thesis upon prostitution. She declared that in her research with prostitutes in several cities, but not including Bristol, she had been told repeatedly of their being 'hounded' by and highly suspicious of police officers. It had been my experience, ten years earlier when working at Trinity Road in Bristol (Chapter Fourteen) that, quite to the contrary, prostitutes seemed to have some respect for the officers dealing with their soliciting as being that rare male who was not exploiting them. I further pointed out the old problem, noticed at the same station among young men of West Indian ancestry who, despite being dealt with entirely properly, would always claim to have been beaten up when they were released from police custody. The underlying reason for this was that if they did not make such claims among their peers they would be assumed to have been acting as informants while in custody!

In the September of 1991, nine months into the role of Communications Officer and now leading the implementation of the changes from the Scrutiny Report, I was sent on the national Communications Officers' Course, hosted by the Northumbria Police. The course lasted four weeks and I travelled by car, piling mileage on the Rover 820 I had only recently bought, nearly new. On the Monday morning journey I travelled the motorways around Birmingham and up the east route but to break the monotony, on Fridays, I crossed the Pennines to Carlisle and came back down the west route. Those of us on the course were a mixture of ranks from a wide number of Forces and included civilian support members.

The Northumbria Sergeant who was the course coordinator organised a few outings for us to occupy an evening in each week but had nothing arranged for the first week, presumably so that he could make a judgement as to what his latest group would appreciate. We, I think it was all of us, decided on an evening out so asked his advice as to where was worthy of a visit. He immediately offered Whitley Bay. We shared our available transport and set off but soon got separated and, in our case, lost. When we regained the route we ended up with all the cars meeting above the sea front, to find that most of the visible population of Whitley Bay were queuing at the bus stop opposite the layby in which we had gathered. One of our drivers asked where we could spend the evening and was told that they were waiting for the bus to go somewhere else for Bingo! We found an empty pub but did not stay long, returning to the bar at the Police Training School as a much better option.

The trips out organised by the local Sergeant went much better. One was to a large battery manufacturer in Durham, quite a run in the school minibus but with lavish hospitality in a large hotel after the factory visit. Another made no pretence to being course-related and was to the brewery famous for Newcastle Brown Ale. The brewing process was explained and we ended up in their own 'mock-up' of a pub where refreshment, solid and liquid, was available. I remade a personal contact while near Newcastle. An old school friend, whom I had not seen since we parted at school in 1962, lives in Washington, not far from Newcastle and I spent an evening sharing an enjoyable meal at their home. A couple of weeks later, to make it different, we went to Sunderland for an evening. I was totally amazed, as I had in my mind's eye the vision of industry and ship-building but we drove along a beautifully illuminated front and visited a really lovely park.

One of the speakers on the course had travelled up from the Home Office and was on a Central Service secondment and in the early stages of starting up what was then known as 'The Major Study'. This project was to examine the future of police, perhaps all emergency service, radio and his presentation was very much exploratory because nothing had yet been 'cast in stone'. The only real declared expectation was to find a more combined system to replace the existing VHF vehicle sets and UHF personal radios then in use in most parts of England and Wales. The questions I raised with this Chief Superintendent from an east midlands force resulted in him contacting me later and inviting me to join the project. Although, somewhat inevitably cutting across the chronological order because it was accomplished by occasional diversions from my 'in-Force' project, I will describe what my participation in that project involved.

Smith's Associates, a communications and computer consultancy company from Surrey, had won the contract offered by the Home Office, to assist the Major Study team. Initially, we had several 'brainstorming' meetings at their offices and established a very 'high level' assessment of what a new radio system for the Service would need to provide. The Chief Superintendent then sent out papers to each of the 43 Forces in England and Wales with the request that they examine the categories we had identified, and any others they considered important, with as wide a circle of police radio users as possible.

I took on the local coordinator role for Avon and Somerset and set up a large gathering at our Kingsweston House training centre to the west of Bristol with requests going out to all parts of the Force to send suitable representatives. The day proved to be most constructive, with force members from virtually every department and geographic area. This gave the opportunity for the real 'end users' to have a direct in-put into what it was they wanted to see improved by a new national radio scheme.

The Home Office based team of a very small number of seconded officers then set up a revised User Group, of which I remained a member. With the information from the responses from the 43 Forces initially being worked upon by Smiths Associates to gather any statistical information together, the revised User Group met in a number of locations. A nucleus of us also convened for several days in a hotel on the Hogg's Back in Surrey. The new group was larger than that for the 'Part One' of the 'Major Study' and included my counterpart from the Gwent Constabulary. We arranged to share transport to the national gatherings to prepare for and support what was achieved at the several day gathering. From this concentrated effort came the first draft of the User Requirement for the revised radio scheme. Although it was to be a few years and after my retirement from the Force, these activities formed the base-line for what was to become the new-generation 'Airwave' Police Radio system.

A couple of years after my police retirement, I found one disappointment with the end-product of our radio user activities in that the 'promise' of a single-tier radio system reaching all users had not, wholly, been realised. There remained, in the rural areas which I had seen it as my role on the User Group to champion, the continued need for 'back-to-back' working. In other words not all areas were fully covered for reception by hand-portable sets and there had to be a 'repeater' facility for officers to leave the more powerful vehicle-based sets just as we had done with the old VHF/UHF repeaters in rural areas and on main-road patrol vehicles earlier. One aspect that had improved, of course, was in respect of the security of the system and the lesser likelihood that unwanted ears were listening in to police radio traffic.

Although it got nowhere, mainly because the newly burgeoning technology which was seeing rapid developments in the mobile 'telephone' industry, I did, individually, follow one line of potential development. With the cooperation of a radio provider from Southampton, I put forward a proposal for the retention of the traditional VHF and UHF schemes in a single-set received/transmitter system. With set internals getting smaller, the company confirmed that there was no reason why a hand-held radio could not be made to operate on either VHF or UHF, responding to the best signal it could identify. This may have brought true hand-held wide area cover but the national die was cast for a cellular system. At that relatively early stage there remained a perceived need for the police system to be discrete but there was already some indication that digital technologies would have securely enabled the combining of any police requirement within one or more of the commercial providers. As with all things technological, timing is of the essence. There was a need for a new system in the mid-1990s that it was thought could not wait but only a few years later the combined approach with commercial digital cellular schemes could have happened. With the current thirst for everything to be 'outsourced' I suspect that the next generation emergency service radio systems will 'share' with commercial providers.

An invitation arrived for me to give a talk to the Filton based Radio Hams' Group. I must confess that I had some concerns about trying to give any sort of presentation on radio to a body of people who would, most certainly, know vastly more about the pure radio technology than I would ever know. With the understanding, strongly emphasised in my acceptance letter and repeated at the beginning of my talk, that I would be speaking about the 'each end user' rather than the technology in between, the session seemed to go well. As I had anticipated, I learned far more that evening than did any member of my audience but they were most appreciative of being given an insight into what was involved in the every-day police use of radio.

Largely because the local volunteer rescue team had, for many years, been provided with radio coverage under the licence held by the Force, they had adopted the title of the Avon and Somerset Cliff Rescue Team. Because of the radio connection, my role included liaison with this very devoted and extremely expert group of people. My role in charge of the Force Communications Department also incorporated our Force representation on the South West Emergency Rescue Association (SWERA), which was, by tradition, chaired by the Chief Superintendent Operations of the Devon & Cornwall Constabulary and the meetings held at their Middlemoor Headquarters.

The Avon and Somerset Cliff Rescue Team, provided cover in both the Cheddar Gorge, where they did most of their training, and the Avon Gorge, when the Fire Brigade equipment (see Chapter Twelve) did not afford access. The Force area also brought ties with the Mendip Rescue Association, which included experts in pot-hole rescue, and had a large group of volunteer Mendip Wardens and a full-time coordinator living high on the Mendips not far from our radio masts at Charterhouse. A similar body, concentrating on wide area searching capability, existed for Exmoor. Although the connection with the river Exe makes many believe that Exmoor is in Devon, geographically far more of it is in fact in Somerset.

All property that came into police hands and was not made the subject of a court ruling or for which no rightful owner could be identified had, under The Police Property Act, to be auctioned off and the proceeds delivered to charitable causes. There was a clause under the act for items to be taken into police use but this was only applied in relatively few instances. The significant sum that these, usually six monthly, auctions realised was split into more suitable sums and it was for Divisional and Departmental Commanders to put forward suggestions as to causes they considered worthy of an award from the Fund. I, invariably, suggested one or other, often all, of these volunteer rescue organisations. Several of the cheque presentations that I made to these groups received some media coverage, thanks to their ensuring that the local press or even television news, were made aware.

On one occasion the Avon and Somerset Cliff Rescue Team staged a 'rescue' abseil down the Cheddar Gorge with their Chairman in a stretcher between two team members. When the TV crew had filmed the descent to the floor of the gorge he was seen lifting his arm from the stretcher to receive from me their cheque for £200 from the Fund. On another, January, occasion, it was the turn of the Exmoor Rescue Team and they chose a remote spot high on the moor. That Sunday morning, I arrived at Minehead and travelled in a Force Land Rover with one of the local Sergeants to meet up with the group. The weather was a bit bleak, with snow high on either side of the roads and a small amount still falling. The reporter from the Minehead newspaper, who doubled as photographer, valiantly reached the spot in his mini car and took a photograph of me handing a scrap of paper to the Team Chairman. We did not want the ink to run on the actual cheque!

The many people who gave freely of their time, expertise and energy to rescue others were, as I suppose would be expected, genuinely nice folk and sought every opportunity to practice their skills with no mean degree of humour. On my first visit for one of the Sunday SWERA meetings at Middlemoor, but not thereafter, I was surprised to hear the massive noise of a Sea King Helicopter arriving with the representatives from RAF Chivenor. The Sea King made the Devon & Cornwall Squirrel helicopter look quite tiny on its nearby helipad. These meetings were always held on a Sunday morning, a couple of times each year, so that they did not interfere with the 'day job' of the majority of those in attendance.

The Chief Superintendent, Staff Officer to Her Majesty's Inspector of Constabulary (Technical) with whom we had contact through the Communications Scrutiny retired and followed up contacts from his final police service role. Affiliated to the American Association of Public Safety Communications Officials, he established the British Association of Public Safety Communications Officers (BAPCO), since having undergone a name change to even more align it with the USA organisation. At the time of my involvement with Regional ACPO its members had been discussing what was referred to as 'subordinate conferences' with a view to cutting down such regional gatherings. One that, subsequent to my leaving the Regional ACPO staff officer role, was discontinued was that of the Region's Communications Officers. This forum had performed a valuable role in terms of knowledge sharing over many years and BAPCO seemed, to me, not a bad substitute. I, therefore, joined and was soon appointed Chairman for the South West Region meetings and representative on the national body.

I now return to the development of the Force Communications structure, which because of the separation that had already occurred between users and providers of equipment I determined we should call Communications Operations. With the broad structure established and much in line with the accepted proposals from the Scrutiny, we established three Working Groups, one for each of the new Communications Centres. I was fortunate in being afforded the full-time commitment of a Constable who was well known to the Chief Superintendent given overall responsibility for the Force Reorganisation Implementation Team (FRIT) with which I was co-housed on the top floor of the New Bridewell building in central Bristol. This Constable had worked most recently in the communications centre for the Staple Hill Division, a facility which would become the northern area centre pending the availability of the

NFHQ suite. I could not have been more fortunate in the choice made for me.

The three Working Groups sat regularly at Staple Hill (including South Gloucestershire and the Bath area), New Bridewell (the proposed Bristol City Districts) and Taunton (for that area, Weston-super-Mare and Yeovil) with police and civilian support members from each existing Divisional (and Force or Motorway) Control as appropriate to each new centre. We soon developed a routine for discussion which allowed for everyone to have their say but where I exercised the control of identifying those items which would not be capable of being realised. We occasionally deferred decisions for further thought or research before the next meeting but, in the main, avoided revisiting items which we had 'signed off'. This process had the undoubted benefit that the people who really knew what was required applied their full input to the way forward.

The new Communications Centre at Portishead Down was not to be operational until some time after I retired but the Support Services Headquarters team moved over the August Bank Holiday weekend in 1995. In view of the occasional difficulties I had encountered because of the separation of the Communications Department from the Information Services Department, who were responsible for the supply and maintenance of the equipment, amid the changes I managed with the assistance of the Support Services Chief Superintendent to create a small unit which we called Communications Operations Support. The new command and control system that was being developed within another project team, led by a Superintendent I had known since we shared the Special Course in 1973/74, would generate a great deal of previously unavailable statistical information and this would require a number of people to monitor that product.

This team, of a Sergeant, two Constables and three civilians had a multiple role within the Communications Operations Department. We had long had two, by then quite old, mobile communications vehicles and I had to expend some considerable effort to get them replaced. The real challenge came from the Operations Department, who wanted a mobile command 'pod' and their Superintendent saw the demise of our old vehicles as a 'budget head' from which to get the mobile command vehicle. After quite strenuous debate we managed to get two large Mercedes vans. A visit, with members of the Support team to Coventry showed what conversion capability was possessed by Tickfords and they got the small contract. I say small because they were, when we visited, converting public order protected carriers for the Metropolitan Police in huge numbers. Of greater personal interest was their smaller workshop in which some quite up-market cars were being personalised for wealthy clients. Among them was the next Jaguar XJ6 being provided with protection for use by the Prime Minister. The availability of the Communications Operations Support team to provide rapid local area communications to the scene of any type of incident was of immense value.

During the time that a group of us were involved with the Force Reorganisation Implementation Team (FRIT) it became a custom for those of us who were about the offices late on a Friday afternoon to have an 'O' Group get-together to review our relative current situations. These opportunities to share what each member was doing helped to secure that we were all moving along progression pathways that would not clash as they developed. One Inspector pointed out that changes in New Bridewell had reached a point at which he had arranged for a number of civilian support staff to come in on the following day, Saturday, 7th December, 1991, to move items of equipment between offices. He pointed out that this had the disadvantage that one of the offices involved was that which doubled as a 'mothballed' Casualty Bureau, with multiple telephone sockets for the call handling such a Bureau necessitates. Another Officer in the gathering asked if anyone could remember the last time we had been required to operate a Casualty Bureau. The Inspector, who had an on-going and periodically exercised responsibility to maintain a corps of trained staff, admitted it had been some considerable time. We left the meeting quite comfortable that we would be likely to escape any dire consequences of the room being in uproar for just one day.

I think what it is called 'sod's law' prevailed overnight for at 8.30a.m. as the staff were assembling to earn their modest few hours of overtime, an Inter-City 125 train travelling between London Paddington and Cardiff Central was stopped by signals at the southern (English) entrance to the huge Severn Tunnel. After a telephone conversation with the signalmen the driver was authorised to proceed with caution. When the train was about three miles into the four mile and 624 yard (just over 7 kilometre) tunnel, proceeding as instructed at a slow pace, it was struck from behind by a Sprinter multiple unit train traveling from Portsmouth to Cardiff. Miraculously there were no fatalities but of the 185 people injured, five of them were classified as seriously so. On occasions what could prove to be a serious failing can be turned, by a bit of quick thinking, into a real success. The Inspector immediately broke out the telephone equipment and forms from the storage cupboard and gave brief instruction to those who needed it.

In record time the Avon and Somerset Constabulary had a fully-functioning Casualty Bureau. On any normal Saturday morning there would, inevitably, have been the delays of getting people from their homes to the room. Thankfully, the operation did not have to last long and the transfer of the equipment originally planned for that morning was easily rescheduled. Importantly, the Force had been in an exceptional position to provide the service that was asked of it to all concerned. More directly pertinent to me was another sequel. This was born of the enquiry that was conducted into the very rare occurrence of a collision in Britain's longest and long established railway tunnel. One of the findings within that, rightly comprehensive, enquiry was that communications inside the tunnel were abysmal and did nothing to assist the strenuous and quite brave rescue efforts on that December morning.

Many months later and arguably far too long, in November, 1995, I was contacted by a Superintendent from the British Transport Police who informed me that Railtrak had completed the installation of 'leaky feeder' cabling through the length of the tunnel. It was hoped that such an arrangement would enable radio transmissions into and within the tunnel. He was seeking our cooperation, with the other local Emergency Services, to mount an exercise to test that the new arrangement was functional. Not wanting to waste too much time, we discussed the matter with Avon Fire & Rescue and Avon Ambulance Service and agreed with the railway authorities that we would have the tunnel free from trains in the early hours of Sunday, 19th November. In view of the likelihood of cold weather I prevailed upon the Force Operations Department to provide the field refreshment vehicle to supply hot drinks to all those attending.

Just after 1a.m. on that morning, I arrived with two of our Communications Operations Support team at the southern portal of the tunnel and found that there were already representatives from all involved agencies arriving. The gated road entry to the tunnel led to a large ledge and a further slope went down to track level. The feeding truck was on the ledge and all non-essential vehicles were parked nearby. At track level there was a large concreted area through which the rails ran but which enabled road vehicles to drive across the tracks.

The Fire Brigade were unloading their mini-train of a powered truck and two trailers with flanged railway type wheels and seating for a total of ten people. This they were placing on a small siding of track. Nearby the Ambulance Service had an inflated field casualty centre which was already up and ready.

The call came down from the ledge that the Constable from Operations had prepared hotdogs with tea or coffee for everyone so, not to let the products of his labour go cold, we all returned to the ledge. Enjoying our warming food and drinks, I was chatting with the man from Railtrak and the Superintendent from British Transport Police. Suddenly there was the familiar sound of the two-tone horns of an Inter-City 125 heralding the roar of the lead engine, a rushing of the carriages and second roar of the trailing engine. I looked at the two railway men beside me and could not stop myself from asking the question with only one, obvious, answer, "What the hell was that?" With their considerable embarrassment obvious, the Railtrak man called the signalling people at Temple Meads. The last train, scheduled for 12.30a.m. had been delayed and nothing had been put in place for us to be warned. The saving of many lives was, so very thankfully, down to operational feeding.

Several weeks before the incident I have just related and mentioned earlier, the Support Services Department Headquarters staff moved, over the August Bank Holiday weekend, from New Bridewell to the New Force Headquarters at Portishead Down. All of the building work, at least that planned up until that time, had been completed but the closing stages of the new Command and Control equipment development had not managed to keep up to schedule. Hence, the Communications Operations Support team and I moved in beside an empty control room space together with the Criminal Justice management, while the communications continued from New Bridewell, Staple Hill and the new facility at Taunton. With the planning and implementation arrangements all completed or well in hand, I had resumed the full-time role in charge of the Department in 1993. The Acting Superintendent and Chief Inspector both took their opportunities to retire while the higher pay rate influenced their pension calculations.

While working in the office beside the principal control room, in New Bridewell, I was able to catch the mood for what was going on beyond my office door which, for most of the time, stood open. It was quite evident when something out of the routine was beginning to brew-up and I could quickly move to find out what was happening. On most occasions the shift Inspector would have everything under control but where the incident started to look as though it would require a Superintendent overview, I would get involved and act, at least temporarily, as the 'Silver Commander'. This had the additional advantage of my assuming that role quickly but also meant that the District Commander could concentrate upon whatever was demanded locally.

The concept of Gold, Silver and Bronze had developed post the 1980s street disorders and became well established in the 1990s. Effectively, someone of ACPO rank was Gold and could be office based at Headquarters, providing policy inputs where necessary. Silver was usually of Superintendent rank and was responsible for the strategic and logistical inputs either from a temporary local mobile communications facility or from one of the three communications centres. Bronze was usually of Inspector rank and was responsible for tactics at the 'sharp' end at or near the scene of the incident. As part of this standing structure plan, each of the three centres, Staple Hill excluded but seen as temporary and New Force Headquarters very much included, had fully equipped side rooms to the main control rooms designated as Silver Control.

I very much enjoyed the distraction from the routine of running the second largest department in the Force, to become operationally involved - at my retirement in 1996 the Department totalled 330 people. I was to lose that to a significant extent with the move to Portishead. What I gained was the largest, and brand new, office I had ever occupied, with the essential advantage of a balcony overlooking the Gordano valley. The balcony was, to me at the time 'essential' as the new Headquarters came with the dictum from the Chief Constable that there was to be no smoking anywhere in any of the buildings. I was able to escape this restriction by moving out onto the balcony for a puff or two of my pipe. Soon, the smokers from the nearby offices prevailed upon me to allow them through my office to join me on the balcony. As had been the case at Chipping Sodbury some years earlier (chapter eighteen), this brought me closer to what was the common gossip of the day than applied for most Departmental Commanders. I carried this over when visiting New Bridewell, Staple Hill and Taunton as I would frequent the smoking area while visiting and all levels from within the Department would share their views openly, much more so than would have occurred in any more formal setting.

We are getting near to the close of my police career, although I have allowed myself a final chapter for summing up, but my final New Year in charge of force communications brought to light the way in which staff who are comfortable in their roles can rise to the unprecedented occasion. On the morning of Saturday, 30th December, 1995, after a night of continuous rainfall, the temperature in the greater Bristol area freakishly nosedived at around 8.00a.m. freezing the lying water on roads and, more crucially, footpaths. All over the affected area people were coming to grief behind the car wheel but more injuriously on foot. The calls to the Ambulance Service through the 999 system became a deluge.

The system within the Ambulance Service at that time was that if British Telecom could not place a 999 call to the local Ambulance Control Room they diverted it to a neighbouring Ambulance Service. On this day, however, the neighbouring Ambulance controls could not get responses on their inter-control room lines because the operators in Avon Ambulance were swamped. Their next port of call, and the next for the BT operators as well, was to forward callers to the Avon and Somerset Force Control facility in New Bridewell, which in the new environment had an overflow facility to the other communications centres. The crisis lasted for about two hours, with police vehicles being deployed to injured people as substitute ambulances. I was informed at home by the duty Inspector, after the crisis had been dealt with, a trait not to be criticised in a proficient middle manager.

On returning to the office on the Tuesday, I got the trusty Communications Operations Support staff to do a quick analysis of the calls handled on the Saturday morning. This revealed a remarkable level of performance. In the mid-1990s the Force was handling an average of about 450 individual 999 calls in each 24 hour period. Between 8.00a.m. and 10.00a.m. on 30th December, 1995 we had taken an additional 450. More remarkable was the fact that our, then recent, target call pick-up times had only been failed on very few occasions. On top of these simple statistics had to be recognised the time and competence at all levels in resourcing and deploying units in support of the Ambulance Service's efforts.

The Force had developed a rather rudimentary, even for the mid-1990s, internal computer messaging system, known unimaginatively as 'Project Seven' and I immediately exploited its capability for me to send a message to every member of the Communications Department. I congratulated those who had performed the miracle and encouraged those not directly involved to take pride in what their colleagues had shown our Department was capable of achieving. Not wanting to hide our collective 'light under a bushel', I copied the Chief Constable into the distribution for the message. Some while later, I trust with his keyboard finger in his cheek, the Chief surmised that for the staff to have achieved this level of performance there must be too many of them!

So, as they say, all good things must come to an end. On Friday, 7th June, 1996, I had issued invitations to all and sundry to join me in the magnificent new bar at Portishead and it was good to see how many turned up. The only slight disappointment was that none of my more senior officers put in an appearance but my praises were sung by the man who was taking my place and who I had first met when we shared the course at Bramshill in 1973/74 (chapter ten). My old friend from the long days in New Scotland Yard (chapter sixteen) made the journey from South Wales and he was joined by quite a crowd of more local colleagues. It was the memorable evening that it should have been and one of the girls doing the driving so that I could enjoy an extra pint.

The two days before my 'do' had been spent with the Communications Operations Support team at the British Association of Public Safety Communications Officers (BAPCO) conference in Doncaster and my final weekend was extended by a couple of outstanding days due to me, so the last week was quite a relaxed affair. I purposely planned it so as I wanted to work on my last day.

On Tuesday, 11th June, I started in the office at Portishead but then visited each of the three communications centres to bid farewell to each centre manager and those staff on duty that morning. I returned to Portishead and pursued the intention to send another all-members message on 'Project 7', thanking everyone for their work and camaraderie. The process, I am pleased to say, was frustrated by a succession of colleagues from all over Headquarters calling in to my office to wish me well. So much was I interrupted that it was well after five o'clock before the message was completed to my satisfaction. At 5.55p.m. I pressed the 'send' instruction and realised that everyone else had left the offices. So, metaphorically and literally, I put the lights out as I shut the door!

22 What Came Next

One of the people outside the Force to whom I had sent an invitation to my leaving 'do' was the Managing Director of the company who, at that time, we were working with to create our new Command and Control computer system. The letter had been for him to pass on the invitation to those alongside whom we had been working at Christchurch in the developing of the product. Instead of passing on the message, he attended. After my old friend had made his speech and I had responded, the MD took me to one side and offered me a job. I had been preparing myself for my police retirement for quite some time, especially since reaching the magical thirty years of service at which I could claim my pension. I had, however, more idea as to what I did not want to do than what I did want. With my fifty first birthday only a couple of days away there was quite a while before real retirement seemed appropriate but, after the long and demanding commitment to the police service I knew that I did not want to start working full-time for anyone. I offered to become a consultant with his company and he readily agreed.

That was the start of another steep learning curve. I now realised, alongside its demanding nature, how cosseted I had been in the big machine backing up policing. I had the good fortune that a neighbour pointed me towards a local accountant who steered me towards becoming a one-man limited company and I spent the first year making periodic trips to Christchurch. Lessons had to be learned along the way and the first came after about ten months. Fortunately, the other big lesson came at about the same time. The trips to Christchurch began to grow fewer as the months went on but I had been careless enough not to have anticipated that possibility and was under an exclusivity contract not to work elsewhere without specific consent. Fortunately, such consent had been forthcoming for a brief involvement that taught me the other lesson.

There came a month in which I was not handed any work and it looked likely that the next month would be just as 'dry'. I had no alternative but to cancel the contract and sit on my hands for a further two months to satisfy the notice element of the contract. The one additional contract in which I had been enabled to engage was for a contact through BAPCO (British Association of Public Safety Communications Officers) and involved only a few days' work, in concert with a London company, to establish a one-day seminar near Heathrow for an American Company. The agreement was that I would be paid £1,000 for the work involved. The seminar took place and the contact arrived direct from the USA and departed back there immediately afterwards. Before he went off to catch his return flight he shook my hand, thanked me and assured me that his cheque would be in the post soon after he returned to his office. He was, to a degree, true to his word and a cheque arrived within quite a short time but, it was for $1,000, at that time worth about £650. A few telephone calls and another cheque arrived for the balance but I had to pay the bank to handle two cheques instead of one.

Not too long after these lessons had been learned, I engaged with another American Company that was looking to get involved in the Emergency Services control room market in the UK. This time, I got it right. The provision existed within their standard form of contract for the consultant to add his or her own conditions. I incorporated a minimum number of days per month and that payments should be in pounds sterling through a UK bank, both were accepted. The contract lasted over a year and brought a lot of travelling around the country. Unfortunately it did not include a need for me to visit the USA as a director made a flight over for a few days each six weeks or so to meet with me and their only UK full-time employee. The rest of the time I worked alongside that employee, often from his home in St Albans.

After expending some considerable up-front investment in their possible incursion into the UK Emergency Services communications market, I could see that their overtures to Police, Fire and Ambulance services around the UK were not looking good. One morning, the man from St Albans telephoned me to tell me that the company was pulling out. The worst aspect was that his services were being dispensed with, not something to which people in that field of employment were at that time unaccustomed. I reminded them of my contract additions and they paid me the two months' notice within the body of the contract for the minimum agreed working days.

By the time that the two months of my pre-paid commitment expired, I received a sub-contract proposal from a company in Chippenham, Wiltshire to work alongside the Royal Parks Police (RPC) in London. My initial visit was to Hyde Park police station and I discovered that the deputy chief officer of the RPC was a, since retired, Metropolitan Police Chief Inspector from my days in the National Reporting Centre (NRC – chapter sixteen). I was introduced to the RPC Inspector in charge at St James Park and was to work with him for about two years. The project involved their 'outsourcing' of their communications and control room requirements to the British Transport Police (BTP) in their facilities above St James Park underground station. In my many times entering and leaving that station, opposite New Scotland Yard, I had not realised what sat on top of it, except to have observed that, from the thirteenth floor of NSY, we overlooked some quite elaborate roof gardens on top of that building.

My role was to act in the best interests of the RPC in the process of transferring their communications control to the BTP. This, it was decided, should include the establishment of a Silver Control facility in a porta cabin type room in the yard at Hyde Park, positioned there because of the periodic need to control resources at concerts. The build-up to the handover was alongside the run-up to the millennium, with all the concerns, much of it subsequently proven to be hype, over what was going to happen to computer systems at midnight on 31st December, 1999. Nothing untoward did happen but many, so called, IT 'experts' earned a lot consultancy fees from businesses panicked by the worries resonating in the couple of years that ended the 1990s. Most public services could not find much money to 'protect' against the suggested threat and it proved to be just as well they could not.

With the transfer of communications control to the BTP accomplished, I was engaged for a few more consultancy days to run training sessions for quite a large number of RPC staff. We ran these sessions in a classroom at Richmond Park Police Station and I called upon my communications and logistics experience from my days in the police to try and equip the RPC Officers to deal with larger scale incidents. There was to be a brief return to the RPC a couple of years later, with the brief to assist the RPC management as the Constabulary was being returned to come under direct control of the Metropolitan Police Service. The outsourcing to the BTP proved to be very short lived but it had worked successfully during that period.

My brief return to the RPC came alongside my last contract as a one-man-band limited company. In 2002 the British Association of Public Safety Communications Officers (BAPCO), in which my status now had been determined as 'commercial', decided to seek a junior executive to be known as the 'Administrative Officer' but in fact more of a coordinator of regional activities. With contract work light at the time, I successfully applied. I remember that on the way to London for the interview I shared the train journey with four Officers going up for the briefing for the funeral of the Queen Mother. The most significant aspects of my two years working with BAPCO were the further development of the BAPCO Journal magazine, in conjunction with a new editor living on the south coast and publishers in Maidstone, and developing the Scotland Region of the Association. The latter involved quite a few journeys to Hamilton, south of Glasgow, where our meetings were held at the Headquarters of the Strathclyde Fire Service.

The principal events of interest to most people in BAPCO were the Annual Conferences. These had developed from the Associations involvement in an annual event known as the Communications in Public Safety Conference and Exhibition but the independent BAPCO event took off well. As the second year of my contract with BAPCO was well advanced, I was informed that the arrangement from the end of my current contract, in May 2004, would require me to become an employee rather than a contracted consultant. I had made no secret of my position that I valued the greater independence I had grown accustomed to since my police retirement so no one was more surprised than I was disappointed when I did not apply for the revised post. The company for whom Gill had worked in Keynsham since 1988 had joined forces with a company in Ireland and determined that her role was to be transferred to Dublin. She accepted the redundancy and finished a month before my last contracted year with BAPCO came to a close. We decided that these almost joint closures should be our signals to fully retire, so in April and May, 2004 we each entered the ranks of the early retired.

While still well engaged with my consultancy work, in 1999 for the third time since my police retirement, I attended the annual general meeting of the Avon and Somerset Branch of the National Association of Retired Police Officers (NARPO). As the meeting was getting assembled, the Branch Secretary spoke with me and told me he was going to ask of me 'a favour'. His conversation was cut short as the Chairman called the meeting to order. Mid-way through the meeting the announcement was made that the secretary was scheduled for some major surgery and that a replacement was needed. The secretary looked at me as though to say, "Well?" I waited to see if there were any other 'takers' but there were not so volunteered my services "for a couple of years". For a while my 'day job' had to take precedence but from 2004 my involvement with NARPO grew to become quite a significant part of my 'retirement' life. A role, at the time of writing, with which my Branch colleagues still entrust to me.

So, second retirement now more than a decade ago, our days remain quite fully occupied. Gill, as well as what she unavoidably does for NARPO, sought some voluntary work and has performed it with the Avon Valley Railway Heritage Trust periodically looking after the shop at Bitton Railway Station. We get involved from time to time in the busy lives of our three daughters, Tanya, Cathryn & Emma, and have delighted in watching the development of our two grandchildren, Abigail & Josh, both now well into their teen years. We, of course, hope that we have many more years left to us. With the story of what this 'Ordinary Copper' did with his Service Years complete, I am taking the liberty of adding a further chapter which I hope will present my inevitably imperfect analysis of some of the aspects to which I have referred and a few which, in the pages thus far, I have not previously discussed. I trust that anyone who has bought this book will not mind that small self-indulgence.

23 Summing Up

The purpose of this book has been to set down a record of what was, for me, nearly thirty one years of working in a service to which I think I can justly claim to have been totally dedicated. My greatest fortune was that the girl I loved, despite many challenges it placed across her path through life, supported me throughout. Perhaps not surprisingly, the greatest influence of Gill's support was during those times when the 'Job' presented the greatest challenges. I will return to this before I close this final chapter but now hope that what has been covered in the bulk of this book will have earned me in the 'eye' of the reader some right to reflect upon where the police service has come from, where it currently is and where it may be going. Some of the matters I have chosen to discuss are within the more routine levels of what policing is about but others are, I believe, of major significance for what the protection of law and order in our country needs to have addressed.

During my time at Chipping Sodbury, one of the ACCs was living nearby and visited the police station on Christmas morning each year with a 'Christmas Box' for those on duty. I emulated his well appreciated actions when I took over the reins of the Communications Department. After we had enjoyed our Christmas Day lunch, I left my family and spent the afternoon visiting each of the three communications centres. Each had a table of fare to which members on the shift had contributed and I added a tin of sweets and spent a short time wishing everyone on duty the season's greetings. Several years after my police retirement, I visited the communications centre at Portishead, which had 'inherited' operators from both Staple Hill and New Bridewell. The Senior Communications Operator seated beside the Sergeant called out as I entered, "Look, it's Mr. Leach. He used to bring us sweets on Christmas Day!" No kind gesture is ever wasted or forgotten.

During my time in charge of Communications we were inspected by a Staff Officer for the HMI (Technical) at the Home Office. He spoke with me early in his day and returned for a 'debrief' before going to his hotel. He related that all seemed to be in good order but he had one concern which he felt sure would be the subject of comment by the HMI should he decide to hold a 'thematic inspection'. He had spoken with several members of the civilian support staff, who comprised about three-quarters of the department, and they had spoken approvingly of me as the boss who allowed them to have a three-quarter hour refreshment break alongside their uniform colleagues (their entitlement was actually half-an-hour). I had wanted to minimise the differences between police and support staff as much as was within my power and this was one small example. The Staff Officer considered that I could only be criticised for allowing this concession. He was, though, at a loss when I asked him whether the staff had related how often their duties on their consoles denied them access to a proper refreshment break of any duration. That the people with whom he had spoken did not refer to their lost refreshment periods told me that I had got that one right and he, then, recognised that fact.

Although with no real expectation of success, later I was to realise no chance at all, I continued to put myself before the annual promotion boards even while on the Bramshill Scholarship secondment to the University of Bristol. When I moved to Bristol I had been surprised at the informality generated by the group system of working and common practice of Constables referring to their Sergeants by their first names. On one promotion board, in front of the Chief Constable and his Deputy, as an Inspector seeking to be nominated for Chief Inspector, this topic was raised by the DCC. My honest answer was that I was aware that it took place but did not approve. It became evident that the desired answer was to deny that it occurred. I shall never really understand why some senior officers feel more comfortable 'not knowing'. Somewhat ironically, two of the Chief Constables who have come to the Force since my retirement have encouraged all ranks to call them by their first name!

In a different context, before the rank was temporarily removed from the structure by the Home Office, there was only one occasion when I applied for a vacancy in the rank of Chief Superintendent. Several of us were interviewed and, unsurprisingly, the senior applicant got the post. One of the applicants was the Superintendents Association representative and he requested that we all receive a debriefing as to why our appearance had not been successful. The only real criticism I received was that I had "mentioned the NRC twice". In many ways, my time in the National Reporting Centre (chapter sixteen) had been the highpoint of my career, so to mention it twice in relevant parts of the interview did not seem excessive. Evident, as had been my frequent experience, was that what I achieved while working elsewhere did not seem to gain recognition beyond the few with whom I maintained contact while away.

In my days as a Constable on Road Traffic, 1968 till 1972, all members of that Department were trained at the Regional Driving School at Devizes in Wiltshire and to a common, high, standard. We were using some of the more powerful cars available from the main manufacturers - the Cortina GT at Williton being an exception but well suited to the local conditions. Certainly within the Traffic Division, which then incorporated the Force Information Room, there was a mood that failing to catch a fleeing motorist was to be extremely rare. In those four years I can say, as could most of my colleagues, that when I set off after drivers who did not stop when required to do so, they did not get away. My later year on Traffic in Bristol presented a different situation and it was possible to 'lose' a vehicle in the more dense traffic situations.

As described in chapter seven, if unable to force the 'target' car to stop the expectation was that we would stick with it until an opportunity to apprehend those on board presented itself. That changed in the mid-1970s when there was a press-driven furore over the police blocking a carriageway with lorries to halt a pursuit that had travelled many miles and, because the driver of the car still refused to stop and collided with the well-lit lorries, passengers were killed. From that time on, the finger of blame has been pointed at the police officers involved rather than the criminals doing all they could to escape arrest. Indeed, there are good grounds to conclude that the excesses of dangerous driving by those wishing to evade capture have become more severe due to the expectation that the police officers will feel obliged to call off their pursuit. In fact, 'pursuit' and 'chase' have been erased from the police vocabulary and replaced by 'follow'!

The regular impact of this weird situation is that criminals evade capture on a regular basis. The more serious consequence is that escaping drivers too often kill or permanently maim innocent members of the public and police officers. Before this situation was allowed to develop, the objective was to stop seriously errant drivers before they could do more harm. It is an irony that media programmers, who are so quick to criticise the police officers when a collision follows their attempts to stop a dangerous driver, also thrive on re-running video images of pursuits to what, I presume, is a significant and receptive audience.

In my latter years, when in charge of the Communications Department, we entered the era in which there arose a perception that anyone who had dealt with anything in any way shocking should receive counselling. A whole industry has built up around the presumption that people cannot deal with traumatic situations without professional help. The cutbacks of recent years seem to have made this concern less of an organisational priority! The main 'safety valve' for police officers was the banter after an incident which, out of the view or hearing of those poor people directly affected, made light of what had taken place. This means of release from the direct stresses of many situations has, so it appears, evaporated in the pursuit of political correctness. I even understand that officers resist letting off their feelings for fear that a colleague will take exception and report the matter.

On one particular occasion, I was required to attend the debriefing of an incident where a worker had been scalded to death by escaping steam from a broken pipe. At the time the contents of that pipe could not be confirmed as to whether it was anything other than water. The officers arriving at the scene could see the body but were warned by the senior Fire Officer not to approach until what was in the steam had been identified. It was, of course, a fact that the officers had encountered a stressful situation but there could be little doubt as to the fatal nature of the victim's injury. The newly arrived ACC chairing the debriefing, having heard from those involved, directed that all officers involved must receive counselling. This was extended by the ACC to include the communications room staff who had heard the serious nature of what was taking place at the scene of the incident. I interjected that I would not be directing anyone to receive counselling but would ensure that any staff within my department who felt it appropriate would be able to avail themselves of the offer. I seriously believe that many, even most, police staff encounter enough of the 'rough' aspects of life to be able to handle the more severe with equal acceptance. Where they find they cannot, help should be available but many will find that recounting what took place in a counselling session some time after the event does no more than reinforce their memory of the trauma.

Not unrelated to the matter of Officers being able to cope with the pressures of the role is the process of recruitment. Indeed, in the early part of the 2000s there was a resurgence of criticism relating to racism within the police that could also be traced back to the recruitment process. In the 1960s and for many years before and after, the appointment process incorporated every conceivable check in the effort to ensure that those offering for recruitment would be up to the demands of the job. By the 1990s, and I know because I had been drawn in to the process as a chairman for recruit interviews, various influences relating to current interpretations of 'equal opportunities' had been brought into play. The concept of checking a candidate's family support for his or her desire to join had been eliminated and limitations upon what interviewers could and could not ask severely limited the ability to 'weed out' weaknesses in any candidate's make-up.

Some of the tales that appear on the media regarding the stresses experienced by officers, or former officers, too often omit the question as to why the individual was in the service. Even more demonstrative of my concern was the television programme in the mid-2000s where a reporter infiltrated a police recruit group at a regional training establishment. Secretly recorded exchanges were said by the producers of the programme to support the contention of a few years earlier that the Police Service was 'institutionally racist'. In fact, the only counter-balance for racist attitudes projected in the programme was from the only experienced police officer, one of the trainers. What the programme did show was that the young recruits seen to be racist were bringing their racist views into the Service from the wider public arena. That ACPO did not strongly make this point was a sadness but that the recruitment system could no longer filter out such unwanted attitudes was even more serious.

In the final year of my Service, there arose some pressure from within the, already largely civilianised administrative offices within Headquarters for the more flexible working conditions being promoted by the long-standing Conservative Government of the day. One aspect of this was the concept of 'job sharing'. When I examined the conditions contained within this new approach, I realised that it had potentially problematic consequences for managing operational staff levels within even the large unit for which I was responsible. I received no applications from members of staff for such an arrangement but shortly after my retirement my successor had to manage such requests. Only a few years later, the opportunity for 'job sharing' was opened up to Police Officers. This must have had an impact upon the earlier flexibility applicable to police resources and must have had some affect upon those Officers and

Staff not enjoying the job-sharing conditions. There is also the side issue to job sharing and part-time working that the raw numbers of police officers within the stated establishment of a Force must take account of how many of those Officers are only available for part of a full working schedule. The term used is Full Time Equivalent and is, in probably all Forces, the true reflection of what police officer availability actually exists.

Gill and I share a strong dislike for a terminology frequently adopted by supervisory police officers of all ranks, often when they appear before a camera or are quoted in newspapers. The first time Gill felt a negative reaction to the term was in a conversation with another officer's wife when she referred to those who worked with her husband as "his men." To give them some credit, a supervisor may wish to describe his or her subordinates as "My Officers" as a recognition of some form of responsibility for their welfare. In too many instances it comes over as a sign of a perceived superiority. One of the key aspects of the role of Constable is that of personal authority under the law and personal responsibility for the exercise of that authority. Hence, each police officer, of whatever rank, is his or her own Officer. Although subject to the direction of more senior officers in many ways, he or she has (at least, had) full independence under the law. If there is any allegiance worthy of recognition it is only that afforded to the Crown. That this independence of legal authority is being eroded, even for Chief Constables, most recently by the terms of reference for the College of Policing, does not bode well for the administration of justice at any level.

During the long lifetime of the Government administration labelled as New Labour, the number of civilian support staff in Avon and Somerset, and I suspect every other Force, grew massively. Avon and Somerset's Support Staff grew by more than four times in about a ten year period spanning the millennium. A significant proportion of this growth was to administer statistics for the Home Office. A smaller proportion of this recruitment purported to replace the visible element of policing with Police Community Support Officers. Although it has occasionally been used as a justification for increasing support staff, none of these changes seem to have resulted in a greater visibility of uniformed police officers in the community. Indeed, the only places in which a traditional police uniform is regularly visible in any noticeable strength is around the Royal Palaces and Whitehall.

Of greater real concern for someone who spent nearly thirty one years acquiring the skills to be a professional police officer is the politicians' obvious disdain for that experience, produced by sustained effort and commitment. When the Coalition Government came to power in 2010, it was hoped by many connected with the police service that it would stop, even reverse, the attack upon the traditional policing model that had taken so many decades to develop. Instead, apparently for reasons deep within the psyche of the higher echelons of the Conservative Party, the situation has worsened. It is difficult to avoid the conclusion when looking at the sad state of all our public services that politicians have, for too many recent years, avoided meeting the true, inevitably rising, cost of providing these services because the taxation really required may hinder their prospects at the next election.

Soon after 2010, and with no mandate or consultation, two measures were taken. We saw the appointment of a new Her Majesty's Chief Inspector of Constabulary who had never seen a day's police experience but who had earlier declared views regarding organisation and remuneration within the Service that ignored the value of omni-competence within traditional policing. Much closer to the people who look to the police for support, we saw the shift from widely drawn and partly elected Police Authorities to the new, single person, role of Police and Crime Commissioners (PCCs). The elections late in 2012 were just about the poorest supported in electoral history, largely because those eligible either did not understand why they were being asked to cast a vote or opted out because they did not agree with the process or appointments. It would have been interesting for there to have been a referendum before these elections, as there had been over mayors in several areas, but that was too much of a risk for the Government to countenance.

The short history of PCCs cannot be said to have been a happy one. The cost of the new system seems to be open to little or no control. The decisions taken by more than a few of the elected individuals show some of the poor judgement that is inevitable when no professional qualifications are required for the job. Unbelievably, there is nothing bar the next elections or sheer criminality, not even within the authority of the Home Secretary, that can remove a PCC from their position. Yet, these individuals hold total sway over appointment and retention of Chief Constables. In future, it seems unlikely that any PCC will appoint an independently minded individual to become Chief Constable, although the former Police Authority seemed to welcome a Chief Constable who displayed such qualities of leadership and command capability.

In recent years the lack of visibility and availability of police officers and their massively reduced routine contact with citizens has been excused by the contention that crime is falling. Perhaps there is a clue to one of the factors that have resulted in reduced levels of crime reporting. Too many people affected by criminal activity seem to have acquired the impression, some with sound reason, that reporting such matters to the police is a 'waste of time'. Anecdotes relating to inability to make useful contact with the police and talk of inattention when contact has been achieved seem uncomfortably commonplace. The mass closures of police stations, initially just the public entrance but latterly the whole building, seems to reflect a desire to capitalise on the real-estate rather than achieve a return to an accessible service. Until a generation ago every locality, down to small villages, had a police station where Constables were not just regularly visible but were known to the local population. Today we are heading toward the only non-confrontational personal contact being, at best, an occasionally occupied desk at the local shopping precinct or council offices.

In the very early stages of the post-Peel police service in this country the positions were often filled from those leaving the military, mainly the army. By the time that the county forces were becoming established in the mid-1850s local Magistrates and Councillors were already looking for those with policing experience from London, other large cities and Ireland. By the turn of the twentieth century, virtually all promotions through the ranks reflected a value placed upon policing experience. The longest lasting exception to this process was the persistence of the view that former senior military officers were the preferred candidates for the roles of Chief Officer, although this did not seem common in the smaller City or Borough Forces. One such notable appointment was in 1931, when Hugh Trenchard was appointed as Commissioner of the Metropolitan Police after he retired from his more widely famed position as the first commander of the Royal Air Force.

In his short period as Commissioner, Trenchard sought to revise many aspects of the police service, his reports to the Home Secretary being instrumental in creating the Metropolitan Police Act of 1933. Trenchard, despite his own background, wanted to set the foundation for the police service to develop its own chief officers and established the Hendon Police College to guide selected young men towards command positions. Although the Trenchard Scheme was as short-lived as was his period as Commissioner, it had set a precedent that would be pursued quite vigorously after the Second World War. No longer only Metropolitan Police focused, in the early 1960s the Service sought a two-pronged approach to finding and training its future leaders. The introduction of the Graduate Entry Scheme was accompanied by access to the same training for non-graduates who could pass the Sergeants' promotion examination within the top 200 in the country. Later, the top 200 requirement was added to and the opportunity to apply extended more widely. Largely thanks to pressure from the Police Federation, the appointment of graduates also brought the opportunity for Bramshill Scholarships to send serving officers to universities. My experiences within this system were described in chapters 9, 10 & 13.

The Graduate Entry Scheme brought promise for those who could 'make the grade' of early promotion to the rank of Inspector but maintained the requirement that all must start at Constable level and prove their capabilities at the 'sharp end'. There was also the requirement that these individuals must pass the Sergeants' promotion examination. The principle was that the training afforded through the Special Course at Bramshill was targeted at Chief Inspector level, with successful completion of the course and a year of operational performance in the role of Sergeant, leading to 'guaranteed' promotion to Inspector. Although I was one of those who had passed the promotion examination to the rank of Inspector, the Special Course incorporated examinations which equated to that qualification for those who had not. In my case there was a benefit in that since my passing the Inspector's examination, the old Larceny Act had been replaced by the Theft Act, while I had been serving in the Traffic Department.

The schemes brought into being by the 2010 Coalition Government are a quantum leap away from the long-established tradition that policing experience is a key ingredient for successful police command (I use 'is' and not 'was' entirely intentionally). Even with the extremely costly induction scheme that is proposed for direct entry at Superintendent level, the capability of police command rank officers in future years will, inevitably, lack that essential ingredient of recognising the potential consequences of decisions from earlier experience gained while 'coming through the ranks'. In the early stages of this transition to the Government's revised scheme, some of the inappropriateness of decisions handed down will be mitigated by the experience of those required to implement them but this will not prevail for many years. Eventually, and the time will elapse all too quickly, there will be no one in the command ranks with any real appreciation of the side issues that almost invariably surround every policing decision.

On top, literally, of the introduction of police commanders with slender real knowledge of policing, there already exists the increasing dilution of policing knowledge among those creators of policy within Headquarters. At the very top now sit the Police and Crime Commissioners, with their unprecedented and seemingly unassailable authority position in relation to Chief Constables. Beside that almost unbelievable situation is assembled a massively increased civilian support cadre who are, daily, pressing home decisions based upon business models, largely economically driven, with precious little recognition of the vital service element of the police that the community values so highly. The focus upon 'targets' and statistical measurement of a long but inevitably not comprehensive list of 'boxes to tick' through the first decade of the 21st Century has totally undervalued the service element. Spending a few hours of police time with a bereaved family or relatives of a seriously damaged victim seems not to 'tick any boxes'. The focus of a few family liaison officers is a mean substitute for every police officer regarding the human caring element as part of his or her everyday role and one that will be recognised and valued by those higher up the organisational ladder.

I am sadly of the view that when the history books are written, a generation or two from now, the policing experience of the twenty or so years from the mid-1990s will be recognised as having lost what the Service had taken over 160 years to achieve. Even before the savage cuts wielded by the post 2010 Coalition Government, oddly more focused upon warrant card carrying police officers than the civilian support elements of the Service which were so exaggeratedly expanded by the previous administration, the cry most often heard when policing performance comes under critical review is that of 'inadequate resources'. That cry has, since the mid-1990s been repeated every time the Service has had to confront accusations that it has not performed adequately.

When I joined the Service in the 1960s we still retained responsibilities for a whole raft of functions, such as the enforcement of diseases of animals legislation, but in 2001 the Army were called in to deal with the Foot and Mouth epidemic. Even with those earlier additional roles the police service was proud to be a 'can do' organisation. The favoured adage was that 'the impossible just takes a bit longer'. The incessant meddling of politicians and massive shift away from the Service being wholly driven and directed by experienced officers cannot be recognised as having improved any element of what people had grown to expect from their police service.

I have spent these last few pages reflecting upon my own Police Service. The Service we see today saddens me and many of my contemporaries when we draw comparisons between what we strived to provide and what we see is currently on offer. The problem, of course, does not lie with the enthusiastic young people putting themselves forward to serve the wider community as Police Officers but the actions of the last several Governments which have created structures and politically driven policing models within which the current generation of police officers have to work. The worst aspect of all this is that it seems unlikely that this process will be reversed.

I trust that the reader has enjoyed this trip down memory lane with me and can excuse the last few pages of my getting a few things 'off my chest'. There is only one appropriate way in which to close these reflections and that must be to return to the central role played in my Police Service required of Gill. When we married in 1967 the topic of the first chapter had happened a few months earlier so Gillian knew a bit as to what my job was about but could have no concept as to how my choice of career would impact upon her. She successfully handled the rearing of two small children while I was absent for much of the year between 1973 and 1974, during which one of them reached her first birthday. This, she repeated with three daughters, while I was largely absent for nearer two years in the mid-1980s. With the exception of the time I was seconded to the University of Bristol, my presence at home, as with all police officers of my era, was never wholly predictable. In addition, on five occasions before we had been married eight years and four with no more than a fortnight's notice, she had to manage packing up our entire home to move elsewhere in the Force area.

Conditions have changed to a massive extent in the intervening fifty years but, even now, the role of the family in supporting any police officer is crucial, sometimes referred to but seldom appropriately valued. Gone, I imagine, are the days when the police officer's spouse responded to enquiries at her door because the nearby police station was, at that time, empty. Much less, it seems, is the unpredictability of when an officer will return home from a shift but the current vagaries of the role must still impact upon an officer's family to at least some proportion of what was our experience.

Gill not only managed our household while I was absent but was an ever-present support, especially during those times I have related when all did not look good and when meaningful support from within the Service was not all it could have been. Tanya, Cathryn & Emma must have experienced some reaction to their father's occupation, probably all police officers' children encounter that at some time, but they never brought it to my notice. They all coped admirably, actually they triumphed, and without their having done so I cannot imagine how I would have been able to sustain my commitment to what I saw as an important role. There were numerous occasions when my enforced inability to meet domestic commitments made other arrangements necessary but only once, thanks largely to Gill's ingenuity, was I really heavily impacted. About mid-way through my 'toing and froing' to New Scotland Yard every week, in 1984, Emma, at the age of eight, was helping me to load the boot of the car. As she handed me another item, she said, "Do you really have to go again Dad?" The 120 mile journey that Sunday evening was probably the hardest of my life. This final sentence must record my heartfelt and loving thanks to all four of them.